WHY WE CLIMB

The World's Most Inspiring Climbers

CHRIS NOBLE

Guilford, Connecticut

To Mark Andrew Davis
1966–2016

An imprint of Globe Pequot
Falcon and FalconGuides are registered trademarks and Make Adventure Your Story is a trademark of Rowman & Littlefield.

Distributed by NATIONAL BOOK NETWORK

British Library Cataloguing-in-Publication Information available

Library of Congress Cataloging-in-Publication Data

Names: Noble, Chris, author.
Title: Why we climb : the world's most inspiring climbers / Chris Noble.
Description: Guilford, Connecticut : Falcon, an imprint of Globe Pequot, [2017] | Includes bibliographical references and index.
Identifiers: LCCN 2016033437 (print) | LCCN 2016035976 (ebook) | ISBN 9781493018536 (pbk.) | ISBN 9781493018543 (e-book)
Subjects: LCSH: Mountaineers—Biography. | Mountaineers—Interviews.
Classification: LCC GV199.9 .N625 2017 (print) | LCC GV199.9 (ebook) | DDC 796.522092/2 [B] —dc23
LC record available at https://lccn.loc.gov/2016033437

∞™ The paper used in this publication meets the minimum requirements of American National Standard for Information Sciences—Permanence of Paper for Printed Library Materials, ANSI/NISO Z39.48-1992.

CONTENTS

Foreword by Conrad Anker vii

Acknowledgments xi

Introduction xii

    The Way Home 1

    Game Theory 17

    Why I Compete by Angie Payne 25

    The Heroic Life 37

    Spirit Matters 47

    Partnership, Love & Loss 61

    Conrad Anker & Peter Croft 69

    Tommy Caldwell 111

    Paige Claassen 131

    Alex Honnold 145

    Chris Kalous 169

    Adam Ondra 185

    Ines Papert 203

    Doug Robinson 221

    Chris Sharma 239

    Raphael Slawinski 261

    Mayan Smith-Gobat 277

    Learning to Downclimb 295

Notes 303

About the Author 306

FOREWORD

by Conrad Anker

Why do we climb? It certainly isn't an easy way to spend one's time—and it can be deadly. The rock and snow that create the mountains we climb are in a constant state of flux. You may have noticed that humans are soft when compared to rock. If we fall on rock or rock falls on us—the rock always wins. Some would say climbing is frivolous. It doesn't solve any problems. Climbers aren't caring for other people. Yet for a certain few, the call of the vertical game of gravity is too great to resist.

When asked the question "Why do you climb?" most climbers respond based on their own predilection. Scenery, exhilaration, challenge, partnership, and exercise are a few of the reasons often mentioned.

George Leigh Mallory, the pioneering climber who disappeared on the slopes of Everest in 1924, answered the question with the comment, "Because it's there." While much has been made of his famous retort (over Scotch and in writing), we really don't know if Mallory was offering a philosophical insight or an easy quip to placate a pesky reporter. Either way, "because it's there" is the most-often quoted reason to explain climbing . . . especially by those who don't climb.

Yet for those of us who tie in, are willing to fight gravity, and seek out the hidden secrets of hand- and footholds sculpted by nature, Mallory's answer might leave us wanting more. There seems to be something deeper.

Does why we climb have to do with humankind's eternal drive for exploration? Maybe this, more than anything, has resulted in our being the dominant species on the planet. In the beginning, our drive was for food and shelter. Eventually it grew into the quest for empire. This explanation might make sense when applied to Genghis Khan, Magellan, or Lewis and Clark—yet it's

Conrad Anker footloose and fancy-free in the California Needles probably not why we hang on the side of a cliff and voluntarily put ourselves in harm's way.

Perhaps some of us are simply hardwired for adventure. Perhaps we have some gene that every so often switches on to drive some of us to risk more. In every tribe there have always been those who left the comfort of the fire to dare the unknown. *What's on the other side? Will I return with success? Will I return at all?* Throughout history, the call to adventure is well documented. Homer's *Odyssey*, for example, is the quintessential story of risk and adventure, the quest into the unknown. Fittingly, Odysseus never arrives at an answer. Perhaps today's modern adventurers are simply a new interpretation of this ancient story.

Could the opening of new routes, the last vestiges of terrestrial exploration, be a climber's grasp at immortality? While Riccardo Cassin is no longer with us, the route he pioneered on the south face of Alaska's Denali lives on.

Perhaps some humans are simply narcissists. Perhaps we want the biggest and the best, so we accomplish daring feats to fuel our pride and create envy among our peers. For superstars, celebrities, and politicians, this outward manifestation of the ego makes sense. They thrive on it, and fame becomes its own feedback loop.

Yet for many of us who seek gravity as a way of life, maybe we do so to be reminded of the transitory nature of life. I think for most climbers, the self-effacing lot that we are, we climb to release the ego.

So while there are many deeper reasons why we tie in, at the end of pitch or at the summit of a peak, it all comes down to joy. If all goes well, we experience the elation of having overcome gravity, figuring out a way get to the top with our own strength and determination.

Problem-solving brings joy: *How do I get to the top? Can my body function without adequate oxygen? What's the coefficient of friction between skin and sandstone?*

Teamwork brings joy. The very act of belaying, our own attention and patience while our partner pushes his or her limitations, speaks to a shared happiness human beings seek.

And adventure brings joy. For me, this is the root of all happiness.

Anker falls under the spell of *The Sorcerer* in the Needles.

I'm reminded of René Daumal and his answer to why we climb from *Mt Analogue*, published in 1952: "You cannot stay on the summit forever; you have to come down again. So why bother in the first place? Just this: What is above knows what is below, but what is below does not know what is above. One climbs, one sees. One descends, one sees no longer, but one has seen. There is an art of conducting oneself in the lower regions by the memory of what one saw higher up. When one can no longer see, one can at least still know."

Climbing is a combination of all of these things.

Chris Noble's images span decades and generations. He successfully made the transition from film to digital and has captured the emotion of climbers' struggles and successes from the Himalaya to Yosemite. Chris's writing is tempered with experience—he is a climber and so is as haunted and motivated by the same questions as all of us who climb. Through word and image, Chris explores the motivation of climbers who by their own volition are lifers. They have no other calling. They have no other choice. They must climb. Perhaps through their view, you'll want to climb as well. To feel the stretch of muscle and tendons, the single-mindedness of focus as you engage a challenging pitch, and the warmth of memory of the journey and a day spent climbing with friends.

Let Chris take you there.

ACKNOWLEDGMENTS

First I'd like to thank all the amazing climbers profiled in *Why We Climb* who have given generously of their time and wisdom, and I'd like to thank my wife, Kinde Nebeker, for her love and support, as well as for being a courageous and insightful reader who kept bringing me back to the bread crumbs when I was lost in the forest. Last but not least, I'd like to thank: Jay Smith, Kitty Calhoun, Jim Donini, and Ron Kauk. The dedicated staffs at *Alpinist*, *Climbing*, and *Rock & Ice* magazines. Everyone at Black Diamond. Ann Krcik at The North Face, Angie Mekkelson, Jeff Leads, Elaina Arenz, Tracy Martin, Evan Lai-Hipp, Jeff Pedersen, Mike Call, Mike Beck, Brooke and Terry Williams, as well as all the van bums, dirtbags, and over-stokers I've met along the way.

INTRODUCTION

When I was traveling around the country promoting my last book with Falcon, *Women Who Dare*, I did a slide show in Ouray, Colorado. A few of my climbing heroes including Jay Smith and Jim Donini were in the audience. Being on stage in front of such experienced climbers always makes me nervous, so I was relieved the next morning when Donini posted on SuperTopo that he had enjoyed the show. Then with customary wit he added, "And Chris is looking for subjects for his next book which will be titled *Men Who Care*. Does anyone out there know any?"

The post inspired many humorous responses ranging from the observation that the new book would certainly be one of the shortest in history to the suggestion that a better title might be *Men Who Stare*, since then there would be no lack of subjects to choose from.

As useful as these suggestions were, I decided instead to take on an even more formidable task than finding men in touch with their emotions, and that was to tackle the oldest and biggest question in all of climbing—Why? Why do people devote their lives to what on the surface appears to be such a dangerous, uncomfortable, and worthless pursuit?

It's a huge question, and I would never be stupid enough to try to answer it on my own. So I recruited some of the most talented and committed climbers in the world to help. As I like to say, if watching elite climbers climb made you stronger, I would be the strongest guy in the world. Pity it isn't so. But even if watching elite climbers and listening to them talk about the lessons they've learned doesn't make you physically stronger, it does provide a template for how to live a fully realized human life. There's no lack of information out there about how to train the body, but this book isn't about climbing's effect on your forearms, it's about climbing's effect on your entire being—body, mind, and soul.

If you're not a climber, be forewarned. If you choose to climb, everything will change. Your entire attitude toward life will shift. Where others drift aimlessly, you will move with purpose. Where others seek comfort and security,

you will seek the opportunities that can only be found in challenge and adversity. You'll learn to set lofty goals, then attain them, or fail heroically in the attempt. You should know that you will inevitably alienate family members and lose close friends—but in exchange you will gain membership in a worldwide tribe who share your passion.

And for those who have already realized their life's true calling is to be a climber—perhaps not the best climber in the world, but the best climber you can possibly be—this book will help chart your course. For to master all the climbing arts requires a lifetime of devotion, and no matter how talented one may be, we all need to learn from the masters in order to make their Jedi mind tricks our own.

Chris Noble

Salt Lake City, Utah, 2016

THE WAY HOME

I could climb for a million years and still not know why I do it . . .
WHY? . . . WHY? Why am I here?

—Chuck Pratt, during the first ascent of
Ribbon East Portal, June 27, 1964

I've tried to quit climbing more than once. I figured it was time to try something new, meet new people, broaden my horizons.

I couldn't do it. In the autumn, when the air cools and the cottonwoods turn gold, my thoughts flee south, to the towers and mesas of southern Utah; to evening light on sandstone; to constellations hanging like lamps above the camp; to waking in the back of a pickup, knuckles bruised, body aching like it's been in a prizefight, but the spirit soaring in anticipation of adventures yet to come.

With its liberal doses of pain, suffering, and fear, the reasons why people climb can seem an enigma—even to climbers themselves. To the uninitiated, climbing appears dangerous, crazy, obsessive. For evidence there are the piles of guidebooks and magazines strewn across the kitchen table. Windblown peaks rather than family portraits lining the walls. The training log, timer, and finger-board down the stairs. The late-night texts: "Dude, Rifle tomorrow?" Three short words with the power to shatter sacred oaths to clean out the garage. My friends and I all like to joke that we would quit climbing in a heartbeat—if only we could find something half as good to take its place.

So what is climbing and why do people do it? Is it a sport or a lifestyle? Is it a frivolous hobby or meaningful quest? Is it a healthy discipline for body and mind or a reckless and selfish addiction?

Perhaps most puzzling: Why, for some, does climbing become a lifelong love affair, while others scratch their heads and wonder why anyone's crazy enough to climb at all?

Milky Way Camp, Indian Creek, southern Utah

And can climbing aspire to be something more? In our secular age, can sport rise to the level of spiritual path—a *Way* in the traditional Eastern sense of the word—like yoga, Zen, tai chi, and the martial arts—a lifelong mental and physical discipline that elevates the mundane to the transcendent?

It would be naïve to think there is a single answer to the question, "Why do we climb?" The truth is, there are as many answers to that question as there are climbers (and in 2015 *Time* magazine estimated that number to be thirty-five million worldwide and growing).

Why do we climb? At the most basic level: Because it's fun. Let's face it, we're primates. Our evolutionary predecessors spent millennia scrambling up trees. Climbing is literally in our DNA. For proof one has only to observe young kids testing themselves on jungle gyms, rocks, trees, and other high places—risk-taking made all the more delicious by its ability to scare one's parents half to death.

Along with walking, running, and speech, climbing is fundamental to the human animal. However, because it's dangerous and for the most part serves no economic purpose, society has typically viewed it with suspicion.

"What are those kids doing off climbing all the time?" asked the farmers of South Tyrol about the young Messner brothers, Reinhold and Gunther, as tales of their mountaineering prowess began to spread. "Haven't they got anything better to do? If they want exercise, they should be chopping wood or fetching hay down from the meadows."[1]

In other words, when your Aunt Hazel asks, "Why do you climb?" what she's really asking is, "Why risk your life and waste your time on such a worthless activity?"

For these reasons, ever since climbing began as an organized activity in the Victorian era, climbers have tried—and mostly failed—to find a satisfactory answer to the question, Why do we climb?

History's most famous answer, "Because it's there," came from George Leigh Mallory at a press conference in 1922 before leaving to meet his death on Everest. And even though Mallory's reply was probably more annoyance at having been asked ad nauseam to explain mountaineering to people who had never seen a mountain, his koan-like response had just

Doug Heinrich gets crazy on *My Daddy's a Psycho*, Murchison Falls, Canadian Rockies.

the right blend of truth and mystery in it to capture people's imagination and to endure.

That kind of mystery clings to high places and the creatures that inhabit them. Because they are largely inaccessible, mountains, towers, mesas, and plateaus pose a question. Somehow of this earth yet standing apart, mountains form a bridge between heaven and earth. To explore them requires abandoning the comfort, security, and support of civilization. In this way, they have come to symbolize renunciation, spiritual growth, and transcendence, offering a fleeting glimpse, through rushing cloud and blowing mist, of a realm pure and unstained by the moral ambiguity of human affairs.

Because mountain regions, protected by their harsh climate, poor soil, and challenging terrain, remain relatively untamed, they are also seen as lying

Jay Smith on his route *Voodoo Child*, V, 11+, Parriott Mesa, Utah

somewhat beyond the control of central governments. Traditionally they have been viewed as the home of outlaws and mountain ascetics such as the Chinese Tang-era poet Hanshan:

I'm happy with my way of life,
living in mountain caves amid mist and vines.
My wild moods are mostly unrestrained;
I'm carefree as my friends the clouds.
There are paths here, but they don't lead to the world.
Emptied of illusion, what can the mind cling to?
I sit alone on my bed of stone all night long,
while the full moon ascends Cold Mountain.[2]

Even in the era of Google Earth, mountains, deserts, and cliff faces retain a sense of wilderness in its truest sense, "a place of danger and difficulty" as the poet Gary Snyder defines it, "where you take your own chances, depend on your own skills, and do not count on rescue."[3]

Out at the end of a thousand dirt roads, living in trucks and vans, rootless nomads searching for the next flash of backcountry satori, modern climbers are the spiritual heirs of Hanshan and other mountain hermits who left the world seeking a life of simplicity, one that is part of (rather than at war with) nature.

As Mallory suggested, by their very existence, *because they are there*, mountains beg to be explored.

Yet when we are honest with ourselves, we see that the truth is not simply because *mountains are there*—it is because *we are here*. As the French alpinist Gaston Rébuffat wrote, mountains provide "a mirror of stone or ice, a mirror, which helps us know ourselves."

In ancient Greece, Apollo's temple at Delphi was inscribed with the injunction "Know Thyself," and three millennia later this remains the central task of human existence. Find a way to know oneself, discover the soul's true purpose, and life flows in joyful play. Fail, and life can seem a wasteland, devoid of any meaning or significance.

Reaching a mountain summit requires that we confront the reflection we find in the stone mirror, working with all that is weak, lazy, and fearful within ourselves. Climbing provides a way (one way) with which to see ourselves more clearly, the first step in personal growth.

Big wall climber Jim Bridwell called it "individual character improvement." Bridwell rated the excellence of different pitches on El Capitan according to their potential to bring out the best in any climber attempting them.

As Conrad Anker states, he and Mugs Stump once practiced what they called "mental toughness training," a discipline that would begin long before a climb. Once, on their way from Utah to Yosemite, they vowed to do the entire drive without speaking, a self-imposed form of silent meditation that devolved into farce when Mug's van died suddenly, leaving charades the only means of dealing with the situation.

I am sitting naked on a boulder in the midst of a stream two hundred miles north of the Arctic Circle. The granite is smooth against my skin, burnished by the passage of amber water flowing down from stone mountains standing against the Alaskan sky like fingers. "Like the fingers of a hand outstretched," the Inuit observed, giving these mountains their name. Arrigetch. The Arrigetch Peaks of Alaska's Brooks Range in Gates of the Arctic National Park.

The cool air raises the skin on my neck and arms, but the boreal sun is warm. I revel in the contrast between warmth and cold, between an exhausted body, and the luxury of basking in the sun. Again and again, my eyes are drawn back to the mountain. Of all the peaks in this cirque of stone fingers, she is the most alluring, a granite arc leading to the sky.

Four days ago we left camp before dawn, believing the climb would take one long Arctic summer day, which should have been 24 hours of continuous climbing. But we were only four pitches up, when Catherine on lead, felt a block shift beneath her grasp. She lunged for another hold, but too late. The block was already falling. It slid over her right hand crushing her index and middle fingers.

Stunned, we watched the block fall free, strike, shatter into a hundred parts, then fall again, like the heavy drops of blood that dripped from Catherine's hand.

We could have gone down. By any measure it was the smart thing to do. But something called from high on that peak, *and* something within us responded.

As gently as I could, I taped Catherine's fingers together. Bravely, she offered to climb with the pack, if I would lead all the pitches. So we began again, measuring out the mountain a rope length at a time. Twenty hours after leaving camp, we threw ourselves on a ledge for a few hours rest. The Arctic sun curtsied toward the horizon, then rose again. We ate a few bites of salami and tried to sleep.

By some gift, the weather held, and by afternoon on the third day the summit was within reach. After 3 days of effort and little food, I was weak and shaky. Yet Catherine's quiet courage sustained me. Her fingers painful and swollen, clumsy and nearly useless, she somehow found a way to pull herself and the pack upward without a word of complaint. If she was frightened, it didn't show. If she doubted our ability to make the summit, it was left unsaid. The mountain had united us, and in the process, we had somehow learned to climb beyond ourselves . . .

We were made for this. We were made to sleep on the open ground, to rise before dawn and set off once more . . . toward what? To discover where the elk lie in the next valley, to press on downriver in search of better fishing, or to discover an elegant parabola of stone that takes us far beyond, and simultaneously deep within, ourselves.

As the Alaskan poet John Haines wrote, "As many have found, having once lived that life, nothing else ever quite satisfies the spirit. It is the original life of people, and there is in it something inexhaustible and fresh. To rise in the morning, look from the doorway of a tent at the early light on the land; to

Alex Honnold dances up the *Salathé* Headwall (13b).

drink from a tundra pool, break fast, and then break camp; to pack one's gear and with encouraging cries to the animals, set off once more to the hunting ground: it may in many ways have been the best life we have known on this earth, clean and unburdened, filled with peril and expectation."[4]

In contrast, humanity now faces an era of unprecedented social, environmental, and spiritual crises. Somehow our long journey from Hunter-Gatherer to Industrial Man has led us into a box canyon. Dark walls rise on every side. It is unthinkable to go back, to abandon all that we've gained, yet the way forward is dark, shrouded in fog.

We find ourselves waking in the night, as the poet Wendell Berry put it, "Afraid of what our lives and our children's lives have become." We have tamed the original wilderness, but now seek refuge from a more troubling, and possibly far more dangerous, wilderness of our own making.

The ecologist Paul Shepard believed the anxiety we feel is the longing of the human genome for its one true home—the world where it evolved—the vanished world of the Pleistocene. We have been exiled, cast adrift, left to run endlessly on treadmills, hunting through strip malls, questing in video games for a world that remains only in fragments.

But if the species has lost its way, at least its individual members can have the pleasure of reclaiming the lithe and powerful bodies, the quicksilver minds, which are our human birthright.

Participating in modern activities such as climbing, surfing, skiing, sailing, and kayaking allows us to rediscover an ancient and intimate dance with untamed, elemental forces. More than just sport, such activities offer a way of being in the world, a practical down-to-earth philosophy, founded on voluntary simplicity and the appropriate use of technology.

Where have the Ice Age hunters gone? We may believe they have followed the auroch into extinction, but their sons and daughters walk among us. They are attempting highball boulder problems in the Buttermilks and *enchaînements* on les Courtes, les Droites, and the Grandes Jorasses. At this very moment they are sharpening ice tools at Rampart Creek, pumping cracks in the desert, then doing evening yoga beneath the cottonwoods. The children of the Pleistocene live on.

"If you're not flyin' you're not tryin.'" Keenan Takahashi dynos at Red Rocks.

In the 1972 Chouinard Equipment Catalog, Doug Robinson wrote, "Technology is imposed on the land, but technique means conforming to the landscape. They work in opposite ways, one forcing a passage, while the other discovers it. The goal of developing technique is to conform to the most improbable landscape by means of the greatest degree of skill and boldness, supported by the least equipment."

This is the climber's manifesto, to seek a balance between technology and adventure. It is based on a philosophy of boldness and grace, discipline and restraint, and as Robinson says, it may provide a bridge across our fraught and perilous experiment with industrialization.

Because the path to a sustainable future cannot be purchased or engineered, the way ahead is to become *more* human—not less. It is to find the

courage to stare into the stone mirror and see ourselves clearly—perhaps for the first time—with all our strengths and weaknesses.

In a world with ever-shrinking options to know nature and know ourselves, skills that return us to the elements become increasingly vital. In a culture ever more preoccupied with *virtual reality*—experiences that reunite us with wind and rock, ice and snow, provide the dash of cold water that shocks us from our all-too-human dreams. Mountains demand all that we can give. Then they ask for more. The summit is always higher and farther than we imagined. But in return they bestow the pearl beyond price—a measure of all the grit, gumption, skill, and vitality we possess.

"We demonstrate in the most stunning way of all—at the risk of our lives—that there is no limit to the effort man can demand of himself," wrote the alpinist Walter Bonnatti. "This quality is the basis of all human achievement in whatever field. It can never be proved enough. I consider that we climbers . . . serve all humanity. We prove there is no limit to what man can do."

In a letter to *Rock & Ice* magazine, a reader wrote, "Climbing is reckless and selfish, it doesn't create anything, change the world, or improve anyone else's life."

In the next issue, Dan Froelich, a climber from Cleveland, Ohio responded, "While I have had this same thought, the evidence to the contrary is staggering. Climbing and mountaineering have significantly changed my life for the better. Last year my father and I along with two brothers-in-law went to Yosemite. Just planning this adventure caused my brother-in-law to quit smoking and drop 30 pounds. My father lost weight, is in his best shape in 20 years, and brags about it being the best vacation of his life. Climbing these mountains changed the entire family dynamic, everyone is healthier, more present, and has a new outlook on life . . ."[5]

On some deep level, even if we find it difficult to express, we all intuitively know why we climb—whether it be for fitness, challenge, competition, socializing with friends, connecting to nature, or travel, or because our girlfriend thinks it's cool.

Melissa Thaw gets "trad" on *Sheila* (10a), Pine Creek Canyon, California.

Veteran climber Dirk Tyler distills climbing's complex appeal down into three simple categories: The What, The Who, and The Where.

The What refers to what we climb, the numbers, grades, and difficulty of routes and problems.

The Who refers to who we climb with, our partners and the broader climbing community.

The Where is the environment in which we climb, the aesthetics of the landscape, which can range from a homemade woody to Switzerland's Magic Woods.

As Tyler says, over time The What matters less and less, and The Who and The Where gain precedence.

Some will say that dissecting climbing to find its meaning is like cutting open the proverbial ball in search of its bounce—a fool's errand. Many climbers will simply shrug, grab their packs, and head for the crag. No need for further analysis of what one instinctively knows to be essential for one's well-being.

So why write a book about the question?

Because first I wanted to better understand why climbing holds such deep appeal for me. Nothing else brings me joy the way climbing does. Nothing else re-enchants the world in the way I felt when I was a child. Nothing else makes me yearn to be young once more, simply so I would have more time to climb.

And second, because by listening to the stories of others, we expand our own vision of what's possible. So when we hear all the remarkable climbers profiled in this book talk about why they climb and what they've learned, our own perspective expands like the view from a mountain summit. Suddenly we can see much farther than we could before and new horizons open at our feet.

This is not a book of answers; it is a book of possibilities. For as Rébuffat suggested, "We should refuse none of the thousand and one joys the mountains offer us at every turn. We should brush nothing aside, set no restrictions. We should experience hunger and thirst, be able to go fast, but also know how to go slowly and to contemplate."[6] Because from time to time, we climbers stumble upon moments of pure grace, when time, space, gravity, and fear dissolve, and we float magically up long vertical passages of stone or ice. Such moments are rare, precious, fleeting. The Japanese have a word, shibui, that strives to express the inexpressible essence of such things: the mastery that flashes like lightning in the movements of a swordsman, the haiku of steam rising from a cup of tea, the fragile elegance of an orchid. It is the epiphany that washes over us when a sequence of moves—impossible only a moment before—suddenly reveals its secrets; when after days of anxiety and effort, the mind surrenders, and the climber soars like a falcon released from the fist.

One evening I was climbing with the alpinist Kitty Calhoun. As she lowered, her face was glowing. "You know climbing is a gift," she said. "We aren't going to be able to climb our entire lives. None of us know what the future will bring. There's no time to waste being consumed by fear, self-doubt, and comparison. Those are all negative emotions. We need to spend the time given us climbing with all the joy possible, all the joy climbing deserves."

I couldn't agree more. Because I had so many questions of my own, because I felt I had so much to learn, I set out to track down people I would characterize as *soul climbers*, those who regardless of age, gender, or background have found their true calling. The result is *Why We Climb*, the accumulated effort of many hands calloused by rock, blackened by 'biner grease and belaying. These pages are a distillation of the wisdom of some of the world's best climbers, people who have spent their lives searching for answers to riddles posed by height and distance, soaring arêtes, and arcing splitters.

As free-climbing pioneer John Long observed, "The way you climb is the way you will live your life." If you approach climbing as recreation, competition, and exercise, then that is what it will be. But for those who choose to enter the temple and dedicate themselves fully to the mysteries found there, climbing becomes a means of connecting more deeply with nature and one's self, a way of living intentionally with confidence, boldness, and grace.

The words found here are a rough translation of a much older language, one which each day grows more distant and foreign to our modern ears—the song of wind and rushing water, the hieroglyphics of the stars, the promise of a waterfall frozen to stillness by winter's cold. If I had my way, when opened, the book might provide a sudden exhalation of sage, sunburned skin, and mountain pennyroyal. Tiny flakes of granite, red sand, and a raven's feather would fall from the sweat and coffee-stained pages. . . .

Belay's on. Have fun up there.

GAME THEORY

Climbing is such a wide activity. You can climb only in the gym. You can only boulder. You can do so many things, but it's still called climbing—it's still based on getting from the bottom to the top.

—Adam Ondra

One reason it's so tough to pin down *why* we climb is because climbing is so many different things. The distance between the hypoxia and wooden fingers of a Himalayan summit and the pounding music, chalk, and musk-laden interior of a climbing gym is vast indeed.

Every day, most of us *climb* a set of stairs. Many of us visit a *climbing* gym a few times a week, where we stand in line for the Green Route or test our mettle on a new v5. But Alex Honnold *climbs* the *Northwest Face* of Half Dome, a 2,000-foot vertical wall, alone and without a rope. All of these experiences are *climbing*, yet they are light-years apart.

In today's world climbing refers to anything from racing up indoor speed routes to running up El Cap in 3 hours or less. *Climb* is a short word that has been stretched to encompass everything from buildering to bouldering to deep-water soloing. The only thing connecting all these dots is, as Ondra says, "getting from the bottom to the top of *something*."

And as Paige Claassen observes, even when comparing similar climbing disciplines—say World Cup competition versus projecting hard routes outdoors—the differences are so profound, many people now spend their entire careers specializing in one discipline or another.

In 1967, Lito Tejada Flores published a visionary essay titled "The Games Climbers Play." "What I would like to propose," Flores wrote, "is not a new answer to the basically unanswerable question, 'what is climbing?' but rather a new way of talking and thinking about it. Climbing is not a homogenous sport, but rather a collection of differing (though related) activities."[1]

Jay Smith enjoying the high-altitude expedition game on the North Face of Thelay Sagar, India

Flores went on to divide climbing into different *games*, each with its own advocates, terrain, and—most important—rules. As Flores noted, at first glance, alpine climbing with all its attendant risks may seem too serious to be considered a game.

But it is—because climbing is voluntary. No one forces us to play. And like all games, climbing has its own rules, which allow us to keep track of who's posing, who's crushing, and who's cheating.

For example, the game of bouldering has far more rules about what's fair than expedition climbing. On Everest in the Khumbu Icefall, using extension ladders to cross crevasses is standard procedure. Yet if we bring a ladder to Hueco to climb a boulder, there's no challenge—and therefore no game.

The same can be said of helicopters. If reaching the summit of a mountain were the only thing that mattered, everyone would fly. But ultimately a mountain summit means nothing without the personal transformation experienced by the mountaineer, and that is something that cannot be purchased. It is earned only through the currency of blood, sweat, and tears.

Free soloing is the purest of all the climbing games and the most serious. Just the climber and the climb. No rope. No partner. No protection—and no hope if one falls. The slightest error can result in the ultimate penalty—death.

Other forms of climbing are more nuanced. This explains the enduring fascination with Everest. Everyone understands it's the highest mountain on Earth. So it must also be the hardest and most noteworthy. Right? Well not really. Because climbing is also about style—the style with which one plays the game.

Yvon Chouinard summed up the embarrassment high-altitude tourism on Everest has become when he said, "You get these high-powered people who want to climb Everest, they spend $85,000 . . . there's a Sherpa in the front pulling, a Sherpa in the back pushing, carrying extra oxygen bottles so you can cheat the altitude. You haven't climbed Everest. The purpose of climbing something like that is to effect some kind of spiritual or physical change. When you compromise the process, you're an asshole when you start out, and you're an asshole when you get back."

The semifinals of the 2015 Briançon World Cup, France

Mayan Smith-Gobat gets her "systems dialed," Grand Valley Climbing, Colorado.

Perhaps the biggest irony of all is that climbers like to think of themselves as free-spirited nonconformists unconcerned with rules.

Yet climbing history, the blogosphere, and countless online chat groups tell a different tale. All are filled with vitriolic rants against people who are perceived as having broken the rules. Take Reinhold Messner for instance. Roughly once in a generation an iconoclast like Messner appears, a visionary who ignores the rules and changes the game forever. Yet in the process such individuals bring down a hell storm of criticism upon themselves from those who've spent their lives mastering the old game, only to watch in horror as it suddenly changes before their eyes.

When Messner learned to climb, there was a war raging over what constituted *fair means* in mountaineering. There were two schools. One believed that massive military tactics were required to climb big mountains. The rules of the Expedition siege game allow tons of equipment to be carried to base camp by armies of porters. Miles of fixed rope are used to connect networks of camps stretching ever higher until a summit party can be deployed. On the highest peaks, liberal amounts of bottled oxygen are used.

But Messner proved that even giants like Everest can be climbed *light and fast* in *alpine style*. Climbing without oxygen, Messner and Peter Habeler reached the summit of Everest as a team of two in 1978. In 1980 Messner returned, this time alone, and again without oxygen, he soloed the peak.

This was high-altitude alpinism, a new game with new rules, one that dramatically moved the needle away from technology, logistics, and overwhelming use of force, back to the red zone defined by the courage, commitment, and boldness of the individual.

In 1971 Messner wrote an essay titled "The Murder of the Impossible" that remains one of the most hotly debated texts in mountaineering literature. It was Messner's response to climbers like Cesare Maestri, who used expansion bolts to engineer routes up what were considered *impossible* mountain walls like Cerro Torre. Messner argued that the indiscriminate use of bolts removes the uncertainty from climbing, which renders the activity ultimately meaningless.

After all, if we can use technology to put a man on the moon, there's no question we can put a human on the summit of any terrestrial peak.

Half a century later, the argument over fair means continues. In 2012, when Hayden Kennedy and Jason Kruk returned to the village of El Chalten after chopping many of Maestri's bolts on the Compressor Route on Cerro Torre, they were arrested and spent a night in jail—*for their own protection*—from an outraged mob.

This is the problem with rules. They're all made up to begin with. Yet climbers, like all humans, become so caught up with how we believe the game *should* be played, we see any attempt to change the status quo as an attack on ourselves.

During the 1980s many traditional climbers became incensed when a group of Lycra-clad newcomers who came to be known as *sport climbers* began adapting radical new techniques such as bolting on rappel and hang-dogging (i.e., hanging on the rope to rehearse moves).

Across the United States, routes were chopped and fistfights erupted. Despite the fact that both techniques are nearly universally accepted today, variations of the "Bolting Wars" continue online and on the rock.

For better or for worse, sport climbing democratized climbing. It allowed the sport to spread to areas that had no mountains and to crags with no cracks. It lowered the threshold of gear, training, and risk required to play the game. Eventually it increased the number of participants to the point where it became economically possible to build modern climbing gyms and design better gear.

The result is that since the 1960s the number of climbers and the games they play have proliferated like lemmings. There are now climbers who only climb indoors. There are mixed climbers who have never sunk a pick in real ice.

As of 2016 a quick (but not necessarily comprehensive) list of modern climbing games includes Bouldering, Sport, Trad, Cragging, Big Wall, Alpinism, Expedition, Ice, Mixed, Soloing (Roped, Deep Water, and Free), and Competition.

But wait—within the Sport Climbing category alone there are finer distinctions—the Red Point game, the On Sight game, the Flash game. Competition climbing is a Pandora's box of subspecialties. Open it and you find Lead, Bouldering, Speed, Mixed, and Psicoblock.

And in perhaps the ultimate irony, those climbers like Messner, who ignore the rules and piss everyone off, are the most likely to become the superstar legends of their generation.

Take a skinny 14-year-old named Chris Sharma for instance. Sharma demonstrated that the traditional rules of rock climbing—moving slowly and statically, always keeping two points of contact on the rock—were great for a bunch of guys in wool sweaters putting up 5.9s in the Tetons—but that those rules had nothing to do with the future—and the future turned out to be 5.15. Hell, Sharma didn't even use his feet—one of the cardinal rules of all time.

And then there are visionary accomplishments like Tommy Caldwell and Kevin Jorgenson's 2015 ascent of *The Dawn Wall*, a big wall game so new, so visionary, it required a whole new set of rules to play in the process

Bridge crossing, Khumbu Icefall, Everest

leaving so-called experts stuttering on television trying to explain what had just happened.

No one aspect of climbing deserves more praise than another. In fact diversity is climbing's greatest strength. There's no way to get bored! Each game is so difficult, most people spend their lives trying to master just one. The beauty and variety of the various playing fields beckon from across the globe.

And at the same time, each game illuminates and informs all the rest.

It's like music. Your first love may be jazz, but your understanding and pleasure deepen as you learn to play all the musical genres. Why on Earth would you limit yourself to just one?

WHY I COMPETE

by Angie Payne

Introduction

As someone who learned to climb "B.G.E." (Before the Gym Era), I knew competition was an important part of why people climb, but I also knew I needed help explaining its virtues. After all, I'm one of those people, as Angie Payne describes, who feels faint at the mere thought of climbing before an audience.

But whether or not we like to admit it, competition has been integral to climbing since its inception. In 1786, once the summit of Mont Blanc was in sight, Jacques Balmat and Michel Paccard literally started racing each other to be the first to stand atop Western Europe's highest peak.

In his interview, Doug Robinson underscores a crucial distinction in understanding why people climb. Robinson points out that *all climbers* are pushed and pulled by two powerful, yet divergent, psychological forces—competition and spirituality. These two gravitational poles coexist within each climber, at all times, exuding a greater or lesser influence throughout their lives. Recognizing the split explains much about how people view, talk, and participate in the sport.

We've all known individuals for whom competition is the primary reason they climb. But where are they now? Chances are the moment they plateaued or got injured, they moved on to triathlons or mountain bike racing. Why? Because it was never climbing that mattered, what was important was competing, and there are infinite ways to do that.

For as Angie makes clear, the mental gymnastics required to compete well in climbing are far more challenging and strenuous than the physical demands. Sharma concurs. Both climbers emphasize that only a deep and abiding love of climbing in its purest sense allows one to endure the bruising emotional journey of competition.

Angie Payne races Emily Harrington during the 2015 Psicoblock Masters, Park City, Utah.

Old-school climbers may scoff at the spread of organized competition saying that's not what climbing's all about, but as Conrad Anker points out, in this day and age, it's hard to imagine an elite professional climber without a competition background. Sharma, Caldwell, Claassen, Honnold, Smith-Gobat, Ondra, Papert, and Slawinski—most of the people profiled in this book—have all been involved in competition at some stage. There's simply no other way to access the level of coaching, training, mental, and physical preparation starting at a young age necessary to become one of the world's best.

In the end what Angie made me see is that competition is simply another way to *love* climbing. Competition is innate in all the many games climbers play. It makes us try harder. It makes us better than we are. It inspires us and offers a glimpse of what we might become. And I can't think of anyone more qualified to sing the praises of competition than Angie Payne. I first met Angie when I profiled her for *Women Who Dare*, and I was knocked out—not only by her climbing talent but by how thoughtful, articulate, and fearless she is in expressing the challenges of bouldering at the highest level. In 2003 Payne was the Professional Climbing Association's overall female champion. She has won three American Bouldering Series National Championships and has had more than twenty additional podium finishes during her career. On the rock she's made the first female ascent of twenty-five boulder problems ranging from v9 to v12, and in 2010 she became the first woman in the world to climb a V13, *The Automator*. She's currently the communications and marketing coordinator for USA Climbing. Angie speaks eloquently for the new generation of climbers for whom climbing and competition are one and the same.

—Chris Noble

Why I Compete
By Angie Payne

I walked out of Isolation to face 2,000 sets of eyes. It was the final round of the 2011 Bouldering World Cup and I had a spot in the finals. The judge and I nodded to one another, and just like that, my 4 minutes began. *Step one, look at the problem. Think. Relax.* The holds were sparse. The problem was punctuated by a dyno midway through. *Don't freak out, you know how*

Remember competition's fun! Angie and Emily warm up.

to dyno. This is exactly what you've been training for. Had I encountered this type of sequence a year before, I would have had a slim chance of success. But 7 months of painful reprogramming of my climbing style had increased my chances. 3:35 . . . 3:34 . . . 3:33 . . . *time to try.* I climbed through the first two moves and found myself staring at the dyno. *Breathe, aim, ready, set, JUMP.* A collective sigh passed through the crowd as I fell. *That's okay, you were close. Stay calm.* I paced myself and rested another 30 seconds before pulling back on. 2:15, 2:14, 2:13 . . . *Try harder this time! Breathe, aim, jump, GRAB.*

Doing that dyno didn't secure a win or even a spot on the podium for me, but that moment is one of the most memorable in my 19 years of competition climbing. Confidence, uncertainty, composure, decisiveness, failure, breakthrough—everything I love about competition existed in those 2 minutes.

Winter 1996, age 12. I'm at my first climbing competition at the Rec Center Wall at Ohio's Miami University. My finals route starts on a slab—a challenge for nervous competitors—but I cruise it, because "Hey, it's just climbing, and

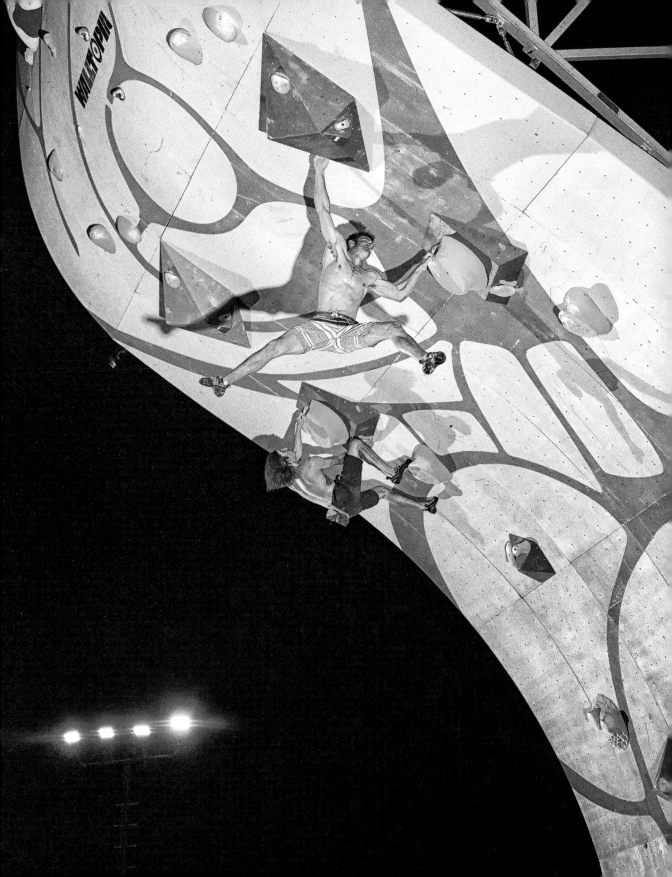

I'm not that nervous. After all, climbing's fun!" And so's winning my first comp.

For me, separating climbing from competition is impossible. As a kid I started climbing in a gym and immediately started competing. Many climbers, especially those from previous generations, came to climbing as a way to escape the rat race and connect with nature. But in the suburbs of Cincinnati, where I grew up, rock was scarce, and competitive sports were commonplace.

I've always been competitive. As a kid I was ninety-nine parts conformist, one part black sheep. I loved climbing because it was different but mostly because I was good at it. My friends had their sports, and mine was climbing. Getting involved in something edgy and obscure appealed to my rebellious streak, while competition provided the structure I craved.

As I grew, so did my desire to break out of the Midwestern norm. Competitions legitimized my involvement in a fringe sport while providing evidence to my parents that I was good at what I was doing. Of course, I didn't realize that all the while, my participation was also building self-confidence, problem-solving, a work ethic, and a whole laundry list of other traits that would serve me well. It was enough that I was naturally good at climbing.

Summer 1999, age 14. I'm at Youth Nationals waiting to compete. I hear the crowd and tears well up in my eyes. I'm not focusing on the enjoyment I get from climbing, or the character-building experience competition provides. I'm only thinking—when is this going to be over?

That was the first time I realized I was competing for others, not for myself. The actual *climbing* was secondary to success, and that wore me down. Competitions can do that. The anticipation and preparation, the enormous self-imposed pressure, and the complete unpredictability of competitions make them a guaranteed emotional roller coaster. When they're over, sometimes you find yourself at the top of the hill—and other times you find yourself a very long way down—in the gutter of frustration. If you stick with it long enough, you will undoubtedly experience every twist, turn, peak, and valley along the way. That summer was my first real low point, and I walked away from competition for several years.

Arjan de Kock gives his all against Daniel Woods in the 2015 Psicoblock.

As a young competitor my first choice was Lead climbing, but when I tired of it, I turned to the shorter stuff. At first I was *horrible* at Bouldering, but it allowed me the independence my teenage personality hungered for, so I kept at it. That's when I really fell in love with climbing for climbing's sake. I have a vivid memory of a night at the bouldering gym when I was flailing, heckled by friends. There was no formal competition. No awards. No expectations. It felt so good to try hard, to fight and push through the difficult moves. As I grappled with a sloper, it struck me. I truly loved what I was doing!

Three more years of flailing on boulder problems led me to Colorado. I was on the verge of actually being good, but I had no way to know. So I returned to competitions, with a renewed psyche and an appreciation of climbing for its own sake.

Spring 2004, age 19. I'm in the finals at the American Bouldering Series National Championship. Lisa Rands, one of my idols, just climbed, and I begin to realize I could potentially win, but only if I finish the final problem. I climb through most of it and find myself staring at the final hold. The crowd is cheering, but for a moment I'm frozen. I hesitate, almost give up, then something comes over me and I realize I have to go. I close my eyes, and for a split second time freezes. Suddenly I'm at the top.

That day I walked away with a win, and the knowledge I was capable of performing well. I rode that wave of confidence through several more big events. Competitions bring out traits I wish I could embody in my everyday life. Many of the moments when I've felt the most confident and fully in charge have been during comps. I try hard to reach my potential. I'm decisive. I move with purpose.

In the climbing gym or out at the boulders, it's easy to give a halfhearted effort. But when hundreds of spectators are cheering, it's a different story. Trying hard is . . . well . . . *hard*. Focusing every ounce of physical and mental energy on a single effort in climbing—or anything else—is something I rarely do. Sure, I like to think I *always* try hard. But in reality, I typically rely on my technique to do the heavy lifting. The kind of effort I'm referring to is the all-consuming, mind-numbing, everything-you-have (and then some), *TRY HARD!* The ability to tap into this whatever-it-takes experience is rare and illusive.

Adam Ondra considers his options during the 2015 Briançon World Cup.

In my life outside of competitions I'm terrible at making quick decisions. However, competitions do not allow the luxury of taking one's time. Decisions need to be made in split seconds. Procrastination is not an option. This forces me to trust my gut, my body, and to act. Sometimes the decisions I make are wrong, but at least they're quick and deliberate. For me this goes against the grain. I was born stubborn. As a rock climber that's often a blessing; it allows me to stick with bouldering projects for months, even years, until I succeed. But being stubborn during a comp isn't necessarily a strength. Comps force me to quickly abandon a method that isn't working and try a fresh approach. I'm more open-minded and creative when I compete than I am when the time clock stops.

Fall 2005, age 20. It was an unusual year when there were three Bouldering National Championships. I managed to win them all, preceded by an overall victory in the Professional Climbers Association Series. I was a freshman in college, struggling with homesickness, and I talked to my mom every day. One night after a win, I sat on the phone with Mom, attempting to understand the anxiety and emptiness I felt about my success. I felt like there was nowhere to go—but down. Winning did not bring me the happiness I thought it would.

I spent years focusing on my placement, comparing my performance to others. Now I found myself on top of the podium—but downhearted. Competitions bring out my best self—the confident, decisive, unattached, open-minded, creative person I wish I could be all the time. But the intensity of competitive situations doesn't discriminate, and with the good times come the bad. Competitions provide a stage to display one's strengths, as well as a very public display of one's weakness. Handing out medals, titles, and prizes can be dangerous. When you stand on top of a podium, you can make the mistake of actually believing you are the best at something—that you really are *the winner.*

But anyone who has competed knows that anything is possible on any given day. A climbing competition simply tests who performs best on *that day* on the particular challenges presented. The results must always be kept in perspective. On some level I have to convince myself that a competition is *very important* in order to do well. On the other, relying on results to provide personal validation and a measure of one's self-worth is a bad idea.

One of the biggest challenges of competition is trying not to compare one's performance to others. Sure, it's easy to say I'm only competing with myself—until the results are in and the prizes are handed out. I strive to remember that I should think only about *my* performance and how it compares to *my* own potential. In theory, this is great.

In practice, it's far more challenging than any of the physical problems climbing presents. There have been plenty of times when the best I could give turned out to be a winning performance, and of course there have been other days when my best wasn't good enough. I would be lying if I said that I focus solely on my own experience. I would be lying if I didn't admit I try harder

And the winners are: Jain Kim (Korea), Jessica Pilz (Austria), Anak Verhoeven (Belgium), Briançon World Cup 2015.

when I know someone else has already completed the problem. But when I find myself at the edge of this deep, dark hole, I try to remember just how great it feels when I climb without the burden of everyone else's performance in mind. I try to remember that moment during the World Cup when I wasn't worried about who else had done the dyno. I only focused on *doing it myself.*

Spring 2010, age 25. I'm climbing on an artificial wall next to Boulder Reservoir. I've made it to the final problem and have entered a sudden-death face-off with Alex Puccio. Whoever sends first—wins. I'm shaking out on a jug, two moves from the finish. Six months ago, I broke my ankle. This is my first comp since the accident. I'm very close to victory, but all I can think about is how happy I am to be climbing again. I turn to the crowd with a smile wide enough to make my cheeks sore, soaking up one of the happiest moments of my two decades of climbing. I don't win, but I've never enjoyed myself more at a competition.

It took 13 years to reach a point where I could leave a comp in second place and still feel like I enjoyed the experience. A lot had to change. I had to fail, succeed, fail again, be unhappy, mature, walk away, return, battle, deal with injury, and—most important—learn to remember that at the center of competitions is something I truly love

Many people get a bit queasy at the mere thought of climbing before a crowd. Growing up in competitions forced me to become comfortable with being the center of attention. After all, it's not those strangers I need to be afraid of—it's the person I know best—myself. To succeed at competition climbing you must embrace a paradox. You must believe in your ability to perform your best, while simultaneously abandoning all expectations. Expectations are the albatross hanging around every competitor's neck. It's not easy to climb with the extra weight, but the best somehow manage to remove the burden of expectation before the clock starts ticking.

After 19 years of competing, I still struggle with that challenge. To avoid being sucked into the black hole of expectation, self-criticism, and fear of failure, I must remain unattached. This is also something I struggle with in life. I've spent hours perfecting the subtleties of short sequences on rock, wrestling with the mental challenges that inevitably accompany repeated failures on boulder problems outside. Competitions force me to work through this process at an accelerated pace. Competitions impose an urgency that isn't present working a problem in the mountains. Outside, there's time to think—typically too much. But during a comp, there's no time to become invested. The problems never remain. While there's immense satisfaction in finishing a problem outdoors that required years of dedication, during a comp there's a certain freedom knowing that one's relationship to the problem has a time limit. In that way competition climbing is an excellent exercise in nonattachment.

Winter 2015, age 30. I'm sitting next to one of my closest friends, Alex Johnson, during the finals at Bouldering Nationals. We're halfway through the round when it hits me: This doesn't feel like it used to. I begin philosophizing to Alex about why things feel different now. Maybe it's because I'm not happy about my performance, or maybe it's because I feel the crowd isn't very excited . . . or maybe we've just been doing this for a very long time . . .

An hour later, much to our surprise, Alex and I found ourselves standing on the podium below Alex Puccio. There we were, three climbers who had competed with one another longer than some of the other competitors had been alive. I was thrilled to be on the podium again, but more than anything I was happy to be looking down with a healthier perspective that was years in the making. It felt like everything had come full circle.

The modern world is incomprehensibly complex, and my mind is a whirling speck in its midst—too often riddled with anxiety, worry, and frustration. Climbing muffles the din of the outer world. Once in a while when I'm climbing, I find an exquisite moment of stillness and calm. I listen to my body instead of my mind. I operate on instinct rather than habit. I block out everything and something magical occurs. It's a moment of inexplicable clarity when all the pieces of the puzzle temporarily align. Climbing competitions provide unique opportunities to tap into that stillness. Competing creates situations that transport me to that moment when the pressure's on, yet everything clicks, and life becomes euphoric.

Winter 2016, age 31. This time I'm on the other side of the curtain, working for USA Climbing, helping to organize the Bouldering Nationals. I'm watching young kids try boulder problems, and I'm seeing lots of tears. I can't help but see myself in these little climbers taking everything so seriously and being so hard on themselves. I want to point out how much climbing they still have to look forward to. "The failure you're crying about now will serve you well in later years! Even though it seems the world is ending now, the outcome of one competition isn't important. What's important is how you carry yourself; how you accept defeat and success; how you interact with other competitors; how you judge yourself; all the lessons that you learn. You won't remember the results of this comp, but you will remember the moments that define everything that competition climbing is—all the places you've been, the people you've met, the lifelong friends you've made. If you don't let the noise, pressure, frustration, repetition, failure, and success go to your head, you'll discover a true love for climbing—which is at the heart of it all. And with a little luck, you will learn that the true key to success is simply remembering what you've known from day one—that climbing is so much fun!"

THE HEROIC LIFE

The heroic attitude requires an endless supply of optimism. You must believe more in yourself than in the strength of what opposes you.
—Stephen Kaplan Williams

When I look up, the cold slaps me and I remember where I am. We got a late start on a long technical ice climb neither of us knew. Topping out at twilight, but unsure of the descent, we started rappelling, but lacking headlamps, it quickly became too dark to see if our single rope would reach the next ledge. So rather than risk a night hanging in space or prusiking up an icy rope, we elected to sit and wait for dawn.

Until you spend a night out without shelter, you don't know how long night can be. Unabashedly, my partner and I hug each other, using our bodies as the only barrier we have against the cold. As the saying goes, adventure begins when everything goes wrong. Yet most of what we believe we know of adventure we learn in the comfort of our own homes. As children snug in our beds, we read stories of Arthur and his knights, Harry Potter, or an island in the sky called Never Land. So it comes as a shock when 800 feet up a frozen waterfall we meet adventure face-to-face. Like a fist to the gut, there's the sudden realization that the adventure we meet in our own lives is not a fairy tale, movie, or video game. It is not someone else's story. It is our own—and happy endings are never guaranteed.

Sheltered behind the fortress walls of our civilization, humans forget that we are only tiny specks on a planet which is itself a speck drifting through the vast firmament of space and time. As Rébuffat wrote, "In this modern age, very little remains that is real. Night has been banished, so have the cold, the wind and the stars. They have all been neutralized: the rhythm of life itself is obscured."[1]

We forget that this is only one night in a billion nights in the life of the planet, and despite all our efforts, it will continue at its own pace. No need to

Tommy Caldwell on the North Face of *The Rostrum*, Yosemite. In a TED Talk, Caldwell said, "Hardship is inevitable, so put your goggles on and face into the wind."

Peter Croft racing thunderstorms in the California Needles

rush—toward sunrise, light, and warmth. Whether the wind rises, whether it snows, whether two climbers crouched on a ledge live or die is of no consequence whatsoever. Shivering in the darkness, I realize the greatest mystery is not death. The mystery is that we live at all. The balance is so delicate. More wind, a few degrees colder, one item less clothing. What loads the scales?

Lost in drugs as a teenager, a friend of mine went by chance to a mountaineering lecture and discovered the path he had been looking for all his life without even knowing he was searching.

"This was Homer," he said, "these stories were the modern equivalent of the story of Troy, the voyage of Odysseus. I realized that through mountaineering I could set out on that voyage as well."

Talk with climbers and you will hear some variation of this story time and again. As Peter Croft says, up until the moment he discovered climbing, "I had always felt like I was drifting through life, then in one instant I realized this is what I'm supposed to do. Everything changed."

What these men discovered was that to climb is to live mythically. That is to say, to live a life flecked with moments of meaning and connection as the night sky is flecked with stars, to feel whole once more, at home in one's own skin, in the natural world and in the universe. Carlos Castaneda wrote that in everyone's life there are many paths—but only one is the path with heart. At first glance, all paths look the same, but the path with heart leads to a life of coherence, integrity, and purpose, while the others lead to a pale and blood-less version of what life might have been.

Everyone dreams of being the hero of his or her own story, so we climbers become alchemists, placing our leaden souls in a crucible of stone and sky, turning up the heat with hunger, stress, and exhaustion—to see if some glim-mer of gold will emerge.

Can I control my emotions or will they control me? Can I handle the stress and gnawing fear? Will I sink into a pit of despair or fly on wings of joy? Who am I? What am I capable of becoming? All the questions of a lifetime are dis-tilled to a span of days.

Living at the northern rim of the world, the ancient Norse saw existence as a mythic struggle between elemental forces mountaineers know well—the armies of light, warmth, and creation pitted against darkness, cold, and chaos.

H. R. Ellis Davidson wrote that the Norse envisioned their gods as heroic versions of themselves:

> Men and women writ large, who led dangerous, individualistic lives, yet at the same time were part of a closely-knit group, with a firm sense of values and certain intense loyalties. They would give up their lives rather than surrender these values, but they would fight on as long as they could, since life was well worthwhile. Men knew that the gods they served could not give them freedom from danger and calamity, and they did not demand that they should. We find no sense of bit-terness at the harshness and unfairness of life but rather a spirit of resignation: humanity is born to trouble, but courage, adventure, and

the wonders of life are matters of thankfulness, to be enjoyed while life is still granted to us.[2]

This is the heroic view—the recognition that life is full of challenges and the way we meet them is what defines us. Yet the time of the Vikings is long past, and we now find ourselves living in a post-heroic age. The sound of wind rushing through a forest has been replaced by mass media's constant litany of despair. From birth we are taught to think small, to pursue money, comfort, and security above all other virtues, and that our highest purpose, our one true calling, is to be a good consumer.

Perhaps this is why the story at the heart of *Star Wars* resonates so strongly. In the modern world, boys and girls of all ages feel as though they have been abandoned on a desolate planet at the trailing edge of the galaxy. Told to scavenge among empty wreckage for anything of value, they wait. While within, an untapped and latent power waits with them—for The Call to claim their rightful life, a life of meaning, purpose, and adventure rushing at light speed through the stars above.

As a boy Peter Croft was in love with tales of adventure, especially Tarzan swinging through the jungle clothed only in a loincloth. Years later, on the day he first soloed *Astroman*, Croft found himself alone at the top of Washington's Column wearing only shorts and rock shoes. As he gazed out over Yosemite Valley, the air alive with swifts, he realized he had found his life's purpose. With a start, he recognized he was actually living his childhood dreams.

Elite climbers like Croft have enormous talent, drive, and dedication, but that is not what sets them apart. Yes, crushing finger strength and the ability to instantly read sequences and shake out on the merest rest are all important, yet more vital still is discovering and embracing one's destiny. Recognizing one's highest human purpose and potential; knowing why we are here on the planet—that is what makes human life meaningful.

And yet most of us don't have a clue. Most modern humans can't imagine why they are here or what their destiny might be. Most of us live a thousand miles from our full potential. But one thing is certain: Surround yourself with

Mayan Smith-Gobat racing nightfall, Shune's Buttress, Zion Canyon, Utah

complacency and fear and you will remain firmly rooted to the ground. Surround yourself with courage and excellence, and you will soar.

As a general rule, elite climbers are optimistic, disciplined, and self-assured. Which is not to say they don't have their share of faults or problems. No one has a perfect life. What's important is not to place one's hero on a pedestal and worship him or her. The key is to study the example of people we admire, then make their best practices our own. Just like us, the people who climb hard are flesh and blood. Just like us, they battle the same inner demons, disappointments, and setbacks, but the challenges they face make them more determined than ever to achieve their goals.

In September 2015, 8 months after his success on *The Dawn Wall*, I spent time with Tommy Caldwell in Yosemite. When I asked him if he ever felt

Doug Heinrich, Upper Weeping Wall, Canada. "It is not the goal, but the way there that matters, and the harder the way, the more worthwhile the journey," wrote Wilfred Thesinger in *Arabian Sands*.

despair after cutting off half his index finger with a table saw, he said no, that all he felt was more determined than ever to be a climber. When one of his doctors told him he might want to start looking for a new way of life, "It just pissed me off," Caldwell recalls. "The minute I got out of the hospital I started training 14 hours a day. I wanted to show him I could be even better than before."

In fact Tommy credits some of the darkest moments of his life—including his accident, being kidnapped in Kyrgyzstan, and a divorce—for leading to his biggest gains as a climber. In his presentations he talks about how his father, Mike Caldwell, taught him from an early age to view adversity and discomfort not as suffering, but as grand adventure, and how that attitude has shaped him. As Tommy puts it, modern humans are too focused on living lives of comfort and security. We are taught from birth to avoid risk and to see challenge as something to be avoided.

A month after Yosemite, I had the opportunity to take Tommy's attitude out for a test drive. It was now late October. My partners and I were 900 feet up a sandstone wall in Zion National Park. We had completed the climb, but it was getting dark, and despite a favorable forecast, a storm was building. We had gotten a late start, and in the interest of moving light and fast, we left our headlamps and rain jackets below.

At the first rappel I waited as my partners simul-rapped into the darkness. As they swung around searching for the next anchors, I thought back 30 years to the time my partner and I had endured a bitterly cold night out on an ice climb. In one crucial way that night, we had been lucky. The wind stayed calm and the cloud cover kept temperatures from plunging. After what seemed an eternity, dawn came. Stiff with cold we staggered up, jumping, stamping, and shouting life back into our wooden arms and legs. When it was light enough to see, we started rappelling once more. This time we made it down.

The memory reminded me of master alpinist Jay Smith talking about his cardinal rule of mountaineering. "The first rule is never to have a forced bivouac," Smith said laughing. "In other words, if you plan a bivouac, fine, but if you don't plan a bivouac, try not to have one, because it's going to be miserable. *So don't do that!*"

Maintaining a positive attitude on Pumori, Khumbu Himal, Nepal

Yet here I was in Zion once again facing the possibility of an unplanned night out. "How many times do you need to learn the same damn lesson?" I asked myself in disgust.

"What if we stick the ropes?"

"It's so dark, we won't even be able to see where they're caught."

"Why didn't you bring a knife? If the ropes stick, we won't be able to cut off a section so we can keep descending."

"What if it rains?"

"Then we're screwed! We'll spend the night hanging like a stringer of fish— soaking wet with no rope, no light, and no jackets."

But suddenly this mental tirade was interrupted by the memory of Tommy sitting calmly along the Merced River talking about his philosophy of looking for adventure in adversity. I remembered him talking about the weeks he had spent on El Cap, where the worse the weather grew, the more excited he became. How when other parties were bailing off the wall, he would remain snug in his portaledge reveling in the raw power of the elements.

"Okay," I asked the night sky, "what would Tommy do?"

I couldn't be certain, but I was pretty sure he wouldn't waste time and energy worrying about all the things that *might* go wrong. The difference was immediate and profound.

"Yes, it's possible we could stick the ropes," I thought. "Yes, it's possible it could rain. But it's also possible that if we simply take our time and pay attention, we'll soon be back in camp drinking beer."

Which is exactly what happened. We decided the wisest course was to rappel using only one rope. That meant more rappels and a slower descent, but it also meant we would have a second rope in reserve—just in case.

Hours later, when we made it back to the truck and the first raindrops splattered on the windshield, we all laughed with relief.

Zen masters say that enlightenment is only a hair's breadth from normal perception. Shift one's view incrementally and something magical occurs.

Everything changes, while nothing changes at all. Channeling Tommy didn't make the rain clouds disappear or eliminate the very real danger of being trapped high on a rock wall in a rainstorm without proper gear. *So don't do that!* But it did transform my inner experience. It helped me focus on the job at hand rather than the worst-case scenarios playing in my mind.

And it turns out that the research of modern psychology supports this view. A recent study at the University of Toronto has shown that a positive mood can actually improve how our visual cortex, the part of the brain that registers sight, processes information. Negativity narrows our focus and limits our options. We *literally see more* when we're positive.[3]

Nietzsche said it best, "*Amor fati.*" Learn to love your fate. With all your heart, with all your soul, learn to embrace what life brings and find the gift in it, even when it seems nothing remotely good could ever come from it. As Tommy says, "Hardship is inevitable, so put your goggles on and face into the wind."

For me, this is the essential lesson climbing teaches: That only by embracing the entire spectrum of human experience, good and bad, for better or for worse, do we find transcendence and joy. Whether we find ourselves high on a mountain wall or lost within the maze of modern life, the same question confronts us: Do I have the courage to accept my own life? Not the life we wish for. Not the life of the modern fairy tale that says we could all be happy if only we had more possessions, were more glamorous, or more famous. Not the life we feel entitled to, or should have had, but this one rare and precious life—the day-to-day, messy, screwed-up, and chaotic existence each of us has been given as a blank canvas.

Because we always have a choice. We can respond like victims and blame others. We can whine, complain, and make excuses. Or we can become the heroes of our own story and go forth bravely. After all, what would Tommy do?

SPIRIT MATTERS

I. Everest 1987

When I first saw her, I was startled—a westerner with a pale face sitting among the Sherpas in the teahouse kitchen speaking rapidly in Nepali. Later that evening she was in the dining hall, and I took a seat across from her. She told me she was French but she now lived at the monastery near Thame, a few hours walk from Namche up the Bhote Koshi river gorge. In my mind's eye I saw the *gompa* set among the cliff facets, the monk's quarters stacked like children's blocks upon the mountainside.

"There's a very ancient cave there," she said. "Did they show it to you? It's said that Padmasambhava himself (the patriarch who brought Buddhism to the Himalaya) meditated there. And now there is a great yogi living in it, a remarkable man."

I told her I felt something in the Khumbu different than any place I'd ever been, that in the way water quenches the body's thirst, the Himalaya seemed to quench the thirst of the spirit.

"There are many people meditating here," she answered. "Surely that is what you feel."

I told her I had come to climb Everest.

"What does it feel like climbing mountains?" she asked. "Does it bring you pleasure?"

I laughed. "I'm not sure pleasure's the word. I suppose you could say there's pleasure in overcoming pain and resistance. Often, climbing's an ordeal, but there's pleasure in pushing beyond one's limits."

"That's not what I mean," she said. "Do you not experience a certain lightness of being when you climb, a feeling that body and mind are one?"

"Yes, but only occasionally, when things are going well. I've done some meditation, and certainly there are similarities. After all, climbing requires long periods of intense concentration. Certainly it clears the mind. But these

A climber above the Mediterranean. James Hillman wrote, "An archetypal requisite of the soul is to live a life with passionate purpose."

mountains are so beautiful. Doesn't just the sight of them make you want to explore them for yourself?"

"I used to feel that," she said. "I lived near Chamonix and I climbed and hiked. But now I find all those feelings you describe in meditation. The mountains are only mountains. I feel no need to go up into them. I have everything I need sitting in my tiny hut."

I believed her. I believed that all the wisdom I would ever find humping loads through the Icefall, paying for each meter gained with willpower and searing breath, could be found by relinquishing all such striving—by simply sitting still, accepting life exactly as it is. But at the same time, I also knew I didn't have the courage to turn my back on the world. Not yet.

"Even if it's all illusion," I said, "I still need to find out what's hidden in those shining peaks."

She nodded with her Mona Lisa smile and we parted ways—she back to her meditation cave, and I to the wind, cold, and distance that awaited me.

I've often wondered how climbing might have been different if it had been practiced first in ancient India or feudal Japan. We moderns like to compartmentalize. We place spirituality in a box along with religion but separated from business, education, science, sports, and the arts. In the past the East made no such distinctions. In ancient India, China, and Japan any activity, no matter how mundane, was seen as an opportunity for spiritual growth—making tea, arranging flowers, doing calligraphy. From one perspective carrying water from a well is drudgery, but with a slight shift in attitude it becomes spiritual practice.

One of the most interesting aspects of modern climbing is that it shares many qualities with traditional spiritual practices, yet those similarities are rarely acknowledged. Climbers are reluctant to assign a higher meaning to what they do lest they sound religious, pompous, or preachy. But anyone who has practiced *One Legged Awkward Pose* balancing on a granite foothold while trying to fish an uncooperative stopper into a crack, recognizes climbing's similarity to yoga.

Dawn Glanc seeking "one-pointed focus" on *Flying Circus*, M8+, Ouray, Colorado

And while sitting with aching knees in a meditation hall is one way to calm the "monkey mind" and attain "one-pointed focus," another way to develop laser-like concentration is dry tooling on Camp Bird Road where every tool placement is overhanging and blind. Here seemingly solid placements skid across rock without warning, and the slightest outward pressure on the ax can send a climber blasting into space. Progress is gained by shinnying up the tool shaft with a physical and psychic stillness worthy of a Zen master.

In North America the Plains Indians once practiced the Vision Quest. Individuals would leave their community and go without food, water, and shelter to prepare for a visitation from the spirit world. Today alpinists travel to the Himalaya, Baffin Island, and Alaska to climb in situations where there is never enough of anything—warmth, food, water, rest, even oxygen—in order to distance themselves from the carnival atmosphere of modern society.

"Climbing acts like a kind of 'Big Broom,'" the Polish alpinist Yoykek Kurtyka said. "You experience fear, as well as the beauty of the mountains, which borders on ecstasy, and most of all, you have this feeling of great pride in your ascent. These powerful sensations sweep out, just like a Big Broom, all that neurotic garbage and all that shitty entanglement with the shitty world. Good climbing allows us to attain an inner freedom."[1]

Just as every climber has a different opinion about what climbing is, every human has a different take on what spirituality *means*. In 2016 Wikipedia offered this: "Traditionally, spirituality has been defined as a process of personal transformation in accordance with religious ideals. Since the 19th-century spirituality is often separated from religion and has become more oriented on subjective experience and psychological growth."

As Peter Croft observes, "There are times when you feel like there's so much more going on than science can account for. I don't go to church. I don't buy into that kind of thing, but at times it feels like, whether you're talking about "The Force" in *Star Wars* or some other term, that there is something more to the Universe than we understand. Maybe the word *spirituality* is a way to put a name to it."

For the purposes of this book, I define *spirituality* as connecting with something greater than ourselves, in order to transcend our personal limitations. I believe spirituality is a striving with all one's body, mind, and soul to achieve one's highest potential. In fact, all that we are, and all that we can ever be, can be seen as an expression of the spiritual energy we possess.

Like Buddhist practice, climbing offers a way or path, as well as membership in a community (sangha), which supports that way of life. Like most spiritual traditions, climbing cultivates beneficial qualities of character—focus, discipline, commitment, humility, and courage. And like all true spiritual practices, climbing heals the rift between body, mind, and spirit which is the central affliction of the modern world. When viewed from this perspective, climbing can be seen as *autotelic*—that is, an end in itself, not a tool or instrument of something else, but the expression of an elegant and noble way of being in the world.

II.

The cliffs smoke with spindrift. Blowing snow fills my eyes, burns my face. So much snow is spiraling down the frozen waterfall I feel a trace of vertigo as though I am falling—upward. The whole world is in motion. Ice dissolves into snow. Snow blends with mist. Sky flows into rushing cloud.

Only three things seem real: the sound of my breath, the tools gripped in each fist, and the exposure—the air beneath my crampon points, the distance to my last ice screw, the Day-Glo rope running down to my belayer.

I swing an ax and the ice shatters with a sound like crumpling glass. A cobweb of cracks materializes around the tool's pick. Suddenly I hear the blood drumming in my ears; feel the cramp of exertion in my forearms and calves.

The urge is to rush. To hope the tool placement is "good enough." To punch it past the vertical to where the angle softens and I can recover. But instead I ignore the fire alarm clanging in my head and force myself to slow down. I hang from the solid tool. Drop the other hand and shake. Gently I ease back on the throttle.

Slowly. Deeply. Relax. Release. I pull up on the good tool, shuffle my feet a few feet higher, and swing above the shattered ice. This time I'm rewarded by the wooden *thunk* of a solid placement. *Ahhh . . . move the feet. Now again . . .*

Five hundred years ago a Japanese Buddhist monk named Takuan Sōhō recognized the paradox lying at the heart of all dangerous activities. Takuan is famous for his essays on sword fighting written for some of the most renowned swordsmen of his day. For the samurai, the way of the sword was *literally* a game of life and death, one in which the slightest error could be fatal. Takuan pointed out that in battle those who cling most dearly to life, *those who are most afraid of dying*, are the most likely to be cut down. In climbing, the corollary is to say that the more afraid the climber is of falling, the more likely it is he or she will fall. No amount of training, no technical mastery can be effective, without the spiritual discipline necessary to overcome this *suki* (Japanese for a psychological gap in one's defenses).

Dealing directly with matters of life and death is warrior spirituality. It leaves questions about the existence of God to the theologians. It's not concerned with the hereafter, only the here and now—with doing dangerous things well. Climbing is not war, but at times it feels like it. High on the walls of Changabang, British mountaineer Peter Boardman observed: "This was like war: We were living under constant threat and danger, our cunning and stealth were being stretched as exactingly as if we had been commandos beyond enemy lines. Except here there could be no victors or conquered— but perhaps we could sneak up and down whilst the enemy was sleeping?"

As the psychologist William James said, the primary challenge facing modern man (especially young males coming of age) is to find a moral alternative to war. James realized that after basic needs are met, humans crave challenge. The trick is finding challenge that is not destructive to one's self, other living creatures, or the earth. Climbing offers an alternative to battle, one in which the war is waged internally, between different aspects of the self rather than externally, against enemies real or perceived.

Jim Bridwell concurs, "In many ways climbing is a peaceful substitute for war. Peace is the social yardstick to measure civilizations' advancement, and although peace is productive and positive, it can be boring. During our

Arjan de Kock attempting *The Nest*, v15, Red Rocks, Nevada. The climber Kryzstal Wielicki said, "To experience pleasure when you have everything against you, you must have some kind of warrior philosophy."

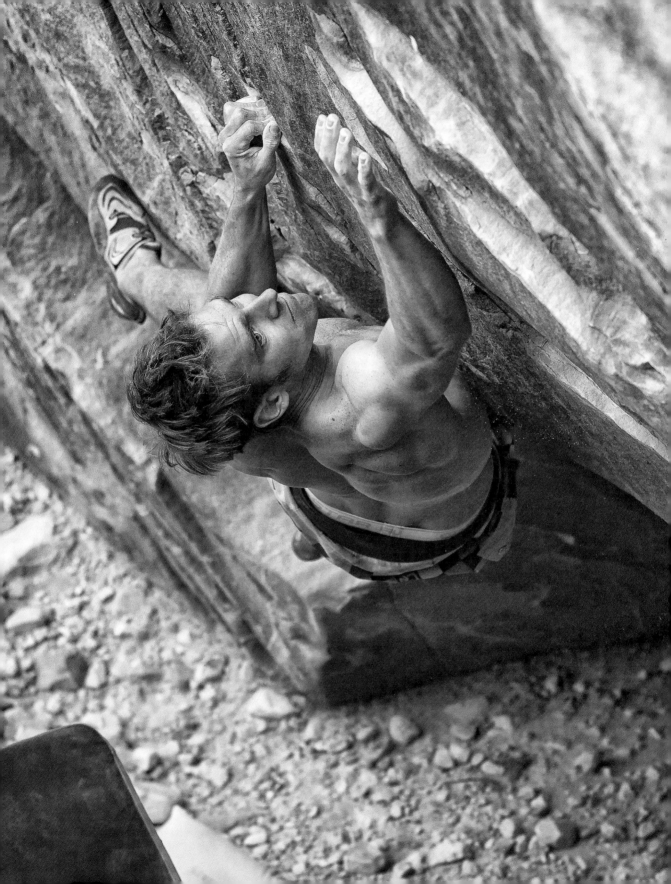

stone-age days we climbed to escape danger. Paradoxically, now that we are at the top of the food chain, we climb to expose ourselves to danger, filling one of our basic emotional needs and one component missing from modern civilization—real excitement."

Even climbers with decidedly nonmilitary personalities, like Sharma and Caldwell, talk about the *struggle and battle* of climbing. Both men have spent years battling gravity along with their own limitations on the hardest climbs in the world.

III.

What would happen if we did not condemn the world as a state fallen from grace, but viewed it as a realm voluntarily entered into as a game or dance, wherein the spirit plays?

—Joseph Campbell

In his book by the same name, British mountaineer Paul Pritchard refers to climbing as *"Deep Play."* The insight is brilliant because climbing is a form of play, yet it is serious—play with consequences. As Raphael Slawinski says, it is "a kind of game where the rewards are not necessarily commensurate with the potential losses."

Whether one climbs in the gym or the Karakoram, gravity never sleeps. Gravity and its allies—height and exposure—are formidable opponents. The risks are real.

"If you believe you know exactly what's going on, and that you know exactly what's going to happen—you're fooling yourself," says Slawinski about the dicey game of technical mixed climbing he likes to play.

Slawinski's right. The most dangerous gamble of all is to think it is we who control the board when the truth is, we are all pawns within a larger game played between Life and Death.

In her own book titled *Deep Play,* Diane Ackerman writes,

Deep play is that more intensified form of play that puts us in a rapturous mood and awakens the most creative, sentient, and joyful aspects of our inner selves . . . The savage is what we sometimes long to be, living by cunning and raw emotion, attuned to nature, senses alert, eluding danger, thrilled by challenge . . . One might even argue that all play is a contest of one sort or another. The adversary may be a mountain, a chess-playing computer, or an incarnation of evil. To play is to risk; to risk is to play . . . In Indo-European, *plegan* meant to risk, chance, expose oneself to hazard. A *pledge* was integral to the act of play, as was danger (cognate words are *peril* and *plight*). Play's original purpose was to make a pledge to someone or something by risking one's life.[2]

By risking life and limb climbers make a pledge to themselves to discover who they really are and discover what life really is. Because it's inescapable—the suspicion we might all be sleepwalking through our one brief and precious life. That existence is somehow a dream obscuring some deeper, more vivid reality.

Climber Will Gadd writes in his blog:

The most important thing in life for me is to see life as it is. Whether I'm in a relationship, climbing, skiing, building a set of stairs, working on a video, that's the goal for me. To strip away all my own filters and those I have been taught and to try and see things as they truly are. To be an attentive, caring, and switched-on human being. In the mountains I often feel like I operate close to this ideal; I never come close to it in the city, it's too energy sapping and mentally spinning. Time outside slows me down, filters my blood of aspirations and junk, and leaves me less cluttered physically and mentally. The mountains don't respect nonsensical prayer or cherished rosy beliefs, they just are. To see them cleanly and clearly is as close to the divine as I'll ever get.

Climbers are not alone in this quest. As Joseph Campbell observed, "I don't believe people are looking for the meaning of life, as much as they are looking for the experience of being alive."

The high-wire walker Karl Wallenda put it this way, "Walking the wire is life, everything else is just waiting."

And in his obituary for climbing partner Gary Hemming, with whom he made the first ascent of the *American Direct* on the Dru, Royal Robbins wrote, "He seemed to want, so much, to be alive. That's why he picked the route on the Dru. He wanted to live fully. And for those few days—amid the lightning, the wind, and the burnished stone—we did."

IV.

I come to a place where the ice forms a hollow shell less than an inch thick. Through holes in the ice, I see the living stream rushing over moss-covered rock. When struck, the ice booms like a drum. No bashing here. Gentle as a surgeon I hook my tools. Quiet as a burglar I tiptoe the monopoint of one boot out onto a dagger of ice hanging in space. I reach out with an ax and peck softly. A quarter inch of steel slides home. I drape the second tool over my shoulder and take a deep breath. Grasping the seated tool with both hands, I step out onto the dagger. It holds. In a few more moves, I've reached the anchors on the ledge above. Off belay!

Pop culture is like a raging river a million miles wide, but only a single pixel deep. There is no depth. How could there be? To find depth one must stay and dig in one place, perhaps for years, and the modern world is far too ADD for that. Instead we are all blindly rushing ahead looking for the next big thing. But when there are immediate and spectacular consequences attached to our actions, we are forced to slow down and pay attention. As Sharma says, "I've done meditation retreats, but the fact is, when I go climbing I can tap into a meditative state of mind so much easier than I can sitting in a room with crossed legs."

Everyone pays attention to something. The question is to what? We can spend our lives paying attention to Taylor Swift's Twitter feed, playing Fantasy Football, or batting emojis back and forth with our friends. Or we can use that same time and attention to compose a song, write a book, or, as Sharma did when he was 17, walk for a thousand miles alone through rural Japan.

The Grand Charmoz, French Alps. Alpinist Anatoli Boukreev said, "Mountains are not stadiums where I satisfy my ambition to achieve. They are the cathedrals where I practice my religion."

Legendary climber Ron Kauk in Yosemite. In his book *Letters from Sacred Rok*, Kauk writes: "The movement of my body through physical space requires the coming together of my body and psyche with the spirit of the natural world."

For the goal of all spiritual disciplines, and the key to high achievement in any field, is the control of consciousness. As psychologist Mihaly Csikszent-mihalyi wrote in *Flow: The Psychology of Optimal Experience,* "We have all experienced times when, instead of being buffeted by anonymous forces, we feel in control of our actions, masters of our own fate. On the rare occasions that it happens, we feel a sense of exhilaration, a deep sense of enjoyment that is long cherished and that becomes a landmark in memory for what life should be like."

The flight of a falcon skimming a cliff's edge. Silver mist wreathing an unknown summit. The fragrance of snow, cold metal, and wet leather that rises from the pack at the end of a day of ice climbing and with it the feeling of wholeness knowing that for a time, I was able to master myself. For one brief and magical moment, body, mind, and spirit became one.

Again and again, in mountaineering literature and spiritual texts, we find the longing to transcend ordinary consciousness and merge with something vast, beyond words, concepts, or limitations. According to the sacred texts of India, "There is a spirit that is mind and life, light and truth and vast spaces."

This is the spirit climbers are hopelessly in love with. This is the mystery, the fact that a physical act can somehow lead us beyond the ordinary. As Chris Kalous says, "Everyone fantasizes about living close to the edge, but climbers get to do it. That's what we're really up to. We're living mythical lives!"

Humans are continually pulled by two competing urges. On the one hand, the spirit longs for height, transcendence, and the eternal. On the other, the soul loves the world and all its attachments, the benediction of normal hours. Just home from an expedition, a hot bath and warm bed seem the only heaven we could ever desire. No need to visit the stars, one can become lost for hours in the constellations of dust swirling in a shaft of sunlight. Climbing simultaneously opens our minds to a vast world full of potential and grounds us in the deeply personal; in friendship, love, and loss; in longing and com-munity. Living with all these seemingly disparate and unruly impulses under one roof is what it means to be human. Uniting it all in one consciousness is spiritual practice.

PARTNERSHIP, LOVE & LOSS

A ship in port is safe, but that's not what ships are for.

—**Grace Murray Hopper**

It's early Sunday morning when a call from an unknown number wakes me.

"Who could be calling so early?"

I click off the phone and roll over. Moments later a text arrives.

"Chris, it's Mariel. I have urgent news about Mark. Please call."

It's the call that climbers, and those who love them, hope will never come. In the next few minutes I learn that one of my dearest friends and my closest climbing partner, Mark Davis, has been killed in Indian Creek. He was descending a route and rappelled off the end of an uneven rope. He died on the scene from massive head trauma.

I set down the phone and suddenly am transported. The edge of the bed becomes a granite shelf above lucid water. I watch a single trout floating in a shaft of light. Uphill from the lake, Mark lets out a shout. I chuckle, knowing its part of an ongoing war he's waging against chipmunks determined to steal his food. I gaze up at the Elephant's Perch wreathed in mist and cloud. Yesterday we climbed *The Fine Line,* topping out in alpenglow. Today it's stormy. Mark's put out, but secretly I'm glad to have the rest.

Someone's sobbing. I realize it's my wife beside me in the bed. Her tears snap me back to the present, to the call, and a reality I want no part of. Impossible! In a few days I'm driving south to meet Mark in Moab. Look—the guidebooks, the cams, the ropes are already laid out, ready to go. We're going to take care of unfinished business on a desert tower, then head to the Creek. This summer we're going to the City of Rocks, back to the Sierras. Someday we're going to the Dolomites, Alaska, the Canadian Rockies . . . We have a lifetime of plans. I stare at the phone willing it to ring again, to hear this is all some terrible mistake. That he's up. He's walking. He's laughing. He's fine.

Kindred spirits Conrad Anker and Peter Croft, the Needles

But somewhere in the basement of my heart I know the second call will never come. Death is final. It torpedoes life, then leaves we survivors struggling to heal the breach as the sea rushes in.

Eleven years younger, Mark was continually schooling me about climbing and life. Growing up poor in Georgia in his youth, he wrestled with alcoholism. After high school he discovered the film business and AA. He got clean, moved to LA, and began climbing during breaks from work as a Hollywood cameraman. Seeking a calmer life, he eventually moved to Salt Lake to teach filmmaking at the local community college. I liked him from the moment we met. With most people I'm guarded and reserved, but there was something about Mark, his easy laugh, the fact he didn't take himself too seriously that drew me. He was the finest climber I know—who didn't look like a climber. I might have been slightly better at redpointing limestone, but on granite and sandstone he moved with the grace and precision of a dancer half his size. He would waltz up granite puzzles that left me scratching my head, and once he used hand stacks to hike a wide crack in the desert I could barely toprope. For years he talked about how he was going to lose weight and climb 5.13, about how he was going to Baffin Island to put up new routes. And for a long time I believed him.

For Tibetan Buddhists the Bodhisattva Manjushri is the embodiment of discerning wisdom. In his hand, Manjushri holds a flaming sword he uses to cut through all illusion. I have now learned that death is such a sword. The moment I heard of Mark's passing, many things I had not seen before became clear.

First, that a good climbing partnership is a rare and precious thing. It is a gift from the gods of high places that should never be taken for granted. Like a good marriage, a climbing partnership is more the result of luck and serendipity than reasoned purpose. It is a subtle alchemy arising from a million possible combinations of personality, temperament, and inclination. Second, that death rips away the veil obscuring those things we would rather not see. "Fool," it says, "what are you waiting for? Life is fleeting."

Physically Mark and I were quite different, but we were well matched. I'm tall and thin. He was short and stocky, but we weighed the same. More

"Thatta girl!" Madaleine Sorkin and Kate Rutherford, Black Canyon of the Gunnison, Colorado

important, the stars of our interests aligned. We were both stoked for sport, trad, or ice—at a moment's notice—it didn't matter as long as it was climbing. I looked forward to the hours we spent driving. When I told him what was driving me nuts, we always ended up laughing about it. I returned home feeling clean and unburdened.

Last year unknown to one another, in a single week, we each bought a copy of *The Rock Climber's Training Manual* by Michael and Mark Anderson. I suspect we both hoped to surprise the other with a demonstration of crushing new strength (I know I did) before revealing the source. We were competitive, but in the low-key way middle-aged men can be. It was fun to have a partner interested in the same lowly projects. It was fun to occasionally win a race—by inches rather than a mile. We supported each other's successes as much as our own, and after reading the book, we both agreed that now that we finally knew how to train, we no longer had any time or energy to climb.

We trusted each other's judgment, but even more important we trusted each other emotionally. The youthful days of having a pissing match to see who was the bigger man were gone. We knew we would support each other regardless of who shouted "Take!" and that trust gave us the courage to go farther than we had gone before. As Peter Croft says, a true partner is "someone who inspires you to be better than you are."

Damn it, Mark! I realize now how much I wanted to see us grow old together. I had assumed there would always be one more trip, and that there would be plenty of time to sit, talk, and reminisce about all we had done, and to bullshit about all we were about to do. I probably could never have told you this when you were alive, but now I know how much I loved you. Yes, I'm mad you're gone, but I'm not mad at you. I just wish our journey could continue. I wanted to watch your footwork. I wanted you to show me how to climb off widths, and I wanted to show you everything I've learned as well.

I could say that if it weren't for climbing, Mark would still be alive. But without climbing it's unlikely we would ever have met, and without a shared passion we would never have become as close. As I age I realize the only thing

Best friends Tommy Caldwell and Alex Honnold, Leaning Tower, Yosemite

"You've got this!" Arjan de Kock supporting Paige Claassen during a project in the Virgin River Gorge, Arizona.

we truly control is our response to what life brings. May we find the gift in it. As painful as death is, its gift is to open our eyes to what the heart treasures— the love that we share.

I once attended a Native American ceremony where I was shocked to see a grown man, a Lakota, stand up and weep openly before the crowd. He wept for what had been done to his people and he wept for what was being done to the earth. Then he said, "Don't ever be afraid or ashamed of your tears. Tears cleanse the heart, they prepare it to receive even more love than before."

That was one of the bravest things I've ever seen.

The last day we climbed together, Mark and I were working a route with a bouldery start. After clipping the first bolt, Mark flew off the rock, lifting me in the air. We slammed together like two hands clapping, our chalk bags trapped between. There was a tremendous explosion of chalk.

When the cloud finally cleared, we were left hanging, looking like we'd been dipped in flour.

Croft and Anker in the Needles. As Croft says, "A true partner is someone who inspires you to be better than you are."

"Good thing I'm wearing all black," I said, and we laughed till we cried.

As someone wise once said, nothing lasts forever, or ends completely. Mark, you left us in the spring just as the light was beginning to linger in the desert and the cottonwoods were turning green. The rest of us will go on. But know that I will miss you when I enter the canyons. When I see the light upon the cliffs, I will think of you always.

CONRAD ANKER
& PETER CROFT

How often do any of us get to hear climbers of the caliber of Conrad Anker and Peter Croft riff on why they've devoted their lives to our crazy sport? In the spring of 2015, I accompanied Croft and Anker on a climbing trip to the California Needles. Since I had both of them together in one place, I decided to conduct their interviews as a conversation. All the other profiles in this book are based on individual interviews with the featured climber.

Introduction: Conrad Anker

I laid my head on the snow and coughed. Coughed until I thought my lungs would burst and my ribs would crack. A deep interstellar cold penetrated every fiber of my being. Climbing in the Himalaya, every step upward is a victory of will over weakness, every pause, an invitation to turn back. The climber continues, driven by a single desire, laughable in its absurdity, simply to finish what he or she started. To stand at the apex of a tower of ice, rock, and snow and gaze out.

It was 1990 and Conrad Anker and I were making a winter ascent of one of the world's most lovely peaks—Nepal's Ama Dablam. Suddenly the fluted snow we were climbing ended. We found ourselves suspended in a turquoise sky, encircled by all the peaks of the Khumbu: Kwangde, Thamsersku, Makalu, Lhotse, Pumori, Cho Oyu, Cholatse, Taweche, and above them all, the black pyramid of Everest, with its eternal plume of wind-driven snow.

The High Himal is a world apart, inhuman both in its beauty and its severity. It's a world few visit, but Conrad Anker calls it home. Anker's résumé reads like a syllabus for a PhD in mountaineering. He has partnered with many of the most brilliant alpinists of his generation: Galen Rowell, Mugs Stump, Seth Shaw, Alex Lowe, and most recently David Lama. Anker has literally spent

Yeats asked, "How can we know the dancer from the dance?"
Peter Croft, *Airy Interlude* (10b), The Needles

years studying in the world's greatest open-air classrooms: Yosemite, Zion, Alaska, the Karakoram, the Pamirs, Antarctica, Baffin, and Patagonia. In the Khumbu, along with Ama Dablam, he has summited Everest three times. On his first ascent, he discovered the body of George Mallory, and he completed his third without supplemental oxygen, making him a member of one of the world's most exclusive clubs.

I first met "Rad" in the early 1980s when he was still a kid, a member of a pack of young motivated climbers getting after it in Utah's Wasatch Range. At the time he was endlessly happy, enthusiastic, keen, and perhaps a bit silly and goofy.

Even though many years and mutual friends have passed since those days, and even though he has matured into one of the most recognized and respected mountaineers in the world, I'm happy to report that when you get him out in the hills—nothing's changed. Conrad is still the same hyperactive kid in a candy store I knew decades ago. Which is all the more remarkable considering his chosen path. As many climbers in this book observe, climbing big glaciated mountains is an exceedingly dangerous game. Some of Anker's closest friends and partners—Stump, Shaw, and Lowe—are all gone.

In 1999 I was in Bangkok on my way to Bhutan. The elevator door in the airport hotel opened and I was shocked to find a bruised and bandaged Conrad standing before me. He was on his way home from Shishapangma, where Alex Lowe had just been killed in an avalanche. When the slide hit, Alex jumped one way and Conrad jumped the other. Alex was swept away, and Conrad survived. That night we spent hours sharing memories of Alex, whom his friends call *The Fiend* due to his supernatural energy. Losing a friend to a climbing accident is a life-wrenching experience. It makes individuals question their assumptions about acceptable risk. But when an icon like Stump or Lowe is killed, it makes the entire climbing community stop and question why we climb.

Anker has had to grapple with those demons far more than most, but to paraphrase what he says in the following pages: Yes, pursuing a life in the mountains can be touched by sadness and loss. Yes, mountaineering involves suffering and deprivation. But the biggest tragedy is to never try at all. The biggest sadness is to never discover one's passion. The biggest loss is wasting our one rare and precious life.

Conrad was mentored by the best, and now, as captain of The North Face athlete team, he is passing his experience on to a whole new generation. He is an outspoken witness to the calamity of climate change, and he has helped spread the gospel of adventure through films like *The Wildest Dream* and *Meru*. A chronic overachiever, Conrad is deeply committed to giving back. He serves on the board of the Conservation Alliance and the Rowell Fund for Tibet, and he spearheads the Alex Lowe Charitable Foundation, which trains Sherpas in the skills of mountaineering. He embodies the words of his motto: "Be good, be kind, be happy."

—*Chris Noble*

Career Highlights

1987 Gurney Peak, *Southeast Face*, Kichatna Spires, Alaska VI 5.10 A3, New Route

1989 Mt. Hunter, *Northwest Face*, New Route

1990 *Stump Anker* Route, Streaked Wall, Zion N.P. VI 5.11 A4, New Route
Ama Dablam in winter

1992 *Stump Spire*, Sam Ford Fiord, Baffin Island, IV 5.11, First Ascent

1994 *Badlands*, Torre Egger, Patagonia, VI 5.10 A3, New Route

1995 *Russian Shield,* Russian Tower, Ak-Su, Kyrgyzstan, VI 5.10 A3, New Route

1997 *Continental Drift,* El Capitan, Yosemite N.P. VI 5.10 A4, New Route
West Face Latok II, Karakoram, VII, 5.10 A3, New Route
Rakekniven, Snow Petrel Wall, Queen Maud Land, Antarctica VI, 5.10, A3, First Ascent

1998 Spansar Peak, Karakoram, Pakistan, VI 5.11, First Ascent

1999 Summited Everest. Discovered the body of George Mallory, who along with Sandy Irvine disappeared there during a summit bid in 1924.

2007 Summited Everest for the second time

2011 Meru Central Peak, Karakoram, New Route

2012 Summited Everest for third time, without supplemental oxygen

2015 *Latent Core*, Zion N.P. 5.11 A1, New Route with David Lama

For me, climbing truly is "freedom of the hills," Anker says. "You're out there and you're able to interact with nature. Climbing is a creative space where you're living in the moment."

Conrad Anker in the Needles. Anker points out that exploration of the inner and outer worlds remains one of the primary reasons people climb.

Introduction: Peter Croft

Stand around enough campfires drinking beer, and you'll notice that when veteran climbers start talking about those they admire, Peter Croft's name always comes up. Croft is a climber's climber, someone who has never sought the spotlight, but whose accomplishments blaze with a light all their own. The first free ascent of *Moonlight Buttress*. The first linkup of *The Nose* and Half Dome in a day. The first free solo ascents of *Astroman* and *The Rostrum*. Epic traverses in the High Sierra.

Doug Robinson calls Croft "the most joyful climber alive today," and I would have to agree but with the small caveat that Peter can be a bit grumpy until he's had his twin fix of climbing and caffeine. Croft embodies the archetype of the *lifer*, someone who climbs for love and does so with a childlike enthusiasm and humility that's infectious. As Peter says, "I take climbing *very* seriously, but I don't take myself seriously."

Even at age 58, Croft can't get enough. As he says, he started soloing because in the early days when his partners wanted to spend afternoons at the Squamish bakery he couldn't bear wasting the remaining daylight.

On our last day in the Needles, a storm was approaching, but we wanted to pack in one last climb. Peter and Conrad hiked around to the southwest flank of the pinnacle known as *The Witch*, while I rappelled from the top to photograph them. We had planned to shoot a route Peter was familiar with, but I ended up too far to the side. The wind was howling. The horizon was a mass of clouds. It was clear there wasn't time to jug back to the top and reset the ropes.

To my right I spotted a promising line with a random scatter of bolts, a few old buttonheads. The Needles are infamous for heady and runout climbing, and this route appeared to end at a bolt with a bail biner—never a good sign. I shouted down that our plan wasn't going to work. "What about that route to my right?" I asked. "I don't know what it is," Peter shouted, "but I'm willing to give it a go. If I don't like it, I can always climb back down."

What followed was a master class in the climbing arts. In a wind that batted me around like a piñata at the end of my rope, Croft slowly, patiently made his way upward, tiptoeing swiftly across blank sections, linking the calligraphy of flakes, ridges, and incipient cracks. Deciphering cryptic gear placements, looping runners over flakes then weighting them with cams so they wouldn't blow off. When he reached the bail biner, I shouted that he could lower off if he wished.

"No way," he responded. "That would be terrifying! I'm not sure this old bolt would even hold body weight."

So he continued, running it out 60, 70, finally 150 feet to the top of the spire. When Conrad reached the belay he was smiling. "RESPECT!" he said with enthusiasm. "That was an incredible lead."

"How can we know the dancer from the dance?" asked the poet Yeats, and watching Croft climb, it's clear we cannot separate the two. Grace. Economy of motion. A relaxed calm presence, whether the route is 5.7 or 5.12, regardless of how run out or dicey the pro. Even after 4 decades of devotion, sheer delight in moving well in mountains.

—Chris Noble

Career Highlights

1982 *University Wall*, Squamish Chief, British Columbia, V 5.12, First Free Ascent with Hamish Fraser and Greg Foweraker

1984 Solo linkup of four big routes in the Bugaboos, Canada

1986 Linkup with John Bachar of *The Nose* on El Cap and *The Northwest Face* of Half Dome, Yosemite

1987 First Solo Ascent of *Astroman* and *The Rostrum*

1992 *Moonlight Buttress*, Zion National Park, First Free Ascent with Jonny Woodward

1998 Spansar Brak, Karakoram, Pakistan, First Ascent of 8,000-foot knife-edge ridge with Conrad Anker, 5.11

1999 *Evolution Traverse*, The Sierras, VI 5.9, First Ascent Solo

2004 *Airstream*, *The Incredible Hulk*, Sierras, V 5.13, First Ascent with Dave Nettle

2004 *Venturi Effect*, *The Incredible Hulk*, V 5.12, First Ascent with Dave Nettle

2012 *Valkyrie*, Angel Wings, Sierras, V 5.12, First Ascent with Dave Nettle and Brandon Thau

2014 *Wind Shear*, The Incredible Hulk, V 5.12, First Ascent with Dave Nettle and Andy Puhvel

A Conversation with Conrad Anker and Peter Croft

Why don't you two introduce yourselves?
Conrad: Hi, I'm Conrad Anker. I was born the 27th of November, 1962, and I'm a climbing enthusiast of all types and disciplines.
Peter: And my name's Peter Croft. I was born in 1958, and I'm not really a specialist, I'm just a climber. Mostly rock, but I like all types.

So Conrad, how long have you been climbing and how did you get started?
Conrad: I was introduced to climbing by my dad and a couple of his buddies. Climbing was sort of an offshoot of being outdoors backpacking and things

like that. My first climbing experiences were with my family in California. My family is from Big Oak Flat near Yosemite. Every summer we would go peak bagging in the high Sierra with a mule train carrying supplies. Then during the eighties and nineties, I was a student living in Salt Lake City and I climbed as much as I could.

Was it love at first sight?
Conrad: My first technical climb was in Boulder Canyon in Colorado. A friend took me up *Wind Ridge,* a steep and airy 5.6 and I didn't have climbing shoes. I thought, 'Wow, this is a whole new level." It's beautiful and there's this exhilaration when you have to rope up and the risk is far more imminent and part of the equation.

How old were you?
Conrad: I was 16 or 17. That was about the same time I climbed Mt. Rainier. I thought that to be a mountaineer you had to have glaciers and crampons and wear knickers and be able to yodel. So I needed a rite of passage like Rainier to bring all that together.

Peter, what about you?
Peter: Well, I never wanted to be a climber because all I knew about climbing was what I saw on TV, and it looked like some kind of daredevil thing. But at the same time I never connected to any sports, I just loved being outside.

Then a friend turned me on to a book by the British mountaineer Chris Bonington, *I Chose to Climb.* At first I didn't want to read it, but eventually I picked it up, and reading about Bonington's adventures made me realize that it wasn't a *sport* I had been looking for—it was *adventure.*

I loved watching Tarzan movies when I was a kid, and as soon as I read about climbing, I knew I had to try. My first climb wasn't even in a real climbing area. It was on some junky rock on Vancouver Island where I lived. But the very first step up onto stone was like discovering who I really was. It was that intense. Up until then I had always felt like I was drifting through life, then in that one instant I realized this is what I am supposed to do. Everything changed.

How old were you?
Peter: Same as Conrad. Probably 16 or 17.

Why do you think you had that initial resistance to reading Bonington's book?
Peter: Because I didn't really get it. I thought climbing was like bullfighting or jumping out of an airplane. It seemed like a way to show off, and it didn't seem connected to nature. I suppose that's a fairly common point of view. The general public sees a film like *Cliffhanger* and they think that's what climbing's all about.

But for me climbing became a way to find out who I really was—through action that was under my control. I got to say what I wanted to do, when I wanted to do it, and how long I wanted to go.

How did you two meet?
Conrad: I was living in the Bay area and I had met Galen Rowell, who was a photographer, running companion, and climbing partner. Galen was always finding younger climbers to get out with, and for a few years I was that guy. He and I dreamed up the idea of making a trip to the Charakusa Valley in Pakistan. Galen knew Peter, so we invited him.
Peter: But the original plan was to go to a place in India called the Bilafond Valley, which is disputed territory between India and Pakistan, and a week before we were due to fly, there was some kind of skirmish and the whole place closed down. So just as we were ready to board the plane, we had to come up with a whole new plan. We ended up going to the Charakusa with virtually no prior knowledge, just hoping something would pan out.
Conrad: Yeah, Galen was sure he could get us permits because he had friends in high places, but they all said no. So we ended up in the Charakusa, and it was beautiful.
Peter: As it turned out, it was even better than we'd hoped, an incredible place.

But you didn't have an objective? Just went in thinking, "Oh well, we'll find something"?
Peter: We didn't have a clue. Before we arrived, I had never even seen a photo of the place. But we hiked for a couple days, turned a corner, and our jaws just dropped . . .

Croft climbing *Wicked West of the Witch*, 5.10+X, The Needles. "I take climbing very seriously," Croft says, "but I don't take myself seriously."

Conrad: Yeah, it was a trip where double boots, crampons, and ice axes were not part of the equation. We wanted to go rock climbing, and if you add all those other things, suddenly the grade of the climbing drops, and you're wallowing in snow, and fiddling with your stove . . . Our goal was to climb harder stuff on rock at lower elevations.

Peter: We were hiking and suddenly I charged ahead, because I had seen this perfect knife-edge ridge on Spansar Peak. It was like nothing I'd ever seen anywhere, not even in pictures. It was what I had been looking for—kind of an ideal climb. Galen didn't climb it with us, but he checked it out from a number of different angles and estimated it was about 7,000 vertical feet.

Conrad: Yeah we climbed it in a day—I mean a full 24 hours.

Peter: Yeah, it was just under the magic 24-hour mark. But the whole trip was short. As soon as we arrived in base camp, I came down with some sort of lung infection. With only a few days before we had to leave, I was still coughing, but I felt good enough to go. Then Conrad hikes up valley and visits an Italian base camp. He eats something bad and in the morning he's lost his dinner—all around his tent. So we lose another day. And now it's getting very close to our departure. In fact, we have only one day left. So we wake up at 3 in the morning and we're ready, but it's raining. We go back to bed, wake up, and it's still raining. Finally, we're just hanging out, bummed that we can't climb, so we start drinking coffee. We start pounding the coffee, and finally we drank so much caffeine we *had* to do something—so we went for it. And once we got a third of the way up the ridge, we were too far up to rappel back down. We only had one rope and not a huge rack. It was the most amazing ridge climb I'd ever done. We topped out just as the sun was setting. No one had ever climbed the peak before, and the summit was a blade of granite. We each did a pull-up on the summit, then we hand traversed down to a ledge where darkness found us, and we started rappelling through the night.

So have you been climbing together ever since?

Conrad: Yeah, we get together about once a year. I'll come to Bishop, we'll watch Colbert, then get up at 4 in the morning, and climb until 2. We'll have margaritas from 2 to 6, go to bed at 8, and wake up and do it all again. We're both on the same early morning schedule, so we can get a bunch of climbing done. Some of our Sierra adventures have been really good—like the time we went to *The Incredible Hulk*. Others we've tried, like *The Eternal Traverse,* got dogged down by trying to bring a camera crew along. So we will need to go back and do that one again without cameras.

Peter: Definitely. Get Hollywood out of the picture.

Conrad: Yeah. Just go climbing.

What has shaped and influenced you as climbers?

Conrad: Hopefully this won't sound too much like a cliché, but I would say that climbing for me truly is *the freedom of the hills.* You're out there and you're able to interact with nature. Climbing is a creative space where you're living in the moment.

It's the same spirit my dad and his buddies were searching for when we first went peak bagging, and being in the high country is an important part of that.

Then as I matured and started climbing all the time, there was this one fellow, Mugs Stump. Mugs was an alpine climber who in the mid-1980s made visionary ascents around the world, but especially in Patagonia and Alaska. He played football at Penn State, and he was a very intense and driven man. And being 13 years older, he became a mentor. He got me going and helped me find my focus.

Eventually I transitioned to climbing with people who were more my peers. Guys like Peter, who's a better climber than I am, but we're peers in terms of age, and our different climbing abilities complement each other. That's key.

Climbing is a deeply personal thing. We all choose to participate, and when you're out there, you're relying on your partner and he is relying on you—that sense of trust is unique. I don't know if there's anything like it in any other sport.

I mean sure, tennis is fun. But at the end of the day, you still want to beat the guy you're playing with. You still want to beat the other person, then hop over the net and . . .

Peter: . . . whack them over the head with your racquet!

Conrad: . . . and humbly shake their hand. But inside you're thinking, *I cooked that guy!* But if you cook your partner while climbing, then both your lives are at risk.

The late, great alpinist Mugs Stump mixed climbing in Utah

No doubt. What was Mugs like?

Conrad: Mugs had an outsize forceful persona. He came from a family of four boys. He played quarterback in high school, played at Penn State, went to the Orange Bowl, and after college tried playing semipro. When he gave up football, he moved to the Snowbird Ski Resort the year it opened in 1971. For Mugs there was never a single moment that wasn't good for training in one form or another. He was always doing something to get you to that aspiration you had in mind. It didn't have to be anything big—it just had to be good and worthy of your time and dedication.

For instance, there was a time when we drove from Salt Lake to Yosemite. We would go to Yosemite every spring, then we would go to Alaska. It was a seasonal migration.

As we're getting ready to leave, Mugs says, "Okay, this is our next step. We're going to drive all the way to Yosemite without talking."

And I thought, "Cool." After all, what's the big deal? You jump on the freeway, pass Wendover, and eventually you get to the Valley without ever saying a word.

Peter: Was this training?

Conrad: Yes, this was Mugs' idea of mental toughness training, not to talk during an 18-hour drive. Maybe he was just pissed at me. Maybe he just wanted to be in his own headspace. I have no idea.

So we got to Reno, and we're driving south, and all of a sudden the alternator goes out. Just like that it's gone, and the van dies along the side of the road. We tried to tough it out for a while. We bivied in the van overnight, then in the morning we hitchhiked back to Reno to find a rebuilt alternator and install it. At that point we had to break training and start talking. After all, this was before smartphones. We couldn't just ask Google what to do.

What was your most memorable climbing experience with Mugs?

Conrad: The most memorable climbing trip I had with Mugs we didn't even make a summit. It was a route on *The Eye Tooth* in Alaska, the east dihedral that had first been climbed by Tom Bowman and Jack Lewis. Mugs had missed out getting the first ascent but they were buddies, so it was all right. We went back the next year, and it looked like a great line. So we were working on freeing it and we were having a good time. But when we got to the top of the dihedral, a storm hit—a huge storm. Seven days straight. It snowed 9 feet.

We just sat on our portaledge for a week, and when the storm was over, we didn't have the strength left to screw a fuel cartridge into the stove. It was clear we weren't going up.

The whole time we were stuck on the portaledge, Mugs was reminiscing about the time he was on Gasherbrum 4 in Pakistan with Michael Kennedy. They were perched on the edge of a spire of ice. They'd chopped out room for their tent in this completely improbable place. I remembered seeing a photo from that trip in a magazine when I was a kid, and it seemed like one of those iconic events in mountaineering history that feels bigger than reality. So to have Mugs relate that experience to our mini-epic on *The Eye Tooth*—it made me feel worthy.

What's the most important lesson you learned from Mugs?
Conrad: Probably that, *"It's not that bad."* Whenever I would start whining or cringing, Mugs would say, "It's not that bad. I've seen worse."

And years later I was with Jimmy Chin. We were trying K7 and it was storming, and getting dark, and I was leading a pitch, and this chunk of ice came down and nicked my face—and of course you're exercising and the blood is hyper-oxygenated—so when Jimmy reached the belay, I had blood all over me and he was like, "Oh man! Everything's coming unglued. We can't make it up."

And I said, "This? This isn't so bad. I've seen worse."

And that's what you want a mentor to say at times like that—that they've been in similar situations. That *you've* got this. *We've* got this. Whatever we're facing, we can handle it.

I was 29 when Mugs was killed on Denali (May 21, 1992), and I thought, "Wow! You think the world is great, that you and all your friends are invincible, and nothing can happen, and then all of a sudden *kaboom*, everything changes." That was a pivotal moment in my life.

Peter what has shaped and influenced you?
Peter: I got into climbing to connect to the outdoors in a gritty way, where you're actually touching rock, getting bruised and cut up. But the other side

Anker treading on *Thin Ice*, 10b, The Needles

Every day's a good day when you're climbing.

of that experience is to feel inspired. I had tried various sports—hockey, baseball, all that stuff—but they seemed more like work to me. What I had found was that I was pretty mediocre at everything I tried. But when I was climbing, I would see a beautiful ridge or rock face and suddenly I could go to a different space in my mind. I could become someone, different. I could go from being mediocre to being inspired by something greater than myself.

That's not something I can control. I suppose by definition that's what magic is. It comes and it goes, and when it appears, it's unexpected. It's an experience that brings back half-remembered childhood memories of something you can't quite grasp. You know, when you're a kid and there's a magic about everything?

I talk to people who are able to summon their top level on demand. Whether for competitions or hard climbs. But it's not like that for me. The climb has to be beautiful. Something so compelling it's like a spark goes off. If I see a really hard climb that I want to do just for my ego's sake, I'll probably fall. Or maybe I'll manage to struggle my way up, but that's exactly what it feels like—a struggle.

But when I think of the hardest climbs I've done, in virtually every case what I remember is feeling relaxed, not really trying too hard, feeling like I was flowing. I wish I could summon that on demand. Yet at the same time I like the mystery of it. It makes it that much more special.

What elements need to be present for the magic to appear?
Peter: Usually something in nature. One time I was in eastern Canada and a friend was showing me around. I tried a route that I think was hard, 5.11, and I got super pumped and fell off.

Then we walked around the corner, and there was a climb that had never been done. It was a crack splitting 10 meters of roof, fully upside down.

I'd never seen anything like it. I remember looking at the line and I had my arms crossed on my chest, and my heart started beating so hard my arms started visibly moving.

My buddy had tried it over a period of years and hadn't been able to do it. And he said, "Look Peter, if you can get it first try, it's all yours. But if you feel like you're going to have to work it, I'd prefer you leave it alone."

I went for it, and it felt like I was absolutely flowing. There didn't seem like any effort was involved. And it was *much* harder than the route I'd just fallen off, but it was so beautiful. So it can be a one-pitch route like that or it can be a big wall or mountain. It doesn't really matter—and sometimes no one else thinks it's special except me—but when it hits me, that's when the magic occurs.

Very cool. Did you have any important mentors?

Peter: I started climbing at Squamish with a handful of friends, and we all learned together. There were no mentors. We just figured stuff out on our own, usually by reading books by Walter Bonnatti, Royal Robbins, people like that. But the one person who had a huge impact on me, and who in some ways eventually became my mentor, was John Bachar.

By then (1986) I had been to Yosemite a lot, and in those days Bachar was the king of Yosemite. And at that time Yosemite was the center of the climbing universe. So I believed that John was the best rock climber in the world. And he definitely had that aura about him—for one thing he was the first climber I'd ever seen in an actual television commercial. But in those days I did my best to avoid the hotshots. I felt totally unworthy, so I just cruised around and did my own thing.

On the day John and I met I had just driven down from Canada. Seriously, I had just pulled into the parking lot. And I didn't know Bachar. I had never spoken with him. But he pulled in right behind me. I don't know how he knew I was there, but he walked up and asked if I wanted to do a bit of climbing, some free soloing.

Then as soon as we were alone, he asked me if I wanted to try linking *The Nose* on El Capitan with *The Regular Route* on Half Dome in a day—which at that time had not been done.

As it turned out, the El Cap/Half Dome Linkup was something I'd been dreaming of for years! It wasn't just a *cool* thing to do. I viewed it as absolutely *the best thing* I could ever imagine doing. It was *The Thing*, light-years beyond any alternative! So when Bachar asked me to do it with him, it felt like fate, the gods, and all the planets had aligned. It was this moment that was practically sizzling with destiny.

I truly felt like everything I had ever wanted was being handed to me right there, and if I failed, it was okay, because I was going to try to do this huge thing with the best climber in the world!

And right away John gave me some advice, which was that I had to take 2 *full days of rest* before we made the attempt. And in those days I never took rest days. Growing up in Canada if you took rest days when the weather was good, you'd lose out on a big part of the climbing season. So I just climbed every day.

When Bachar told me that, I was like, "Wow, really? Two whole days? I'll get out of shape."

I really thought that.

But he said, "No, no. You've got to take 2 days off and sleep as much as you can and eat as much as you can. Just lie in your tent, and if you can't sleep, pretend to sleep, and when you're awake, eat."

"Great," I thought, "now I'm going to get out of shape, *and* I'm going to get fat."

But this was John Bachar talking, so I figured I would give it a go. So I lined the walls of my little pup tent with Nabisco crackers, because I had hardly any money and that was all I could afford.

When the big day came, sure enough I was super charged from being well rested and fed.

Then halfway up El Cap I dropped our second rope. I don't even know where it went. I thought I clipped it to the back of my harness then it was gone. So now we only had one rope, so we were committed.

I felt like shit. I was so apologetic, but John said, "Forget it. Don't worry about it."

Then we passed two other parties—five people total. I had just followed a pitch, and I was swinging into the lead. And I jumped off the belay and grabbed this big flake as tall as myself, and the whole thing started tipping over.

In that instant everything went into slow motion. I remember letting go of the flake and jumping back to the ledge. This huge piece of rock was falling off the wall and I'm thinking it's going to bust all to pieces, and all those people we just passed are going to die—all because of me.

And at the same instant John, who is dressed all in white—white pants and a white t-shirt—is a blur beside me. He jumps forward and he pushes this *huge* flake back into place like he was a superhero. And you know, in that moment he was Superman to me.

I'd just screwed up and almost killed people, and John saved the day. So I'm fully expecting him to give me a dressing down and make me feel exactly like the idiot I was.

But instead he simply said, "That block was loose. It was ready to go. Don't worry about it. Stuff happens."

He could have crushed me with a single word, but instead he showed me what a real hero is, someone who inspires you to be better than you are.

That's impressive, especially considering that many people believed that Bachar was highly competitive.

Peter: Yeah, I know. I've heard from a lot of people that John could be competitive and really tough on people. But it never occurred to me to compete with John. I held him in such high regard it would have seemed ridiculous. I admired him too much for that, and after the Linkup we climbed together many times over the years. I never felt any competition between us.

I also heard he could be a sandbagger, but once I was climbing with him and I was going to solo a route I hadn't done before, and he said, "Well you know Peter it's graded 5.10, but it's really solid 5.11."

It's also worth noting that I thought the El Cap/Half Dome Linkup was going to be this huge ultramarathon of flogging ourselves and barely being able to crawl over the top.

But instead it was like we were riding a wave that got bigger and bigger. We climbed *The Nose* and then we got over to Half Dome and it seemed like we were climbing faster and faster, and at the same time getting stronger and stronger.

El Cap and Half Dome in a day—that's a lot of climbing. But it didn't take anything out of us, the day, the rock, the partnership—everything energized us.

About three quarters of the way up Half Dome a thunderstorm complete with lightning hits, and the air is full of electricity and our hair is standing on end. It's raining, and the situation should have been serious and scary.

But instead, it felt like the storm was adding energy to us both. We pull up onto the summit, the storm dissipates, and we're standing on top amped like crazy.

And at that moment a perfect double rainbow forms over Half Dome. That's about as magical an experience one could ever hope for.

That's awesome Peter. Conrad you've had amazing partnerships throughout your career as well. Can you talk about how important partners are to the climbing experience?

Conrad: Yeah, there are a lot of people on this planet, and a lot of good climbers you can go with. But when it comes to making your dreams and aspirations come true, you need to find people you are comfortable with, with whom you have a sense of trust, and the innate understanding that you're both in it for the same reasons. So I've had plenty of partners who have been fun to be with, but for one reason or another I didn't climb with again. And with others, there's this special connection, a bond that grows stronger the more you share.

Alex Lowe was one of those. I was fortunate enough to spend a decade climbing with Alex, and he was one of the most energetic, enthusiastic, and creative climbers I've ever met—and a truly exceptional ice climber. He was the first person to climb *The Fang* in the Vail Amphitheater, which is a sustained freestanding pillar of ice with an intimidating aura. He brought mixed climbing to Rocky Mountain National Park with *Hot Doggie* and other challenging mixed routes that were protected only with traditional gear. When he lived in Salt Lake, he ushered in an era of hard mixed in Provo Canyon by climbing the limestone up to the lip of the cliff then climbing out onto free-hanging icicles. He was in the forefront of that kind of climbing, and he even survived a ride on a shattered ice pillar when it collapsed as he was climbing it in Montana's Hyalite Canyon on a route that was subsequently named *Airborne Ranger*.

But the fun part of Alex was his sense of motivation and his excitement. We had a couple of really fun trips. One of them was a speed climbing competition in Kyrgyzstan organized by the Russian Climbing Federation. We raced up Khan Tengri, a 7,010-meter peak in Kyrgyzstan, with a field of international competitors. Done in traditional style, the West Ridge has four camps, but we ran up and down it in a day. Alex took first and I came in second, which really upset the locals. We were fueled by coffee, which subsequently led the organizers to question whether it should be banned.

What qualities do you both look for in a partner?

Peter: High energy and a sense of humor. Not the kind where you laugh at other people, the kind where you can laugh at yourself. Because when you're doing big climbs, you're out there for long periods. Things are going to go wrong. And if that isn't met with a sense of humor, it's going to devolve into "Let's just get this done," instead of, "Let's see how much fun we can have."

It's like one plus one equals four, because there's some sort of synergy in a good partnership. You both become better because of one another and because of where you are. Sometimes when I'm getting close to the top of a climb, I feel a kind of disappointment it's going be over. Those are the best climbs and the best partnerships.

Conrad: I look for a similarity in physical capabilities and motivation, and as Peter says, a sense of humor. You can always measure the seriousness of any situation by how much humor is present. If no one can even manage a smile, you know things are grim. But if you can still joke about the fact that, "Oh well, all we have left to eat again today is oatmeal—for the fourth day in a row!" then it's not so bad. You can still be happy with what you have.

Peter: I think another important element is optimism, even if it's delusional. I have one partner who even in the worst conditions, will say, "This is perfect! This is the perfect time to do this." He just rubs his hands together and gets after it. That's optimism. It breeds more optimism, and sometimes, it sets the stage for great things.

Peter, what do you think your biggest strength is as a climber?

Peter: Being an early riser! I could always get up early, but there was a time early in my climbing career in Canada when I came down from doing my first 5.10 (which was something I thought I'd never be able to do). I was living in a cave at Squamish at the time, and when I got back, all my stuff had been stolen—sleeping bag, pack, everything. They had even stolen my last can of plums!

Anker leads the way to the summit during a winter ascent of Ama Dablam, Nepal, 1990.

And I was poor. It took me ages before I could rebuy all that gear. So for the entire next season all I had to sleep in was a canvas duffle bag my dad got in the Navy and some old blankets my mom was throwing out. I'd wrap myself in the blankets, wriggle into the duffle bag, pull the drawstring tight, and shiver the night away. It was so cold I could only sleep a little, so I'd wake up even earlier than usual to try to get warm. I don't think I've ever recovered from that. So I'm the freak who always gets up super early, and that has meant I could go for bigger days. Honestly, that's probably my biggest strength, because I've never thought I was gifted athletically. I've just been willing to get up early, and I love climbing.

Conrad?

Conrad: Well, like Peter I'm optimistic and an early riser. I like to make the most of the day, because this is the only life we get. We need to make the most of it. But from a mountaineering standpoint, my biggest strength is probably situational awareness, the ability to take in all the information from a given situation, look at it objectively, then do a kind of risk analysis. What could go wrong here? If I don't protect the second and they fall, they could *fly swatter* into that dihedral over there, and that wouldn't be good. If I forget the fuel canister, we're not going to have water. Good planning, awareness, combined with optimism, that's my strength. Being aware of what's going on right now and what could go wrong in the future. How can I prevent things from going wrong with my actions in the present? That's key to survival and longevity in an alpine environment.

If you're an alpine climber, the Himalayas are the youngest, most active, and tallest mountain range on the planet, so eventually you're going to want to go there to test your mettle against facets of the planet that are unexplored. I think that's another thing Peter and I have in common, we're drawn to explore. When you do a new route, that's one of the few places left on this planet where there remains true exploration. Maybe it's relatively small terrain but no one's been there before. And that ability to see a line, then figure out whether it's doable—will it all connect? What type of gear do we need? How much food? All those sorts of things—some climbers are good at that and love it, and other climbers are perfectly happy repeating existing routes, and there's nothing wrong with that either.

Peter, what's your biggest weakness?

Peter: Geez, I suppose watching too much TV. But one thing I've learned is that rest days are really important, so in some ways I think of watching TV as a weakness, but our weaknesses are often connected to our strengths. And I like to recover by watching really good action flicks. Certain movies inspire me, *The Right Stuff* for example, and inspiration counts for a lot. As I said, when I'm inspired, that's when I get the best out of myself.

But another weakness is my fingers. I've never had strong fingers. I've always been better at endurance. And I'm really disorganized. Some climbers are scientific about how they train. They schedule their entire year. I've never been like that.

So that's a weakness, but on the other hand, it's also one of my strengths, because I can be spontaneous. I go to bed thinking of nothing in particular and I wake up at 3 a.m. with an idea, and I go huge! I think, "Wow, today's the perfect day to go do that long traverse I've been thinking about." So strengths and weaknesses are always connected.

Conrad: Oh, there's the physical weakness. I don't train enough, and the body certainly doesn't have the strength it did when I was 20. It doesn't knit back together nearly as fast after a long day. So I'm always working on increasing strength and flexibility. But from a personality standpoint, I take too much on. I'm always saying, "Yeah, let's do this or try that." My sister calls it "a slight case of over-scheduling."

I'm also trying to get better at being in the public eye and not letting all the attention bother me. The way people communicate today is different than in the past. People are entitled to their views, but I've had to learn not to take criticism personally and allow it to distract me. Especially when it concerns my family. I married Jenni Lowe after Alex died, and I became a father to Alex's boys. And there are people who believe that was selfish, and that Jenni's a fool for putting herself and the boys in another risky situation. People argue that I'm harming my kids because I still go climbing. I try not to let that bother me, because I know the boys have had a good upbringing. Obviously, they had no choice in their father dying, or a new dad who is also a climber coming into their lives, but I believe we've all benefited.

Peter, why do you climb?
Peter: It's the combination of things. Ever since I was a kid, I've always loved the outdoors and I really loved watching gymnastics. And climbing combines the two. Climbing is gymnastics 1,000 feet up—kinesthetic feedback in a spectacular setting. When you've practiced that long enough, it becomes part of who you are, you become just another animal up there, responding to its environment.

Conrad: When humans find their one true calling in life, that's when they are happiest. It becomes your work, your purpose, your vocation. The discovery of what you were meant to do—not too many people find that.

Peter: I never thought I would. At 15 I felt like I was just dabbling. I wasn't depressed, but I wasn't connected to anything either, and I thought that was what life was going to be. As I grew into a teenager, I realized it wasn't going to be easy moving to Africa, living in the jungle, swinging around on vines like Tarzan. When I was 7, I thought that was possible, but slowly you find out, "Well, I can't do that, and as much as I'd like to fly like Superman, I can't do that either." So as the years went by, I started thinking maybe there isn't that one great thing, so when I found climbing, it made it that much sweeter.

And in the climbing world, you are with other people who have found it too. You surround yourself with people who have this passion, and you start to travel and realize that most people on the planet don't have anything remotely like climbing to give them purpose . . .

Conrad: Yep. I think that's why I connect with professionals in other fields, for instance musicians who are so talented they make a living from their music, because they've been able to turn their greatest source of happiness into their livelihood, and that's a rare combination. To me the biggest tragedy in life is missing your calling and squandering this brief period of time we've been given.

Croft enjoys being *Lost At Sea* (10+) The Needles.

With that in mind, how do you define climbing? Is it a sport, a lifestyle, a profession, or something else?

Peter: For me climbing is simply life. Whenever I hear climbing described as a sport, I think, "Well, that's not what it is for me." People will ask what else do you do besides climb? It's all connected. My wife and I live in Bishop because we're beside the Sierras. Even if I'm hanging out at some mountain lake, to me that's related to climbing. I'm there because climbing brought me to the mountains—and to an appreciation of nature. The physical act of climbing is only part of the attraction. It's being outdoors, relating to the mountains and the people you're with.

For example, I recently went back to Canada to visit a good climbing buddy I hadn't seen for a while. After having lots of problems with his knees, he recently had operations on both. And when I got there he said, "Ahh, this is great. You're back. Whatever route you want to do, let's go."

So we went for an old favorite, which requires a couple of scruffy pitches to a ledge where the real climbing begins, this huge overhanging dihedral that runs up the rest of the wall.

And we get to the ledge, and my friend said he couldn't go any farther. His knees were killing him. He was worried the operation had not been a success. And he was totally bummed out, because I had come all the way from California and now we weren't going to be able to do the climb. So we just sat down and started talking. We chatted for ages. We had been really tight for years, but that was one of the best conversations we'd ever had. And I remember months later, at the end of that climbing season, I had done some great climbs. But when I thought back over the season and asked myself what was the best day, immediately I realized it was that day hanging out on the ledge with my friend. We did two crappy pitches, then we just talked, but it was a fantastic day. How do you call that a sport?

Conrad: Climbing is a way of life. It's all encompassing. Most of my friends climb and have a deep connection to nature. And it's humbling to go out climbing, because if you make a mistake, you're going to die. That direct knowledge of the frailty of life makes you appreciate it all even more.

Most climbers, myself included, don't subscribe to the common view that humans have been given dominion over the earth, that all creation was put here only for our use and pleasure. In fact I love that moment when you leave the constructs of civilization behind. One of the best aspects of the last couple of days here in The Needles was when we were up on that ridge, and we looked out over all those valleys right to Mount Whitney. And I thought, "Wow, that's a big expanse of wild out there, and I'm intrigued to think about how many bear, deer, and birds might be in it." Whereas when I look out over the LA Basin, which is probably about the same size but teeming with humanity under its layer of smog, it depresses me. Climbing makes me feel alive. In competition climbing they've placed time and physical parameters on climbing, which for me kind of misses the point. For me it's far more about personal experience than beating others.

Do you think climbing has any higher meaning or purpose?
Peter: I think one of the reasons I like really big climbs is that you often reach a point where you can't go any farther—and then what? I feel like boulder problems and short sport climbs are more like a pop quiz. You either do it or you don't.

But on really big things, you often find out there's more to you than you thought. You have to dig deeper, and that's when you find out who you really are. If you don't experience times where you are so far down you don't think you can ever climb back out, you never get to discover those hidden parts of yourself.
Conrad: It's only through hardship that you gain insight into who you are, and climbing is one way of doing that. It's not that we seek out suffering for its own sake, but climbing mountains is not sitting on the beach, lying around getting sunburned, enjoying cocktails. You have to put one foot in front of the other. It's arduous. It's hard. It's a calling, and other people who haven't heard that particular drummer think that climbers have a few screws loose.
Peter: The concentration changes you. That's happened most often when I've gone for really big, intense solo climbs, because then my focus isn't broken by talking with anyone or dealing with gear. It's pure. I'm focused on what I'm doing. That's necessary on the climb, but once the climbing is over, that

intense focus and the ability to see things clearly doesn't immediately go away. It fades over a period of time.

So topping out on some big solo climb where I've had to be ultra-focused, I get to the top, and I can see the texture of the rock. I see detail I would otherwise overlook. And I turn my gaze to the sun streaming down into the valley, to a river sparkling in the distance, and it's an intensity that's almost . . .

Well, it's not psychedelic because it's not warped by drugs. For lack of a better word, it's heavenly. It's a bit unbelievable. There have been times when I've done a big climb and I don't want to go back down because the beauty is so startling.

Can climbing be a spiritual practice?
Peter: I think so. There are times when you feel like there's so much more going on than science can account for. I don't go to church. I don't buy into that kind of thing, but at times it feels like, whether you're talking about "The Force" in *Star Wars* or some other term, that there is something more to the Universe than we understand. Maybe the word *spirituality* is a way to put a name to it.

Conrad: Climbing connects us to the oldest parts of our planet. I've always been interested in the earth sciences. Is this sedimentary rock? Metamorphic rock? Igneous? How did it form? How long has it been here? Here in The Needles we're climbing on rock that's 90 to 110 million years old. Put yourself in the context of that span of time and you realize how insignificant humans are.

And when you're on the highest peaks, far from a city, and you look up, the night sky is filled with stars and planets. The sheer enormity of the cosmos is astounding. It fosters humility and awe. What good fortune allowed us to reach this point in our evolution where we can scamper over rocks hundreds of millions of years old?

Do you think climbing is an addiction?
Peter: Probably. Doug Robinson has written about what a big difference there is in your body chemistry between when you're dozing off in a business meeting and you're amped on endorphins and other neurotransmitters high on a wall. So putting yourself in situations that are active and have potential risks,

if you're used to having those experiences regularly, I have no doubt they can become a type of addiction.

Conrad: Yeah, the people who study that stuff would probably say that we're addicted, but at least to a marginally acceptable activity that isn't too harmful.

So if climbing is an addiction, how do you guys handle yours?

Conrad: I just go climbing more.

Peter: Yeah, keep feeding it!

Peter, you were known for years as a soloist. Can you talk about the rewards of free soloing?

Peter: Well, I've never really thought of myself as a soloist. But at times I've really gotten into it. A whole year might pass when I never used a rope, even though I climbed a ton. And there are other periods when I only rope up. And I think that's one of the things that's kept me safe, the fact that I never called myself a soloist—so if it didn't feel right, I wouldn't do it. The rewards tie back into some of the other things we've been talking about. The kinesthetic feedback and the feeling of flow. Things that can be interrupted when dealing with a rope and partner. Am I on belay? Off belay? Watch me here. You're putting in gear. You're focused on your last piece, or where your next one is going to go. How safe is it? How dangerous is it?

But with soloing, from the start you are in a *Can't Fall* situation, so you're completely focused on what you're doing. It's climbing distilled to its essence. There isn't rope work. There isn't anyone else. It's purely about you and the rock. And there are obvious advantages. For instance, in a given period of time you can climb a lot more! In fact I started soloing just so I could do more climbing. In the early days in Squamish my friends would all want to go to the bakery in the afternoon and hang out. Not me! There was so much daylight left, so I would keep climbing on my own.

Conrad, you've had such a long and varied career. What really stands out for you?

Conrad: The time Peter and I had on Spansar Peak stands out. Being out all day and descending all night. That was memorable. And finally succeeding on Meru, after having tried it three times. That felt good.

But my next memorable climbing experience will be when we all go out tomorrow. Trips to Antarctica, to the Himalaya, I cherish them all, but I don't let any one trip be the end point of my life. I don't want to live life in the past tense. Sure, I'm slowing down, but I want to continue living with the same sense of discovery and excitement I always have.

There's a classic scene in the movie *Napoleon Dynamite* where one of the characters is talking about being a quarterback in high school. This guy's middle aged and he's still living in the moment he threw a touchdown pass 30 years before. And you meet plenty of older climbers like that. People who did one great thing back in the day, but they're still eager to meet some young climbers so they can remind them of their greatness. Personally I would rather say, "Today's great, but tomorrow's going to be even better."

Which brings us to life lessons. What are the most important lessons you have learned from climbing?

Peter: Pick your battles. At times I've been too unfocused. Just throwing myself at things all over the place.

Conrad: I would say being humbled by the mountains and how fleeting life is. Treat that with respect. Far too many people think the details are no big deal, so they're not enjoying the sunshine, the aspen leaves, and the birds . . .

Peter: Yeah, be open to appreciating the unexpected. For example, on Spansar Peak when we were descending, there was just a sliver of moon floating above these incredible black spires. And way down in base camp our cook Ibrahim was worried. He didn't know what was going on. We had been gone all day and nearly all night, and he assumed we should be back. So it's just barely getting light. Maybe around 4 in the morning. And we're descending this really steep moraine. Super-ragged, you needed both hands just to slip your way down.

And Ibrahim sees our headlamps, and he knows we're coffee fiends, so he brews up and he comes up this sketchy moraine with two big mugs of steaming coffee. To me that was an incredible act of kindness.

We all need to appreciate moments like that, to be receptive. Because crazy beautiful stuff comes your way—often when you least expect it.

Do you think climbing has lessons to teach society as it confronts the challenges of the twenty-first century? For example, Conrad, you've been involved in the issue of climate change. Can a climber make a difference?

Conrad: Climbers need to support their partners. They need to work together as a team and be unified in their goals. That's a good model for all human interaction.

I've done some work with troubled teens. They have issues with trust, so they're hard to connect with. But you take them climbing, and they realize that they have to trust the person belaying them. Suddenly there's an immediate connection. There's a good lesson in that.

And another way climbers can contribute is like the joke I saw once on one of those old Bazooka bubble gum wrappers. The riddle was: "How do mountains hear?"

Peter: What? How do mountains hear?

Conrad: Yeah, and the answer is: "They hear with *mountain-ears*." Get it? Sure it's a dumb joke, but the point is we climbers serve as the ears of the mountains. We need to listen to the peaks, the glaciers, and the ice caps, and at the same time we also need to be the voice of the mountains. With the climate climbers are seeing things change quite rapidly and dramatically—especially in the alpine and high latitude areas.

But if you're a politician in Kansas, playing golf on an irrigated golf course that you drive to in an air-conditioned car—you're not really connected to the environment, and especially what's going on in distant regions like the Himalaya or the Arctic. You're not seeing the changes, so it's much easier to say climate change is a bunch of baloney.

People say that to think that humans could have an impact on something as big as the planet is arrogant. Which to me is itself an arrogant statement. Scientists have proven that, given the size of the planet and the current human population and the amount of industry and agriculture—we're having an enormous impact.

The only real question is what's the tipping point we can survive? At the end of the day, this is not about the dodo or the spotted woodpecker, it's about us. It's about saving humanity.

In the future the planet is going to be vastly different than it is now. And we climbers have seen things most people will never see. So in a sense it's our duty to tell people about the things that are changing forever and that we need to be mindful.

Peter, you do a lot of guiding. You bring city people into the mountains. Do you think that has an effect?

Peter: Well, I do remember one time I was teaching a class. There were five students, four of them athletic guys, and the fifth was an overweight young woman. And at the end of the day everybody had done all the routes except the woman. She was halfway up the last route and she just couldn't do it. So I climbed up beside her and she said, "This is impossible for me. You know, I'm just too heavy."

Everybody else was ready to go get a beer but I stayed with her, and eventually she did the climb.

And afterward we were walking back to the car, and she said that she knew she wasn't going to be a climber. It wasn't her thing. That she had grown up in a household of brothers who were all really good at what they did, but whenever she tried something it always seemed impossible. And time and time again, she was proven right. It was impossible.

But that day, on the last climb, she had finally done something she had thought was impossible. And for her that was a huge breakthrough. "I'm not going to continue climbing," she said, "but today was a big turning point for me. I found out that thinking something is impossible doesn't mean it is."

And I was getting fully choked up. It was so powerful. This girl, who on the surface didn't appear to have much going for her, but who had a lot inside that wasn't getting expressed, because she was stifled by people saying, "Don't even bother trying."

Everyone can learn something from striving toward a goal that might seem unrealistic, or beyond what he or she thinks is possible. People have always viewed mountains as symbolic of that kind of striving, even if they've never visited them.

As Anker says, "The biggest tragedy in life is missing your calling and squandering this brief period of time we've been given."

Conrad: At the root, we're talking here about building character, and in the past a big part of education was devoted to building character. But we've lost that. Video games don't build character. You might have faster eye-thumb coordination, but you're still just blowing up make-believe zombies on a small screen. That's not very helpful. But people who participate in outdoor experiential learning of all kinds come back with a sense of respect for other humans and a reverence for all life.

Peter: That's right, and there's also the whole idea that everyone today needs to be a winner, and that winning is the only thing that counts. When I was soloing a lot, I had to be really honest with myself, and I had to reconsider what it meant to fail. I knew that backing off would be important. I might climb the first 600 feet of an 800-foot route. I'd get three quarters of the way up and I'd realize, "Hey, the weather looks bad, the climbing looks too hard, there's loose rock, or whatever. Bottom line, I'm not going for it." And I would climb all the way back down.

But I didn't consider that failure. I would think, "Cool, I just climbed 600 feet up and 600 feet down. That's 1,200 vertical feet of climbing so far today!" Turning back wasn't a negative. It was the right thing to do. Those experiences helped me change the way I look at success and failure.

Do you think climbing has a heart or soul?

Peter: For some people climbing has no heart or soul. It's just a sport. They want to beat other people and be better than other people. But for me the soul of climbing is about my relationships—with the environment, with the people I climb with, and with myself—being true to myself.

Conrad, this question is for you. How do you balance the demands of professional mountaineering with the responsibilities of having a family?

Peter: Yeah. It must be horrendous.

Conrad: I make a to-do list. A list allows me to realistically visualize all the various demands on my time. Then if I'm spending time with my sons, I commit to being there 100 percent—it doesn't matter if it's doing homework or something outdoors.

And if it's time to work, I'm fully present for that too. If I'm going to be with my wife Jenni—that's all I do. If I'm cooking breakfast burritos, I commit 100 percent of my attention to making the best burritos I can.

And it's climbing that has given me that focus. Yes, we're hyperactive people. Yes, we're scattered. There's always something going on. But climbing teaches us moment-to-moment precision, how to pay attention when you can't afford to make a mistake, and that translates into other aspects of life.

Peter: I wish I could say that! I'm way too scattered. I think Conrad has a real talent for managing his time. He impresses me. In contrast, I'm just wandering around bumping in to things.

If you guys weren't climbers what would you be doing?

Peter: Prison?

Conrad: I think if I hadn't been introduced to the mountains I might have been a sailor. There are definite similarities—in climbing we're surrounded by an ocean of air and gravity, and at sea we're surrounded by air and water, both of which can be beautiful and dangerous. Or maybe I would have been a helicopter pilot. I think that's kind of cool.

Peter: Boy, I can't think of anything that would be second best. Maybe surfing. I've done a little. Actually I'm so terrible at it, I'll be out there for hours just trying to catch a wave, and finally I'll be so exhausted, I'll think, "I'm just going back in and flop on the beach." Then by some fluke I'll catch a wave and immediately I have to keep trying. There's something about surfing that can take you from being so exhausted you can barely paddle to an exhilaration so great you have to keep doing it. And the whole time you're thinking, "What just happened?" The bad thing about surfing is that it's condition dependent. With climbing, the cliffs are always there.

What do you think you'll be doing in 10 or 20 years?

Peter: More of the same. Back home I've got a hard sport project I've been working for a while. And there's still big stuff in the High Sierras I want to do—big wall free climbs. You know a long time ago I had some weird health issue. I saw this TV show on Jacqueline Onassis, who died of some horrible type of cancer. And during the show they were describing her symptoms, and I thought, "Holy shit, I have some of those same symptoms!" So I went to a doctor to get tested and it turned out I just had to change my diet. That was all. But while I was waiting for the test results, I was so scared I didn't even tell my wife. I remember thinking that I might be dead within the year, and that was going to be such a bummer! I was really looking forward to being some old dude, walking with a cane on a mountain trail, looking up at the Sierras, just taking it all in. That's the idea you know, we're supposed to reach old age and find out what that's like as well.

And there was another time when I had a really bad shoulder injury and I thought I'd never recover. Never climb again. And I remember when I did come back and I did my first climb, it was 5.7. And I thought, "Even if I can never do anything harder than this, it's okay—because this is awesome!"

Conrad: Well, you get a bit slower, you're not as strong as you once were, but it would still be nice to do two or three more big objectives in the Himalaya. But the key is enjoyment. It doesn't have to be at the same level as when I was younger—and to gracefully accept that.

Peter: On one hand, as you age you do change. But that shouldn't become an excuse. "Oh, now I need to pack it in." Or "I need to slow down more than is really necessary." Because the truth is, I climb harder now than I did when I was 20. That doesn't mean there isn't an aging process, it means that when I was 20 I was really stupid—for instance about how to warm up properly. My reasoning was that I should always do the hardest pitch of the day *first*— before I got tired. I did a lot of things wrong . . .

Conrad: That's another thing climbing's taught us, that being more efficient is where you find your gains. Rather than just having more, going bigger, it's about being efficient with your time and your energy . . .

Peter: And learning from your own stupidity! I think only certain people were born to be lifers. For many climbers, there's the feeling that as soon as they can't be competitive, they quit. As for myself, I've had plenty of ups and downs, but I never considered quitting. I really appreciate easy climbing, hard climbing, the sheer variety of the different kinds of climbing. I love cruising a mellow alpine ridge, and I still love hard sport climbs. I love it all. If I think of the ten best climbs I've ever done, some of them were quite easy.

Conrad: It's an innate feeling . . . .Jenni says, "You don't climb because you want to, you climb because you *have* to." So there's that.

Peter: Yeah, it's like breathing. Certainly you can look at it as a compulsion or an addiction. But that's missing the point? Do you love someone because you *have* to? No, you're just in love . . .

Conrad: Let it be a mystery.

What's your advice for the youth of tomorrow?

Conrad: Find a mentor to go climbing with, and get outdoors! Don't limit your experience to the gym. There are so many cliffs in the world and each one is unique. And don't make mistakes. Gravity plays for keeps. Put safety knots in the end of your ropes. Check your knot and your partner's knot. Double-check everything. I mean it. Climbing is very healthy. It's a good way to live. It has plenty of positive attributes, but if you're a young kid and you deck . . . well, your parents are going to think climbing is the worst thing that ever happened to them—so be careful out there.

Peter: Definitely. I believe there are shrinking opportunities for kids to be active these days. There's less physical education, and there's more emphasis on organized sports, but a lot of us don't fit into that mode, we don't respond well to structured activity, and competition doesn't necessarily bring out the best in everyone. So find something like climbing you can do for the rest of your life that connects you to the outdoors.

I was up in Tuolumne one time, in the high country of Yosemite, and this big van full of inner-city kids arrived, and when the doors slid open, you could hear all this commotion, all these kids fighting and dissing each other. Then they tumbled outside and there are all these little black kids spinning in circles.

I heard them say they didn't think anything like that country really existed. They thought that when they saw it on TV it was all CGI. That maybe once upon a time it existed but not anymore. So we climbers are incredibly privileged to go to the places we go and experience what we have. We shouldn't take places like Yosemite for granted, because if we do, in the future they might not exist. The more people who experience nature, the more people will know these places are worth saving.

Thanks so much to you both!

TOMMY CALDWELL

Tommy Caldwell may well be the most universally liked and respected climber in America. As Chris Kalous put it, "Tommy is America's poster boy climber." And after Tommy and Kevin Jorgenson succeeded in free climbing *The Dawn Wall* on El Capitan, a climb that has been lauded as the hardest big wall climb in the world—he's also one of the most famous.

Tommy is climbing's everyman. Even his name sounds like the boy next door. He begins his presentations with a photograph of himself as a kid, and the audience can't help but laugh at the quintessential nerd that he was, a 90-pound weakling with glasses, the kind a bully would call "four eyes" or "doofus." But the joke's funny because everyone knows that Tommy has grown up to be a real-life superhero—the kind who when taken hostage in Kyrgyzstan escaped by pushing his captor off a cliff; and who, when he cut off half his index finger with a table saw, never thought of quitting. It's a story everyone can relate to.

The Dawn Wall received unprecedented attention from the mainstream media including CBS, NBC, the *Guardian* and the *New York Times*. A few days after summiting, Tommy and Kevin appeared on the *Ellen Degeneres Show*, an unusual venue for dirtbag climbers. As Tommy discusses below, all the attention was a bit of a fluke, a perfect storm created by two intersecting trends—the rise of social media and the growth of climbing as a mainstream sport. But it was also an indication of something more profound, a thirst for inspirational stories in a culture drowning in cynicism and despair. It turned out that the story of Caldwell and Jorgenson prevailing against heavy odds high on a sheer rock wall was a story that everyone *needed*.

In climbing there is an unspoken ethic of self-deprecating humility. No matter how talented, no matter how impressive one's accomplishments, let your actions speak for you, and no one embodies this quiet virtue more than Caldwell.

Tommy Caldwell climbs the third pitch (13a/b) of Todd Skinner's
***Wet Lycra Nightmare*, Leaning Tower.**

When he talks about *The Dawn Wall*, it's not about the struggle or the heroics, it's about how the strong updrafts that form on big walls can hold pee suspended in midair. How when you relieve yourself you can actually reach out and pluck an individual golden droplet from space. That's kind of cool, but the result of peeing in such conditions for weeks on end is that clothing, skin, and hair all become saturated with the smell of urine, a fact that becomes uncomfortably clear when preparing to meet a huge gathering of press and well-wishers at the top of El Cap.

Tommy doesn't even consider himself a talented climber. In his mind, his accomplishments have been the result of starting at an early age; climbing an insane amount; and a singular drive, the same stubborn tenacity he first demonstrated as a 3-year-old when he embarked on a multiyear project to dig a hole to China in his parents' backyard. That type of focus (what some might call obsession) has found a perfect canvas for expression in El Capitan. Few, if any, have spent anywhere close to the amount of time living on El Cap as Caldwell. He has been free climbing routes there since he made a repeat free ascent of *The Salathé Wall* in 1999. He and Beth Rodden were the first to repeat a free ascent of *The Nose*, nearly 2 decades after Lynn Hill succeeded. He then built on those experiences by establishing free ascents of *Lurking Fear* (VI, 14a), *The Dihedral Wall* (VI, 14a), *The West Buttress* (VI, 13c), and *Magic Mushroom* (VI, 14a). Caldwell has now climbed twelve of El Cap's fourteen free routes culminating in *The Dawn Wall*. But in order to put *The Dawn Wall* in perspective, it's important to note that it took 10 years to complete—more than all Caldwell's other El Cap routes combined. In fact, Caldwell freed *Magic Mushroom* as a kind of vacation from the stress and frustration of working on *The Dawn Wall*.

And *The Dawn Wall* is unlike any other free route on El Cap because rather than following prominent crack systems it stitches together ephemeral aid lines with large expanses of featureless granite. The route has twelve pitches of 5.13, six of 14, with back-to-back pitches of 14d, which by themselves are now the hardest climbing in Yosemite. And as anyone who has climbed in the Valley knows, it's humbling—5.14 on glacial polished granite is nothing like bolted 14 at the local sport crag. Success on *The Dawn Wall* required repeated leader falls zippering through beaks and copperheads on existing aid lines; it required entirely new techniques such as "thunder-clinging" (using only one's thumb to undercling), as well as paradigm-shifting strategies such as climbing at night—in January. As Caldwell says, big wall climbing at this level "is an art form." And if that's so, Tommy is big wall climbing's Picasso.

Roots

My name's Tommy Caldwell. I was born August 11, 1978, and I'm an all-around rock climber—everything from bouldering to alpine rock. I'm probably best known for big wall free climbing. In a way, I grew up in Yosemite. Some of my earliest memories are of floating the Merced River looking up at El Cap and cruising around the base of cliffs watching my dad climb. Those are my roots. My dad's major passion in life was always climbing, and he's a pretty obsessive personality, so I spent my childhood as a *crag kid*, before that term even existed. My dad made the tenth or fifteenth ascent of *The Nose* on El Cap, so I'm just following in his footsteps.

When I was 3, my dad and I climbed Twin Owls, near my home in Estes Park, Colorado. Then every summer we would travel to Yosemite. We did the Tyrolean traverse on Lost Arrow Spire when I was 6. And I did my first lead on Manure Pile Buttress when I was 7.

I don't remember ever being scared of heights. I do have one vague memory, when I was 4, of being slightly scared rappelling for the first time. But other than that, I've always viewed climbing as exciting. I see discomfort as adventure. I think I can do that because I started so young, and my father was a superhero to me. He was this big muscle-bound bodybuilder type who loved being outside, and he was always super enthusiastic. As a child I idolized him. I wanted to be just like him. He was the kind of guy you could look in the eyes and see fire and excitement, and that shaped my idea of how to live my life.

Risk

Most of my injuries have not been related to rock climbing, but when I was 23, I did take a 30-foot ground fall in Indian Creek. I broke my wrist and dislocated my elbow. That's really the only time I've been hurt while climbing.

I would definitely say I'm a safety-first climber. I want to live to be an old man. So I choose climbs that are going to fulfill my need for adventure but I'm relatively confident I'm going to live through.

The Dawn Wall is a great example. It's very sheer and it's very solid rock. When you fall, there's nothing to hit, so I felt like it was a safe climb. I tend to look for projects like that. It's one of the reasons I love rock climbing as opposed to mountaineering. I'm well suited for alpine climbing because I'm great at being cold and suffering, but I like to avoid climbing below hanging seracs and avalanche terrain. I prefer situations where I'm pushing myself on good rock.

I think there's a part of me that thinks I should be more afraid, but the fear's been trained out of me. I don't view danger the same way a lot of people do. I tend to get excited rather than scared. For instance, when a storm rolls in, I immediately go to that optimistic place in my brain and think, "This is just a rad adventure. We're going to get through this, and it will be something we will always remember," as opposed to thinking, "Oh my god, what if we die up here? What if we get hypothermic?" I don't really think about that stuff too much.

I don't free solo. I don't go out into big alpine terrain where the risks are high. I don't BASE jump. I won't even buy a motorcycle. I have my own little vision of what's going to keep this really cool adventurous life going for as long as possible.

Elective Hardship

During my childhood, climbing was presented as a life-energizing, exciting, and fun-filled way to live, and I would contrast that to other approaches that are more defined by competition and a pressure to succeed. There was a brief period when I was a competition climber, and I felt that pressure. To me, competing in order to be better than another person is negative pressure. That's a *man vs. man* struggle. But when it's *man vs. himself*, or man *testing himself* against nature, then competition can be very positive. Those are the most positive aspects of climbing—when you are testing your own limits. That's what I thrive on.

Life post *Dawn Wall*, Caldwell fields inquiries atop *The Rostrum*.

My dad believed in putting his kids into situations he called "elective hardship," which means actively seeking scenarios where you encounter difficulties.

So with my own son Fitz, I don't want to raise him in a padded room. Even at age 2 I let him wander, fall down, get dirty and banged up. And as long as he's not badly hurt, I don't pick him up and coddle him. I just say, "You're all right. Brush yourself off."

I believe climbing is one of the greatest venues ever devised for that kind of learning, because it's fun and exciting. But when you climb, you have to put yourself out there beyond your comfort zone. That's my world. So I'm not going to be a helicopter parent, constantly hovering to make everything better for my kids, I'm going to be the kind of parent who lets them experience the hard things, because I think that's the best way to prepare them for life.

Adversity as Adventure

From a really young age I remember going into the mountains and getting in scenarios I think most parents would be afraid to expose their kids to.

"Oh God, it's storming! We've got to run!"

But my dad never showed any fear. Instead of being scared, he saw bad weather as an opportunity to experience firsthand the power of nature. He taught me that everything in life—good and bad—can be exciting. In situations where other people cut and run, you would see the fire in my dad's eyes.

I remember an experience when I was 5, and my sister was 7. My dad took us to Devil's Tower in Wyoming, and he taught us to climb a multipitch route together—just the three of us. I remember him taking an environment that most people view as scary and teaching us how to make it safe. How to place our feet in the crack so they didn't stick. Checking each other's knots. Experiences like that build confidence, especially since the rest of the world thinks it's a little crazy. Even as a child I recognized we were doing things a bit out there, but we were doing it in a safe way. We were learning to master a vertical environment.

Sure, some people criticized my dad for putting us at risk. But he saw that that as a plus. He wasn't trying to get us killed. He wasn't reckless. He was

Caldwell and wife Becca introduce son Fitz to the wonders of Yosemite.

a mountain guide; he was *very* safe, but he was also ahead of his time. He was a baby boomer, part of a generation that was all about trying to create a safe and comfortable society. I believe my generation's idea of adventure has grown beyond that. We love living outdoors, learning through adventure and elective hardship, using those experiences to fuel us and to turn us into the people we were meant to be.

Growing up as I did, I really understand the inherent need to battle. I love getting myself in situations where there's something big and daunting confronting me and I have to figure out a way through it. That's when I'm most energized.

You don't find that if you believe life is all about trying to be comfortable. Ironically, those are the times when I feel the most anxiety—when things get boring. For example, I once went on a Caribbean cruise, and for the entire 7 days I ran laps around the boat like a rat in a cage. I couldn't deal with being cooped up. So it does make certain things, like family vacations, harder. Those are the times I'm the grumpiest.

The Snowbird Comp

When I was 14, my dad and I spent the summer sport climbing around the western United States. In those days there were kids who were starting to compete in gyms, but it was still rare to see kids climbing outside so I had no way to judge how good I was.

But I was definitely reading the climbing magazines and I had my heroes. We were in Utah climbing in American Fork Canyon when we heard there was going to be a comp at the nearby Snowbird Ski Resort. This was a few years after the first US World Cup had been held at Snowbird. The organizers were calling the event an International Invitational, and all my heroes—climbers like Christian Griffith, Steve Hong, and Pat Adams—were competing. It was a big deal, and Dad and I decided to go. I wanted to rub shoulders with some of the best climbers in the country at that time.

Then I found out that there would be an amateur comp before the main event, so I entered and ended up winning. That qualified me for the more elite level of competition. Suddenly I found myself in a room with many of the people I'd read about in magazines. I was so shy I couldn't talk to any of them. When the comp started, I was the first to climb because I was just this little kid and was unlikely to do well. I came out and climbed all the way to the top of the wall.

My first reaction, was, "Wow! The route setters have really blown it! They've made the route way too easy."

Then I sat and watched as all my heroes came out, and they all fell lower than me. I was shocked. I had won. And that was when I started to think that maybe there was more to climbing than just having fun, that maybe I was good at it.

Strengths & Weaknesses

My biggest strength is my mental approach. I excelled when I was young, because I climbed more than anyone else. That's why I got good, because I was one of the first people to start from a really young age and climb so much. As it turns out, that's crucial. But in terms of freaky natural talent, compared to a lot of climbers, I don't have that. My main strength is being willing to stick it out, work on a project for a long time. I get very obsessed.

In terms of weakness, my fingers are weak. After all, I'm missing a finger, and that's a weakness. And I don't build muscles the way some people do. Even mentally, when it comes to competition climbing, I was never that great. After that first comp at Snowbird, I started having expectations about how I *should* perform, then I would get really nervous and not climb well. But strangely enough, when I find myself in the mountains, it's the opposite. When everything's on the line, that's when I perform my best.

Home Improvement

Yeah, I chopped off the end of my index finger with a table saw trying to build a washing machine stand for my cabin in Estes. I didn't know how to use a saw correctly.

So I immediately went to the hospital with the end of my finger in a bag and they reattached it. But it never took. I spent 2 weeks in the hospital. I went through three surgeries and several transfusions. I learned that it's pretty easy to sew a finger back on, but you can't sew veins back together. And my fingers were fat and strong from climbing, so too much blood was flowing into the reattached digit, and it wasn't able to drain. The tip got congested and the tissue died.

If I had been a nonclimber, the procedure might have worked, but in the long run it was a good thing, because there was a high probability I would have ended up with a half-functioning finger. Some people think I went back to the hospital and asked to have the finger removed, but that wasn't the case. I had no alternative.

I never experienced a long period of depression. I knew that climbing was everything to me. And I've always had this capacity to use hard experiences to fuel my motivation. Chopping off my finger simply forced me to step it up a notch. People don't understand what they're made of until they're put up against something that really challenges them.

At that time I was trying to make it as a professional climber, and I was kind of doing it. I was living in my Honda on the road, but it wasn't a sustainable way of life. Then I chopped off my finger and that ignited this fire. It focused me. That's when I became fascinated with El Cap, and I started training super hard.

Weirdly enough, chopping off my finger was the point in my life where I made the greatest gains in my climbing. Which is not to say that staring at my finger in a plastic bag on the way to the hospital was not a moment of complete despair.

"Oh my God, what is this going to do to my climbing?"

But I spent 2 weeks in the hospital digesting that, and by the time I got out, I was determined not to let it stop me. I loved climbing so much I couldn't give it up. There was no choice. And the reaction from my doctors was mixed. The doctor who was on call when I first came in, and actually did the surgeries, was not a climber, and his view was, "Yeah, people chop off their fingers all the time. Everybody finds a way to adapt."

But ironically his partner was a dedicated climber, and at one point he told me I should start looking for another path in life. And that just pissed me off. I left the hospital with this very powerful idea to prove him wrong. Maybe that was his plan all along.

After the accident I started looking for inspiring stories about people who had undergone catastrophes, for instance people who became paraplegics but then became the most psyched people in the world. I found a study that monitored happiness in people who had won the lottery vs. people who had become paraplegics. It turned out a year later the people who were paraplegics were happier than the people who had won the lottery. There's something to that. I have a deep-seated belief that challenge brings out the best in people.

The Dawn Wall

From start to finish *The Dawn Wall* took 10 years. The first time I rappelled down it, it seemed way too hard. Then once I fully committed to the project, it took 7 years of dedicated effort. In order to put that much time and effort in one project you have to be incredibly inspired. When I took on *The Dawn Wall*, I had already been climbing most of my life. I was totally in love with the process of finding something that was beyond me then trying to rise to the challenge. *The Dawn Wall* became the pinnacle of that approach. It's really all based on curiosity. Can I really become the kind of person I need to be to climb something that difficult? Can I get better and stronger and stick with something that long?

And the other side of the coin is that I simply love the life that pursuits like *The Dawn Wall* provide. I get to come to Yosemite for 3 or 4 months a year. I get to live in my favorite place in the world, up on a wall. It's an excuse to be doing what I love.

It was the times I would focus on the possibility of failure when it all felt crushing. I would go up on El Cap for 2 weeks hoping to accomplish something, and I would fail. And part of me would think, "Man, you are wasting your life on this thing. It's never going to happen."

But I tuned that out and focused instead on the benefits the life provided. Even if I wasn't in Yosemite, I would think about *The Dawn Wall*. I was super motivated. I trained continually. Climbing the route was the light at the end of the tunnel. And I reached a point where I knew that even if I never made it to that light—it was okay. The reward became the pursuit itself. That's how I stuck with it all those years.

During that time I went through an entire process of becoming fascinated with *The Dawn Wall*, then giving up, thinking it was too much and moving on to other things. For example, during that time I climbed *Magic Mushroom* on El Cap (May 2012 with Justin Sjong, Grade VI, 14a). I'd look at *The Dawn Wall* and think, "I'm never going to be able to do this. I should step it down a notch." So I'd go climb something else—but I would always come back.

And other people helped fuel me. I would be feeling down, thinking about giving up, but my family and friends would say, "We know you really want to do this, so how are we going to make that happen?"

That made it feel like a team effort, which was very motivating, because I felt if I failed, I would let them down as well.

A huge turning point came when I brought filmmaker Josh Lowell of Big Up Productions up on *The Dawn Wall* to check it out. That was a pretty dark period. I was up there suffering all by myself. I was asking questions: Who am I? What do I want from this project? And I was thinking that this kind of single-minded pursuit was a pretty selfish endeavor.

Then Josh came and it all switched to finding a way to share this incredible adventure with others. And suddenly it was super fun being up there with friends. Having that community made it feel less selfish. It made all the manual labor more manageable. When you do that stuff with friends, it goes from being something that's punishing and pushes you down, to something that's enlightening and lifts you up. When I was up there alone working the route, I was wondering if I was crazy. So when other people came and saw the potential and were inspired by it as well, it helped me know it was worthwhile.

And yes, now that it's over it has left a bit of a void. Throughout my life, I've always gravitated toward the next big thing, and I imagine I will this time too. But those years working on *The Dawn Wall* were intense in so many ways. I felt like I was doing exactly what was right for me—what I was intended to do—and now in a way, that's gone.

But what I really love is the pursuit and the challenge.

So I just have to find it again in an altered form, and I'm confident that's going to happen. It's already happening. I'm writing a book about my life, and that's a huge, daunting task. I feel incredibly challenged. And I'm doing tons of speaking engagements, so I'm developing parts of myself I've neglected. That feels good and fulfilling.

I'm not comfortable with ever being satisfied. I like the idea of always wanting something more. For instance, people are working toward retirement. But to me retirement sounds incredibly scary. I always want to find something new that challenges me and pulls me. But another project the same magnitude as *The Dawn Wall*? I don't know if I need something *that big*.

The Fitz Traverse

(Note: In February of 2015, Caldwell teamed with Alex Honnold to make the first successful ascent of *The Fitz Traverse*, a one-push traverse of all the peaks of the Fitzroy Massif in Patagonia: seven summits spanning 4 miles, with 12,000 feet of vertical gain and 100 rappels.)

It's funny comparing *The Dawn Wall* and *The Fitz Traverse*. Everybody likes to do that because they were done in close proximity, and they were done in very different styles. The old-school mountaineers come up to me and say, "Man, *The Dawn Wall* was cool, but *The Fitz Traverse*, now *that's* what it's all about."

Caldwell practicing "elective hardship" on the *Alien Roof* (12b), North Face of *The Rostrum*

But the more physical climbers, the sport climbers and boulderers, they look at *The Dawn Wall* and think it was far more impressive.

So it's hard to say. I felt like *The Fitz Traverse* was a really beautiful experience in the mountains with tons of adventure, but it was also quite dangerous. And some people who value risk are going to think that's more impressive. But I don't. I believe that being dangerous is selfish.

So I would say that in my heart I value *The Dawn Wall* more—partly because it was a process that drove me for 7 years. Whereas *The Fitz Traverse* was this very cool thing that just happened. I didn't have to pursue it.

I think *The Dawn Wall* spoke to a lot of people because it tapped in to some large themes that inspire everyone—themes like brotherhood and having a big dream. Everyone wants to live that way, but not everyone's bold enough to do it. So Kevin and I became examples of two dudes having this great adventure, living that kind of life. We're all in. We aren't holding back. And we're loving it, having this amazing time up there. Everyone wants to live that way.

But the fact it became this major media event—I think that was just a fluke. I've basically been doing the same sort of things for 20 years, and this was the first time it became so public. I think it had a lot to do with the rise of social media. The climb took place at a time when technology allowed us to project our experience to the world in real time, then it caught fire and went viral.

Right in the middle of the media frenzy I dropped my phone off the wall. I dropped it by accident, but I instantly thought, "This is probably a good thing." We were having the experience of a lifetime, and I wanted to appreciate it. I wanted to be fully in the moment. I could have had another phone brought up, but I didn't want to.

Kevin had his phone the whole time, so he sat there on his portaledge following the media and getting incredibly stressed.

And I just stayed in the moment. I loved doing that. It was a great lesson. I felt my creativity coming to life. I felt my connection with my friends and the environment much more acutely than if I had had my phone.

It made me realize that my motivation to do these things is deeply personal. I don't need to broadcast it. It's all about the things that matter most to me. That becomes the foundation everything else is built on.

And that's something that's changing in climbing. It used to be about going out with your friends building a connection, but that's fading, because it's growing harder to separate your personal experience from how other people view it. Your life is projected for everyone to comment on.

I never thought about it before, but maybe that's part of why *The Dawn Wall* connected with so many. Perhaps people saw it as this genuine, positive, personal thing—in a world where there's not that much that's genuine or positive anymore.

Why I Climb

Every time I think about the reasons why I climb, it hits me differently.

But I think I touched on it when I said it's because I'm in these beautiful places doing something deeply personal. I'm doing something that feels right. The further I get from those things, the less grounded I feel. For instance, if I feel I'm climbing for others—or when I was competing—it doesn't feel as right as when I'm here in Yosemite, living in a way that people might have lived hundreds of years ago. In other words, out in the mountains—just me and my friends—without all the technology, just having a good time, building deep and lasting connections—that's what feels right. And it fulfills the need to battle, which is built into some of us at least. Bottom line: It's a great way to live.

Lessons

In a recent TED talk I gave, I said the greatest gift my dad gave me was to learn how to reframe adversity as adventure. So one of the most important lessons I've learned is to look at challenges as positive, life-driving events. In fact, those kinds of challenges are something I actively seek. And if you learn to see things in that way, life gets a bit easier. What I mean is, people who are always avoiding challenges or looking for excuses have a harder path. If you can learn to tackle life head-on, things are going to be less scary. Climbing has the ability to connect humans with the way we were meant to be. We're not meant to be in an office all day staring at a computer. Climbing provides a path back—to nature and to really connecting with other people face-to-face. It feels like we're losing those experiences as the digital world takes over. I'm

In his presentations Caldwell says, "The greatest gift my dad gave me was to learn how to reframe adversity as adventure."

biased, but in my opinion climbers live life at a higher level than the norm. When you meet climbers, they have a fire in their eyes. They are positive. But when you visit the business world, you meet people who have been sitting inside all day, who are not really that psyched about their lives.

Spirit Matters

By itself I don't think climbing has any higher meaning or purpose. At its most basic it's just another way to play. But the fact that it brings you outside, close to nature, and helps you build connections, there's a higher meaning and purpose to that. And when something in life is inexplicably positive, I think people see that as spiritual. For example, when you have an experience that transcends what you can understand, that's spirituality. And I believe climbing has a way of creating those experiences.

The Future

I feel absolutely spoiled. I feel like I'm living this incredible life. I've found something I'm totally passionate about. I love every day, and the fact that I can raise a family doing what I'm doing? That's rare. So I feel unbelievably lucky.

I'm not sure what the future will bring. I know I won't be a pro climber forever. But I believe in letting life grow organically and not making plans too far in advance. I have tons of dreams, and any one of them might take me in all kinds of directions. So I let motivation be the driver. Listen to your gut. I believe that if you're paying attention, really being genuine about what you know is right, that will lead you in the right direction. People talk about following your passion, but that's also a form of pressure. For instance, you tell a group of kids in high school to follow their passion, and they're like, "Oh my God, what's my passion?" So I would say that it's more than just passion; it's also listening to your instincts and motivation and following your heart.

Relationships

I'm lucky that my parents provided such a great example for me to follow. And I'm lucky that climbing has evolved to the point where I can actually make a living *and* raise a family—that was something that created tension in my past relationships. For example, the idea that if you pursued climbing with everything you had, it meant you were ignoring your family, that you weren't going to be the breadwinner, and all that. But that's not how things have turned out. My job is my passion, and it's the way I raise my family. All those things have merged in a great way. And that makes it so much easier.

That's not to say there aren't tensions. That's part of any relationship. Tension can be especially high on those days I feel stretched in a million directions, and I think I have another kid on the way, and part of me just wants to forget everything and simply spend time with my family, living in some kind of balance. But I believe you have to view life in a positive way—including all the opportunities that come your way. You embrace it all and you realize it's not going to be perfect. That's the only balance I've found.

Partnerships

I feel that everything's better when it's shared. Maybe that's another reason I never wanted to be a soloist. Sure, I want to gain understanding for myself, but at the same time I believe climbing is an inherently collaborative thing. I've been very blessed to have great partners. A good partnership has a way

"Climbing has the ability to connect humans with the way they were meant to be," Caldwell says. "Climbing provides a path back to nature and to connecting with other people." Caldwell and Honnold on Leaning Tower.

of bringing out the best in each person. The negative challenges fade and the positive things become more memorable.

So I look for someone who can put up with a lot and still stay positive. Obviously, I look for someone with the skills that help me believe that whatever we're taking on can be accomplished. And I look for partners who are dreamers, people who think differently and are in some way better than me—because I want to learn from them.

So Kevin saw the first video we made about *The Dawn Wall* and emailed me and asked if I would introduce him to the world of big wall free climbing, and at first I was skeptical. I knew he was primarily a boulderer. I wasn't sure if he had ever climbed any multipitch at all. But his letter also made me think about Todd Skinner. Skinner was the first "outsider" to come to Yosemite and really excel. He grew up in Wyoming and climbed all over the world, so he didn't have preconceived notions about what was possible in the Valley. Todd once told me he thought the people who had done the best in Yosemite were those who didn't live there. They had the creativity to see outside the box. And I needed that. It made me think that maybe a boulderer would have exactly the skills required to climb something as hard as *The Dawn Wall*.

Plus I had watched bouldering go through this great evolution. People are climbing things on boulders I can't even conceive. In Estes there's a bouldering area on the mountainside right above my parents' house. I grew up walking through those boulders, but I didn't think it was a bouldering area. The rocks were too blank. But in the past 15 years that area has become one of the highest concentrations of hard bouldering problems in the world.

If I didn't have the vision to see that potential in my own backyard, I thought maybe Kevin could provide something I couldn't see on El Cap as well.

Yet at the same time, I wasn't sure, because one thing boulderers don't necessarily have is the ability to suffer it out, and that's really what big wall free climbing is all about. So I had to test him. On the first day he showed up, I prepared an 80-pound haul bag full of gear for each of us, and we hiked to the top of El Cap carrying those bags.

I figured if Kevin could handle that, then maybe we had a chance. And absolutely, he manned up and made it happen. From then on our partnership blossomed.

PAIGE CLAASSEN

To paraphrase F. Scott Fitzgerald, the rich are not like the rest of us, and neither are the world's best climbers. Up before dawn. Drive 2 hours in the hope of jumping on The Project before it gets too hot. Three burns and the sun's too high. Drive home. Rest. Repeat.

One's entire existence becomes focused on minutia. Waiting until stone cools and skin tightens enough to provide optimum contact. Esoteric rituals with massage bars, rollers, and muscle probes; filing down calluses; brushing holds. Intricate calculations involving thermometers, humidity gauges, tick marks, beta, and one's ape index, worthy of a NASA moon shot.

Elite projecting requires one to literally believe in the impossible—to ignore the overwhelming physical evidence that the holds are simply too small and too few to use. To somehow cultivate the faith that given enough time, effort, and desire, a few tiny edges a body length apart can be transformed into a path to victory. But first, the swirling constellations of fitness, skin care, nutrition, and mind control must all come into perfect alignment.

Whether competing inside against other climbers or outside against herself, Paige Claassen has been playing the competitive climbing game, and playing it well, since she was 9 years old. When combined with Angie Payne's essay "Why I Compete" (page 25), she provides a primer not only on how to survive, but also to flourish, when navigating the treacherous reefs and shoals of competitive climbing.

I first met Paige when I was working on *Women Who Dare*. At the time she was still in college, commuting on weekends 400 miles between her home in Colorado to Moab, Utah to work a notoriously sandbagged route in Millcreek Canyon. I was immediately impressed not only by her obvious dedication, but by her humor, poise, and calm approach to a form of climbing that can easily descend into obsession. And although scheduling conflicts prevented me from including her in the first book, Paige was the first climber I contacted when starting *Why We Climb*.

Paige Claassen gathers her resources to fight *Necessary Evil* (14c), Virgin River Gorge, Arizona.

In her competitive career spanning more than a decade, Paige made the podium in twelve different competitions, winning the Junior Bouldering Nationals and the Continental Championships in 2006, the Adult National Championships in 2007, the New Jersey Gravity Brawl in 2008, as well as placing second in the SCS Nationals in 2008 and 2009 and the 2008 Continental Championships.

Outside, Claassen has bouldered v11, and she has twenty-one sport climbing sends 13d through 14c to her credit, most notably the first female ascent of *Just Do It* (14c) at Smith Rock; *Ganesh* (14a) in Badami, India; *Sea of Tranquility* and *China Climb* (both 14a) in Yangshuo, China; *Rodan* (14a) in Waterval Boven, South Africa; *Grand Old Opry* (14b+) in Monastery, Colorado; and *Motley Crux* (14a) in Deep Creek, Washington. She also made the first ascent of *Digital Warfare* (14a) in South Africa. In 2012 Paige combined her climbing skills with an interest in social justice to create *Lead Now,* a program to raise money and awareness for nonprofits worldwide.

Like many elite climbers, Claassen has the refreshing confidence to be herself. She freely admits that she loves to eat—pretty much whatever she wants—even sugar! She's so picky about the routes she climbs, she's been accused of not really liking climbing. And she thinks yoga is stupid. As she writes in her resume: "I travel. I climb. I won a spelling bee in middle school. I enjoy vacuuming, although I prefer baking chocolate cakes. I strongly dislike olives. And I'm very thankful to my parents for introducing me to climbing so I didn't have to spend my life on the sidelines."

Roots

My name's Paige Claassen. I was born June 13, 1990. I grew up in Estes Park, Colorado, and I'm primarily a sport climber. My family moved to Estes when I was 9 and I had trouble fitting in. It was a tough time. I was searching for what made me "me," and I was very shy. My parents saw an ad for an after-school climbing program. They took me to check it out, and I loved it.

Climbing was the first thing I was really good at. For some reason, I wasn't afraid of heights, and I started competing immediately. For the first 8 years, I was a total gym rat. The gym provided a comfortable place to train, push

Bouldering in Red Rocks. "We're climbers because climbing makes us happy," Claassen says. "We live simple lives and make sacrifices so we can pursue the next coolest line."

myself, and build confidence. I was very competitive, both with myself and others, and I think that helped me improve quickly. My older teammates called me the "Energizer Bunny" because I seemed to have unlimited energy and love for climbing. My family provided a great support system. No one ever said, "You must train harder" or "You must perform better." All my motivation was internal. I wanted to be the best I could be.

Plastic vs. Rock

Competitive climbing and outdoor climbing are almost entirely different sports. Climbing well on each medium requires very different skill sets, and climbers have to put in the time and effort to excel on each.

Competing taught me how to train and gave me the drive to progress. After school and on weekends my family would drive to the city so that my brother Sam and I could train in bigger gyms. Sam kept things fun and light, and I kept things focused. We were the perfect duo. Climbing is very much an individual sport, yet it requires a strong support system, especially for young climbers. I had a brother and good friends to train with, and I had parents to hug me after a big win, or a bruising loss.

With the ups and downs of competitive climbing came life lessons that reach beyond the gym or crag. I was competitive and struggled with comparing myself to others. I recall the French Invitational in Serre Chevalier where I qualified for the Adult Open. At the time I was only 15, and I remember having a total meltdown, screaming at my parents, "I don't belong here! I'm just a kid competing against World Cup competitors who are so much more experienced."

But they said, "Paige, you do belong here. You earned your spot. Now go out and try as hard as you can."

So I did. I didn't make the podium, but it was a great lesson. *Work hard, try your best, and be proud of your efforts—whatever you achieve.* That pep talk stuck with me through future competitions and beyond as I began projecting harder routes outside. As long as I felt I had put my best foot forward, I knew I

"Work hard. Try your best, and be proud of your efforts—whatever you achieve," says Claassen, shown here (on left) competing in the 2015 Psicoblock Masters.

shouldn't be disappointed in the results. Projecting outside is much the same, except now I'm competing against myself. I'm trying to beat my own past performance, to climb something more challenging and to climb it better.

My most memorable climbing experiences aren't my proudest sends or the hardest grades I've climbed. They are moments from early in my career, traveling with my family for competitions. Those were the days when I fell in love with climbing so they mean more to me than any major ascent. The specific lines I've climbed are interchangeable, but learning to climb with the support of loved ones helped me develop from a shy girl into an independent, confident adult. Deep down, that's really what climbing has given me.

Failure

No matter what type of climbing I'm doing, whether it's competition or a route outside, falling short of expectations is a big part of the experience. I may fall 100, 200, even 500 times—in order to make it to the top once.

Yet all along the way, I'm making incremental progress, so I have to twist all that failure around in my head. I have to convince myself I'm not actually *failing* each time I fall. I'm learning something, adapting, training my body to perform better. It takes the proper attitude to avoid frustration. I wish I could say I always succeed in finding it.

One year at the Lander Climbers Festival, I did a presentation on failure and success. I talked about my climbing batting average and calculated that my success rate on hard routes is .005 or less. That's the equivalent of 1 hit in 200 times at bat! The point being that if we set high goals, we've got to be willing to put in the time and sacrifice necessary to achieve them.

To do that, it's helpful to set smaller, more attainable goals along the way. But that's the part I'm not very good at. I'll bang my head against the wall all day. I won't be happy. Yet I won't give up! But setting a smaller goal that's within reach? Now that's a real struggle.

Projecting

I have to choose projects in places I love, because I know I'll be spending significant amounts of time there. I prefer routes in beautiful settings a bit removed from the crowds. Some projects will be short, but others can take years. So if I'm battling with a route, I want to enjoy the journey, which means appreciating the place I'm in and the people I'm with—no matter how long it takes.

I have unfinished projects that I've worked for years but am still not ready to give up on. When I'm feeling beat down and frustrated, I'll set that route aside for a while—maybe an entire season—and return when I feel refreshed. Most recently I fought a mental battle on *Sarchasm*, a 14a developed by Tommy Caldwell at 12,000 feet on Longs Peak. For a sport route it requires some effort just to get to—2 hours of hiking—and summer thunderstorms make the timing tricky as well. On that route I put immense pressure on myself, and as a result I made myself miserable each time I fell. I knew I was in a destructive cycle, but I couldn't break it on my own. That is when supportive partners make all the difference. Suddenly climbing becomes a team effort, because the emotional and mental encouragement of your friends becomes the difference between sending or not. With the help of my boyfriend Arjan (Paige and Arjan de Kock were married in May 2016) reminding me of things I already knew, but wouldn't let myself believe, I finally clipped the chains.

The movements on *Sarchasm* flow beautifully once you unlock the beta, and that's a quality I look for. I'm very picky about the routes I choose. In fact, I've been accused of *not really liking* climbing because I can be so picky.

I don't consider myself a particularly physical climber, so I tend to drift toward what some might call *old-school* sport routes. Many modern routes are in steep caves, but I enjoy technical climbing, which consists of solving puzzles made out of holds that at first feel too tiny to use. It's a bit magical; with enough time, effort, and creativity, those intricate sequences transform into fluid movement.

The ability to adapt to a wide range of styles is also something I enjoy. I never want to be limited to a single style or technique. When I'm traveling I want to be able to walk up to any piece of rock and feel confident I can find a way to climb it. Each variation in style provides inspiration and a new challenge, and that gets to the heart of my favorite part of climbing—that each line offers something new to learn and new obstacles to overcome.

Motivation

I climb year-round, and I try to maintain peak fitness as required by projects in different seasons. But I also understand the importance of taking breaks, especially when I'm not feeling motivated. Some people advise to push through periods of low motivation, but I've found it's best for me to take a week or two off and do something else that inspires me. I'll spend time with my family, write, draw, or experiment with new recipes in the kitchen. There are so many things in life to put one's energy into. Climbing is one of those things, but for me it's not the *only* thing, so when my mind and body ask for time off, I happily comply.

Inner fire is essential. I have to love what I'm doing, because if my mind isn't engaged, my body will not perform its best.

Training & Nutrition

I love to cook. Food is my favorite topic, even when I'm out climbing. Between attempts on a project, I'll happily talk about what to make for dinner. I get really hungry, so after a day of climbing I'm always tempted to run home and whip up something fast. But I've learned to put more time into the process of cooking and pay attention to the quality of food, which makes it even more fun.

I've experimented with different diets, but I don't think restricting what I eat is helpful. I tried the starvation approach that unfortunately, many female athletes (and males!) go through, and I didn't find it helpful. I've never felt so weak as when I limited my calories to an extreme. I lost a bunch of weight, but instead of feeling light and invincible, I felt lifeless and unmotivated. Fortunately, I was still living at home during that phase, and my mom worked hard to pull me out of that mentality before it went too far.

The fact is I feel amazing when I eat sugar! It keeps my stomach from hurting, it gives me energy, and it's delicious. I feel strongest—in mind and body—when I'm eating what I want. So bring on the sugar, I'm not afraid!

As for cross-training, I'll go through periods where I enjoy trail running. I'll do floor exercises for my core and to strengthen my weak triceps. I have a theory that doing ten push-ups a day makes me a stronger climber. I've tried

Paige and Arjan make homemade pasta. "I love to cook. Food is my favorite topic even when climbing," Claassen says.

yoga, but I find it boring. I'm quite stiff, and I struggle to even touch my toes. But I also realize that some of my minor injuries like tendonitis and heel bursitis result from my inflexibility. I'm trying to get better at stretching at the end of the day and warming up properly at the beginning. Being kind to the body and helping it recover are essential, especially as I age. I'm only 25, but I can already feel those small aches and pains.

Giving Back

Like any activity or hobby, climbing can be very selfish. We're climbers because we love the sport and climbing makes us happy. We live simple lives and make sacrifices so that we can pursue the next coolest line.

I graduated from university in December 2012, and thought, "Well, if I'm going to put all this time and energy into climbing, why not try to do some good as well?" So I designed *Lead Now* with Jon Glassberg, from the production company Louder Than 11, and over a 10-month period I attempted a

5.14 in nine different countries, creating videos along the way to raise money and awareness for a variety of nonprofit organizations. I climbed seven 14s throughout South Africa, Russia, Italy, Japan, China, India, Turkey, Ecuador, and Chile, and we raised $20,000 for organizations around the world.

Lead Now was very much an experiment. It exposed me to the struggles people around the world face on a daily basis. At home in Colorado, everything's comfortable. Certainly there are people struggling in the United States, but most Americans are somewhat removed from that struggle. It was an eye-opener to see how people live around the world. It taught me to appreciate what I have and give up what I don't need.

One of my favorite experiences of *Lead Now* was working with VE Global, an organization in Chile that helps children who have been removed from their homes because of abuse and neglect. We took some of those girls to a climbing gym, and I was surprised by their willingness to go for it. The experience took me back to my days as a young girl learning to climb. It reminded me of the confidence climbing gave me, and it made me very doubly grateful that my family was able to give me the opportunity to climb, because not every kid is that fortunate. I also came home with a new appreciation for how beautiful my own home is. Even after seeing so many incredible sights, I came home thinking, "Wow, I live in one of the coolest places in the world!"

Why I Climb

One big reason why we climb, which people rarely mention, is because we're good at it. I want to devote my time to something that complements my talents. That's human nature.

Climbing presents a challenge, one that requires a perfect alignment of my physical skills, mental fortitude, and emotional perseverance. I actually enjoy frustration. I don't like to feel stagnant. In order to develop new skills and grow my boundaries I need to be pushed. In some ways I'm never content. I clip the chains on one project. I come down. I'm happy, but soon I'm looking for the next objective. That's exciting, because the challenge never ends.

What I Like Least

I don't enjoy feeling as though everything revolves around climbing. I love climbing, but it can also become very one-dimensional, where conversations, relationships, eating, reading—all revolve around climbing. I enjoy getting out of that headspace, because there are so many other things in life I want to pursue and appreciate.

When I was 20, I chose to stop competing because it was becoming unhealthy. I was extremely competitive, which wasn't bad in itself, but I began comparing myself to others in a way that wasn't positive. If I feel disappointed in myself, it needs to be because I'm disappointed in *my* performance—not in my performance compared to others.

There are healthy ways to compete, of course. The spirit of competition should be about how far you can push yourself; *it should not be about hoping that others fail.* If I want someone to fall just so I can place higher, then it's time for a change. So I chose to compete against myself, by refocusing my efforts on difficult projecting outside.

What Is Climbing?

For me, climbing is a sport. I don't think that by itself it has a heart or soul. We have to pour our own heart and soul into the activities we pursue. Climbing can transform our lives, our identities, and how we relate to people and the world. It helped me develop my identity at 9 years old, and it has given me a strong work ethic, confidence, friends, and the ability to speak in front of an audience without passing out in fear.

Ultimately, climbing is a head game, a lesson in controlling fear and doubt. It requires dedication and sacrifice, and in return it provides exercise for the body and mind. When I'm overwhelmed, climbing is my stress reliever, my opportunity to unplug from a crowded world, and my connection to our planet's most eclectic collection of humans.

What I've Learned

I was a very different person when I started climbing. Climbing took me from a place where I couldn't look people in the eye to feeling confident on camera or in front of an audience. It helped shape my control-freak tendencies into a more productive mind-set. Climbing has taken me around the world, and my travels have taught me to adapt to my surroundings. I've learned to redefine the word *need*. I *need* love from family and friends. I *need* to accept myself, and I *need* freedom to practice my faith. I have those things, so there's very little left to want.

Climbing demands a strong work ethic. At first a difficult route or problem seems impossible. After 16 years, I've learned that if I work hard for something, if I put the time and effort into what I want to achieve, it becomes possible.

Spirit Matters

To me spirituality means my faith as a Christian and my relationship with God. For me climbing is not a spiritual experience, it's a really fun sport. But I do believe God has opened doors for me through climbing. He gave me the talent to climb, the family to support my ambitions, and opportunities to learn and explore. *Lead Now* was one of those opportunities. I wholeheartedly believe that project wouldn't have come together if God didn't have a plan for it. *Lead Now* was a stepping-stone that allowed me to get where I am and taught me things about the world and the people in it.

The climbing community is very open-minded and accepting. Most people who know me know I'm a Christian, but not once has anyone made fun of me (at least not to my face) for what I believe, and I think that's a special thing. People expect Christians to be judgmental, but that's not what I believe. We each have a set of morals, regardless of our beliefs. Ultimately, we're all just trying to go about life and be the best we can be. Just because I don't swear, doesn't mean I'm appalled when someone else does. I would rather someone be themselves and not pretend because I might be offended. I'm accepted for who I am, and I want to accept others for who they are as well.

Climber's Mind

For me the mental aspect of climbing has always been more important than the physical. I've trained my body to perform. My muscles know what to do. But success comes down to convincing my mind that I'm capable. I often find I need to turn my mind off so my body can do what I've trained it to do. Rarely does physical weakness prevent me from achieving my goals. Fear and doubt are my greatest hurdles.

I love the beginning stages of working a project: figuring out the moves, finding new holds, learning how to move my body with precision and efficiency. Everything is new and I'm eager to learn. There's no pressure, because it's not *send time* yet.

But once I flip that switch and it's time to redpoint, then the pressure and stress start to mount. As a competitor I rarely felt nervous before competitions, but once

Claassen belaying in the VRG

I began to work projects outside, I had to find a way to distract my mind. Breathing became my best defense. I try to maintain a steady breathing pattern as I climb. Optimally all I can hear in my head is my breath. That keeps my brain from saying, "Oh no! Here comes the hard part" or "Here's where you fall every time!" It's all about turning those thoughts off.

Advice for the Next Generation

I see how competitive climbing has evolved. Kids are pushed *much* harder than I was—only 10 years ago—by parents and coaches alike. As a kid your body is developing rapidly, so it isn't a great time to push your body to its limit. Enjoy being a kid. Focus on developing your mind and your love of climbing. Don't be afraid to pursue other interests. Try to strike a balance and develop a healthy respect for the sport and yourself. In the long run learning to love climbing is far more valuable and sustainable than any single victory.

ALEX HONNOLD

One of the most surprising things I learned writing this book is that Alex Honnold has size 12½ feet. As Tommy Caldwell remarked when Alex mentioned this during an ascent of Leaning Tower, "Dude, I'm surprised you can climb any cracks at all!"

Because as everyone knows, Alex Honnold *can* climb cracks. Anyone who has climbed Zion's *Moonlight Buttress* or Half Dome's *Northwest Face* will surely agree. For most climbers free climbing either of those routes with ropes and protection is a lifetime crowning achievement. But to climb them without rope, gear, or a partner? Are you kidding? Just the thought of free soloing something at that level leaves most climbers speechless.

Asked by Chris Kalous to describe himself for an episode of *The Enormocast*, Honnold said, "I don't drink. I don't do drugs. Really, I'm like a Mormon who doesn't believe in God . . . I'm well-known because I'm good at a game no one else wants to play. It's true! It's like I'm pretty good at basketball but I'm the only one who plays. If I go sport climbing, I'm never the best climber at the crag. And bouldering? Dude, I suck at bouldering."

In his outspoken, funny, and irreverent way, Honnold attributes his success to a quirk of fate—the coincidence that free soloing, the climbing he enjoys and in which he excels, is so easy to understand. Whether or not you know anything about climbing, all it takes is one photo or video clip of Alex soloing and you get it. If this guy makes a mistake—he's dead. Game over.

John Bachar, Peter Croft, Derek Hersey, Steph Davis, and Dean Potter have all taken the solo game far beyond what the majority of climbers consider sane or reasonable—but Honnold has surpassed them all. The result is that Honnold is one of the best-known climbers in the world. Sure, a majority of *climbers* know who Chris Sharma, Lynn Hill, and Adam Ondra are. But Honnold crosses over into the mainstream. More than 60 million average citizens watched Alex do his thing on *60 Minutes*. He has appeared in ads and

Alex Honnold in his element, high on El Capitan

commercials worldwide, was featured on the cover of the *New York Times Sunday Magazine*, and his book *Alone on the Wall* made the *New York Times* bestseller list.

All of which has led to a strange and surreal *celebrity vs. dirtbag* existence. As he discusses below, when he wakes up in his Ford Econoline in Yosemite and ventures forth to eat a bowl of cereal, Alex never knows what awaits him. Will it be just a hungry squirrel or a busload of tourists, hungry to pose with him for selfies?

When I'm around Alex, what strikes me is not his athletic prowess (as others have noted, until he touches rock, he's more Clark Kent than Superman), it is his clear-eyed intelligence, his candor, and his uncanny ability to be completely himself. The Tibetan teacher Chögyam Trungpa once said the first task in becoming a spiritual warrior is to become fearlessly oneself. But in our age of celebrity and self-promotion, that's increasingly rare. Instead we are encouraged to continually rebrand ourselves, using the sleight of hand of social media to create a more marketable hologram of what we think we should be.

In contrast, Honnold is one of the few who never bothers to put on a social mask. Because of this, he stands out in the way only supremely self-confident people can. His actions speak for themselves, so he has absolutely nothing to prove—to anyone. He has mastered one of humanity's primal fears—the fear of death—so he doesn't have to act like a badass. He is one.

And he's genuinely happy living a life of voluntary simplicity. Yes, he has an agent, but his home is a white van and all the climbing areas of the world. By his own admission his income now makes him one of the 1 percent, but he does his best to offset all the jet-setting by being a vegetarian and living with as few possessions as possible. Shocked by the poverty he's witnessed, he created the Honnold Foundation in order to do what he can to help. As he says, in the end the foundation may be far more important than any climb he ever does; however, climbing is the vehicle that makes everything else possible.

But if you want to piss Alex off, just ask him if he ever gets scared. Honnold believes, or wants to believe, that he's just like everyone else. He gets scared. He's afraid of dying. He does not have a personality disorder or a mutant brain. This is a huge part of his charm, the feeling that he's just like you and me.

And when you hang out with him, he starts to convince you. You start thinking that maybe you've gotten everything wrong—as in your entire grasp of reality. You start thinking that perhaps it's perfectly normal to solo *The Steck-Salathé* or fifty routes in a morning at J Tree. Hanging out with Alex and sampling his version of reality is a bit like living in a dream—the one where suddenly you can fly, you just never noticed it before. Then, when you're standing alone at the base of Sentinel chalking up, you suddenly wake up.

"Hey, wait a minute!"

Honnold has been repeatedly criticized for downplaying his achievements. But really, what choice does he have? The only protection Alex allows himself during soloing is his supreme confidence in his own abilities. His unshakable certainty that the routes he solos are so far within his comfort zone, there's no possibility of falling—so he doesn't need a rope.

"If I have a particular gift, it's a mental one," Honnold wrote in an op-ed piece for the *New York Times*, "the ability to keep it together where others might freak out."[1]

And as his good friend Tommy Caldwell observed, "Most of us think dying is a really serious, scary thing, but I don't think Alex does. He's wired a little differently. The risk excites him, and he knows it's super badass, but he doesn't allow himself to go beyond that in his mind. The other great free soloists always talk about this conversation with death. Alex is like, 'I'm not going to fall, its no big deal.' That's what makes him so good."

As I watch Alex climb *The Salathé Headwall* through the viewfinder of my camera, like the falcon that wheels and calls below him, he seems to be a creature of the air. El Cap—with its soaring granite, rushing wind, and heart-stopping exposure—is his home, his aerie. He's as comfortable and as relaxed as a man might be going for a run in a city park.

Career Highlights

1991 Age 5, has first gym experience

2002 Age 16, can do a one-finger pull-up

2004 Places second in the youth division of the US National Climbing Championships; drops out of college

2007 Solos *Astroman* (11c) and *The Rostrum* (11c)

2008 Solos *Moonlight Buttress* (12+) and *Northwest Face* of Half Dome (12)

2014 Solos *El Sendero Luminoso* (12d), El Potrero Chico, Mexico; *Romantic Warrior* (12b) in the Needles; and *University Wall* (12a), Squamish Chief, British Columbia. Climbs 7 routes on El Cap in 7 days, with David Allfrey, many of them new speed records.

2015 Solos 290 pitches in a day at Squamish in honor of his 29th birthday. First ascent of *The Fitz Traverse* in Patagonia with Tommy Caldwell.

2016 Second Ascent/First One-Day Ascent of *The Torre Traverse* with Colin Haley

Roots

Hi, my name's Alex Honnold. I was born August 17, 1985. My social security number is . . . Oops! Sorry. I define myself as a rock climber. People know me mostly for free soloing, but I climb anything.

When I was a kid, I was always climbing trees and buildings and anything else I could find. I loved to play by climbing. Then when I was 11, a gym opened near my home and from then on I climbed in the gym.

I hate to make broad dramatic statements, so I would hate to say that climbing is my *calling*, or that climbing is my vocation, or that climbing is my life. But it's definitely true that I've never enjoyed anything as much as I do climbing and that I would rather climb than do anything else. So basically it's become my entire life.

Early Retirement

At the moment, however, I'm taking time off from climbing. I'm calling it a "full retirement," because then, when I come out of it, it will be that much more exciting. It's the first time in . . . I think 7 years now . . . that I've taken more than 2 weeks off. And even then it was only because I was traveling to some big expedition, or because I was physically crushed by some kind of climbing achievement. So I haven't really taken any time off just to chill for a *long* time.

Honnold making the second free ascent of *Wet Lycra Nightmare* (13d) on Leaning Tower. "Anything significant I've accomplished will be determined by history," he says.

And I was ready. Motivation was low. I could force myself to do a few things, but I didn't really want to. I just wanted to relax. So that's what I've been doing. It's pretty nice. I can see now why people take vacations. But it's kind of weird too, because basically my whole life is a vacation. I go from climbing trip to climbing trip. I do what I love, and I do it all the time.

So it's hard to justify taking time off, but this past spring I spent a month in Australia with the British climber Hazel Findley, and she was struggling with a shoulder injury. And while we were there, she got an MRI and discovered she had a torn labrum. Then she was super depressed, because she needed surgery, and it would take 6 months to recover. And I said, "I don't know what you're complaining about. You're getting a 6-month vacation."

Here Hazel's all depressed, and I'm thinking, "I would love to take 6 months off!" That's when I started thinking, "Hey, this is messed up." So I've been retired for the past 2 weeks. But each day I have some little flicker of motivation, like maybe I should do something rad, or maybe I should go for some big adventure. Then I think, "No, let's just tamp it down. Let's wait until it all builds up again and I'm really stoked."

So last night rappelling into *The Salathé Headwall,* I was definitely thinking, "This is amazing! This is beautiful! What an amazing place!" And to climb again felt great. So it's possible my retirement might be coming to an end.

A Simple Life

I aspire to live a low-impact lifestyle, and that's tough, because with the amount of travel I do I'm definitely living a super high-impact life. So in all the small ways I can, I try to minimize my impact. And that means not having too many things. It means living in a van and making it last for a long time. It means eating vegetarian. I'm doing what I can.

I haven't chosen to live in a van because I want to be a dirtbag. I live in the van because it allows me to climb wherever I want. The van allows me freedom. Why wouldn't I choose to live in it?

Normal life for me depends a lot on where I am and what I'm climbing. For instance, if I'm in Patagonia, life is dictated by the weather. Basically you go bouldering every day—unless the weather's good—then you go up into the mountains. Your schedule is totally helter-skelter depending on what the wind's doing. In Australia I pretty much did 2 days of hard sport climbing, followed by a rest day, then 2 more days of climbing. And here in Yosemite, it just depends. You might have a huge day, so then you have to rest. But if not, you might be able to climb 5 or 6 days in a row. Normally I try to climb a lot, then on rest days I go hiking or do a light run or some other *adventure-y* thing. Bottom line: When I'm on—I'm doing a lot.

Earlier this season I went to free solo *The Steck-Salathé* route (10b) on Sentinel Rock. I hadn't climbed the route in years, and it was my first time soloing it. I was taking a rest day and I thought, "I'll just go do some casual climbing and get some exercise."

So I took a bunch of food and water because I didn't want to hurry. About halfway up the route, I stopped and was eating my picnic when the phone rang. It was this guy who had been trying to get a hold of me to interview me for a book about fear. So the phone rings, and I said, "Cool, no problem let's talk now." And we chatted for over an hour, then I hung up, looked around, and realized, "Whoa! I'm still in the middle of *The Steck-Salathé*. I still have another thousand feet to climb, and I don't really want to now, because I just ate my lunch and now I'm cold."

But what are you going to do? I finished the route and hiked down. It was fine. But in retrospect I was thinking maybe I shouldn't have taken a business call in the middle of soloing a big wall, maybe I should have just maintained my momentum. But sometimes you've got to get your work done too.

And that story is not even unusual for me. I tell a story like that, and people are like, "Wow, that's crazy." But in my life that kind of thing happens all the time. This winter we were doing a shoot on El Cap, and we had to ascend 700 feet of fixed ropes to get into position. And I had a bunch of phone calls I needed to make, so I was holding my phone with my shoulder while I jumared up the wall. For me it was like talking on the phone while doing a stair stepper at the gym, the only difference being that if I dropped the phone, it would have cratered. And the people I was talking to would say, "Why do you sound like you're out of breath?" And I would answer, "Oh, that's because I'm jugging up El Cap."

But that's what you have to do when you live in Yosemite, where you don't have good cell service: You have to take advantage of the times when you can get a signal.

By the way, I've never dropped my phone—which is pretty amazing. I'll do that in the gym too. If I'm in the middle of an interview when I get to the gym, I'll just continue talking while I'm warming up on v1 or v2, problems where I can still hold the phone.

Another time Ueli Steck (the Swiss speed-climbing alpinist) came to Yosemite. We were supposed to speed climb *The Nose* for a film, but the project fell apart. So instead we just did a lot of climbing. We did some cool free routes, then we decided to climb *Free Rider* (Grade VI, 12d). So we went up on El Cap with super-light sleeping bags, some food, and a gallon of water. We didn't even take sleeping pads. In fact our haul bag was so light I didn't know how to haul it, because I only know how to haul using my body weight. The bag was so light, I would lean back, then basically fall down the wall, and the bag would shoot up.

The first morning, we climbed up to *The Spire*, halfway up El Cap. We camped there, and then the next morning we left our gear and climbed to the top via *Free Rider* and then rappelled back down. Then we climbed *The Sala-thé Headwall* (13b), and when we finished that, we rappelled back to *The Spire* again. We camped again that night, and the next morning we woke up early and simul-rapped down to the ground and went to the cafeteria for breakfast. All in all it was a pretty casual 2-day outing, just camping and climbing on El Cap because it's scenic, fun, and beautiful.

When you can climb that fast, you don't need much, and it's totally different from what most climbers experience. Like when you speed climb *The Nose*, you have very little food or water and you're passing parties who have been up there for 5 days and are completely worked. Maybe they ran out of water a day ago, and you're thinking, "Oh that sucks, I'm going to be back in the meadow in an hour having a picnic. But you guys? I wish we had something to give you."

Honnold at the crux of *Wet Lycra Nightmare*

Training

The question of training is interesting, because I would say the strict definition of training is progressive workouts designed to attain a specific goal. And by that definition I've never trained very seriously. But I certainly do a fair amount of working out. I climb all the time, then I do extra things like push-ups and core exercises and the occasional run or cardio. But I'm not sure a coach would call that training, because it's not periodic. It's not structured in a regimented way that builds, tapers off, then starts building again. So I definitely maintain a high level of fitness, but I'm not pursuing it in the same way as an Olympic athlete.

Actually the question of training is on my mind right now, because I feel like if I want to take my climbing to the next level, I'm going to have to start training in a more systematic way. So I think when I come out of retirement, I'm going to start being a bit more focused. At this stage of my career, I believe there would be value for me to train specifically in order to climb harder routes.

It's true that my primary goal isn't to climb the world's hardest sport routes, but on the other hand, I don't really know what my primary goal is. I like climbing hard big walls. I like being able to do big linkups in the mountains.

Everything I've done I've been able to do while climbing mid 14. Let's call it "14ish." If I could climb 14d or 15a, that would mean I could still do everything I love but it would be a few grades harder. There's huge appeal in being able to do that.

Why I Climb

The thing that got me into climbing as a kid, and that's still a big part of the reason I climb, is the movement.

I love swinging around on holds, dangling from toe hooks, dynoing for a jug, just doing fun maneuvers. It makes you feel like an ape, and in fact you are an ape. So it takes you back to your roots. I just love the movement of traveling over stone or plastic.

And of course now that I'm a professional climber, there's a lot more to it. There's the travel, the adventure, and the people. So it's hard to say what I like most, because it's become the focus of my entire life. It's all encompassing.

The way I climb, there's really no pressure to do anything. So right now I'm not really feeling it. I'm chilling, and it's very relaxing. I like it very much. And I'm in Yosemite, the same place I would normally be. I walk around and look at the cliffs, and they still look beautiful. They're still inspiring. But for whatever reason right now, I don't really want to climb, and that's fine.

I suppose that ties in with what I *don't* like about climbing. It hurts your feet. It hurts your hands. You get really tired. And normally that's a big part of what I enjoy—the struggle is what makes it all so rewarding. But right now, I don't want to struggle.

Free Soloing

Free soloing is weird. It requires more from you, so you get more from it. There is more of an emotional payoff. It's certainly a more intense experience. You are definitely more out there, on the edge. And when you solo something that's difficult, it's very satisfying on a personal level, in that you overcame the challenge.

And at the same time, I don't think free soloing is as simple as people think. It's not like hard soloing is just so *awesome*. It's not like every time you do it, you feel like a hero and life becomes *amazing*. In fact plenty of the soloing I've done wasn't as fun as doing a hard free climb with my friends.

So I don't know. Soloing is like a different sport. It's a different subset of climbing, something that you work on, just as you do bouldering or sport climbing, or trad. It's not better or worse. It's just another thing that I do.

I never set out to become a free soloist. I was simply soloing on the side while pursuing other types of climbing. And there were times when I was soloing a lot because I didn't have a partner, or I would go to a new area where I didn't know anyone, so I would end up climbing alone.

I progressed as a free soloist in the same way I progressed through sport and trad, which is that I basically built up a base, then improved from there. I've always been way into *volume*—as in doing tons of climbing. And with soloing it's the same—you do it a lot, you practice, and you get better.

But unlike sport climbing, when you solo you keep it well below your limit. In other words, if you're sport climbing 5.13, you might solo 5.9, or 5.8. I solo at a very easy level for me physically, and I do a ton of pitches at that level until it feels comfortable. Then occasionally I do harder solos that are more of an event.

A big part of the appeal of soloing for me, and part of what got me into it to begin with, was being able to cover a lot of terrain. I would go to a new area and see a bunch of classic routes, and I'd do them all in a morning. For example, I'd go to Joshua Tree and I'd do fifty new routes before lunch, and I'd think, "Wow, that was super fun!"

So I've always liked doing a lot of climbing and doing all the classics, and soloing allows me to combine the two. That's why I got good at it, because I do it so much. You wind up having a lot of experiences that slowly broaden your comfort zone, and pretty soon you're soloing 11c overhanging fingers.

Okay maybe not *pretty* soon, maybe it takes years, but eventually you get to that level.

Actually, I don't think I've ever met another climber who has said he or she wants to be a soloist. I definitely meet young climbers who want to be professionals, and occasionally I'll see people posting online that they want to be a soloist. But it's not common. It's a very personal path that you have to wander all by yourself. If people are passionate about soloing, more power to them, as long as they put the time and effort into learning to do it safely.

Significant Achievements

I think anything significant I've accomplished will be determined by history. What I mean is, 20 years from now we'll look back and see what's never been repeated and what's become commonplace. I suspect that some of the stuff we think is cool now will turn out to be totally routine. No big deal. And other things will never be repeated. Hard to say.

But personally I think the most significant thing I've done is *The Fitz Traverse* in Patagonia with Tommy Caldwell, partially because it was such a big stretch for me.

I'd never been in mountains like that. I'd never climbed ice like that. It was a huge departure from my normal climbing, and it was a giant adventure.

We were in the mountains for 6 days and we got *worked*. It was a pretty big event. And the other thing about *The Fitz Traverse* is that it really built on all the skills I've learned through my other climbing. For example, I'm pretty proud of (rope) soloing *The Triple*, that is climbing the three biggest walls in Yosemite Valley in a day (El Cap, Half Dome, and Mt. Watkins). But having those skills is also what was required for us to be successful on *The Fitz Traverse*—or being able to set the speed record on *The Nose*. It took all the skills and experiences I've learned from my entire career to be able to do *The Fitz Traverse*. So that was a big climb for me.

Close Calls

People often ask me if I've ever had any close calls. And the answer is, "Yes, definitely." I've had all kinds of close calls, many of which were over before I even knew what was happening. I've pulled loose blocks off the wall while free soloing, and then sort of pushed them back in place before I lost my balance. Once in the Sierras I pulled off a huge block, and I jumped back and fell down two small ledges as the rock fell with me. Eventually the block fell past me and I was fine. I cut my leg a bit and I was kind of shaken, but it felt like Super Mario jumping down those ledges while dodging a falling rock.

Things like that are over before your know it. You operate on instinct. There have been times when I've broken a hold and fallen but I landed on a ledge. Or you're scrambling on steep sandstone with snow on it in Zion— terrible conditions. I wouldn't call that a close call in the same sense, but those are times when you really think you could die.

But the only time I *really* believed I was going to die was in a snowshoeing accident. I was 19. I had just dropped out of college and was beginning what would become my endless road trip. I was in a steep icy couloir wearing snowshoes. I had never done anything on snow. I didn't know what I was doing, and I wiped out. I was sliding out of control down this chute. And I thought, "I'm about to die." Then I hit the talus and was knocked out. When I came to, I was covered in blood. I had broken some bones in my hand, and I was happy to be alive.

Biggest Strength

Honestly, I don't know what my greatest strength as a climber is. I guess there might be some mental component, because it seems soloing comes easier to me than it does for others. I seem to have fewer problems with things that seem dangerous to most people, but maybe that's because I've done so many big linkups and other stuff that I've built up to it.

It's difficult for me to tell what's an inherent genetic strength versus what's been attained by simply following my passion. No one in my family was a great athlete, and I've never considered myself a gifted athlete either. I just have always loved climbing and pushing myself and I've gotten pretty good at it.

Maybe I'm more focused than others, I'm not sure. I've had multiple chicks I've hung out with over the years say that I might have Asperger's syndrome, but I don't. And I'm pretty sure I don't have any major personality disorders either. But yeah, people definitely think I have something different going on. But I think I'm totally normal. It's everyone else who's weird.

Fame

The interesting thing about being "America's most famous climber"—which is crazy, because I'm certainly not the *best* climber by any means—is that I'm not the best at anything. I'm not the best boulderer. I'm not the best sport climber. I'm not the strongest. There's nothing that makes me amazing, except the fact that the type of climbing I do is visually amazing, and it's easy for people to understand. Soloing goes over well with the mainstream. It's total luck of the draw that the type of climbing I like to do happens to be the type of climbing everybody can instantly understand, appreciate, and be impressed by. It's just one of those weird coincidences. I look at someone like Daniel Woods—who is freakishly strong, a super-good boulderer, and an amazing climber—and I'll never be able to climb the way he does. To me the type of difficulty Daniel is climbing is far more impressive than going out and soloing 5.11, because, "Hey, it's only 5.11! Anybody can climb 5.11!"

Yet I solo 5.11, and the footage makes it onto *60 Minutes* and gets 60 million viewers, and I become this famous climber. Thankfully it's been gradual. If I had gone from where I was in 2007 to where I am right now, I would probably have snapped under the pressure. Not just the pressure, but from the general weirdness of having strangers come up and talk to me all the time. The sheer awkwardness of having people so excited to see me. Like, "Oh

"I haven't chosen to live in a van because I want to be a dirtbag," Honnold says. "I live in the van because it allows me freedom."

my God! Oh my God!" And I just woke up in the back of my van. I just got out of bed, and now I'm trying to eat a bowl of cereal, and these people are freaking out. And I'm thinking, "Why are you so psyched?" But thankfully, it's been a gradual process, so now I just think, "You know what, Alex? It's all just part of the job."

Because I love climbing. I love being a pro climber, so I'm totally happy with this. People ask me, "Is it hard being a well-known climber?" And I say, "Well, it's way better than laying brick or being a roofer," because basically, I'm an unemployed, uneducated man. What else would I be doing? So taking photos with a few fans—that's pretty casual.

People ask me whether my sponsors are pressuring me to do these climbs, or are the camera crews pressuring me to do hard climbs on cue? And that's definitely not the case. Nobody pressures me to do anything dangerous. Especially sponsors. They are all people working in a marketing department. They're not elite cutting-edge climbers. They don't know what's hard or what I should be doing next. All they say is, "Keep doing your thing, and doing it well," and I say, "Cool, I'll do my best."

So people see these films and they think, "Oh, that's so extreme." "That's so crazy." "That's hard-core."

What they don't realize is that if they are seeing it on film, I've already completed the climb—that we went back and re-created it for the film. We're posing it after the fact. So I'm only soloing the pitches I feel totally comfortable with and that I'm happy to do for the camera. Even if it looks super hard, it's probably not *that* hard, or at least I feel really secure climbing it. I don't do anything I'm not comfortable with. Ultimately it doesn't matter how many times a filmmaker asks—if it's sketchy, I'm not going to do it. That's all there is to it. If I don't want to do it—I don't.

Life Lessons

Climbing has made me a nicer person. It's given me more character. It's made me more patient, a little more understanding, and certainly a lot tougher. For example, in Patagonia in 2015 Colin Haley and I retreated off the west face of Cerro Torre while trying to do *The Torre Traverse* in a day. We'd already traversed the other three peaks in 20 hours or so and were three pitches from the top when we got stuck in a storm. Eventually we had to bail down the wrong side of Cerro Torre, which meant an epic hike back to civilization.

It was serious. If we'd sat down to rest and had been too tired to get up again, eventually we would have frozen. It was one of the first times in the mountains I realized there was no calling for a rescue. The only option was walking out under our own power.

So yeah, I definitely believe the lessons you learn from climbing can be applied to normal life. Especially learning to work hard, set goals, and then accomplish them. Those lessons apply to anything you do. But maybe you could learn the same lessons from gardening? Anything you choose as your craft, that you devote a ton of effort to, and you really push yourself—you're going to learn these kinds of lessons. What's important is that you challenge yourself—not the way you do it.

Giving Back

A couple of years ago I started the Honnold Foundation (www.honnoldfoundation.org) as a way of supporting environmental nonprofits. The reasons I did that are complicated. In fact I need to perfect a better pitch, because I don't really know why I did it. But it stems from the desire to do something positive in the world, because I've been given so much opportunity. I have this great lifestyle I really enjoy, and yet I go to these places where there are so many people living with so much need. I see so much environmental degradation. So I would like to do what I can to help lift people out of poverty through environmental projects. These are things I would be supporting by donating my own money anyway, but I decided I would do it more publically by starting my own foundation in order to leverage my relationship with my sponsors and, hopefully, encourage the public to support these kinds of things as well.

It's a work in progress. I look at the Bill and Melinda Gates Foundation and they have something like a 53-billion-dollar endowment. With that kind of money they can do a lot of good in the world. And I look at what I'm able to give and think it's not so significant. But what I do have is this small platform to speak from to inspire others and ask them to think about these issues. So the Honnold Foundation is just me, using the small influence I have, to do a little good.

Spirit Matters

If you define a spiritual practice as anything that fosters personal growth, then climbing is definitely a spiritual practice. But at the same time, I would question that definition. I think it's kind of a BS definition of spirituality, that it can be anything that provides growth. Climbers are all over the place on this. If you were to interview Dean Potter (Potter was killed BASE jumping a few days after this interview was conducted), he would go on and on about the spirituality of climbing. Or if you talk with Ron Kauk, he'll talk about his connection with nature and water and that we're all one with the earth. Ron is super spiritual.

But I'm not into that, and a lot of other climbers aren't either. Sure, I feel a connection with nature just like they do. Hey, I'm in the same beautiful place. I'm having the same experiences. I appreciate having nature all around me. I love the rivers, the waterfalls, the cliffs. I really love Yosemite.

But I'm turned off by spirituality's connection to religion. I don't want to go down that path. So if we can agree on a secular definition of *spirituality*, I'm fine with that. Personally, when I think of spirituality, I think of a connection with others, a connection with nature, and a feeling that you're part of a greater whole. And I would say that yes, climbing does give you that kind of spiritual connection to the earth and your partners, because we're all having these amazingly rich experiences in such beautiful places.

Here's a story. In Patagonia this past winter, Colin and I wound up doing this 20-hour death march with no food, after having already made a 24-hour push of continual climbing. So basically we've been going for 44 hours without a break, and we're trudging through the night, and I start seeing things that are not there. I wouldn't say I was hallucinating exactly, but I kept thinking we were stumbling into a campsite, except there weren't any campsites. Or I'd see these glittering stones, and I'd think they were lights. But I was just tired and confused. To me experiences like that are the foundation for all of the spiritual and religious traditions on Earth. People go into the desert with no food for a long time, and they find God. So I'm like, "Wow, we went to Patagonia and we found God by getting extremely tired and trudging through the night." That's what all the big spiritual leaders have done. They get totally worked, then they have some kind of epiphany. And we climbers can do that too. We can just go climb a big wall with no food or water. So just call me Buddha! (Laughs.) If I start a cult in a few years, you'll know what I'm thinking.

I was actually featured in a coffee-table book about atheists. It was called *A Better Life* (theatheistbook.com). It was a book that featured a hundred interesting atheists. It explored how people find beauty and meaning in a secular life. I enjoyed doing it. I've always been a staunch atheist.

Climbing Mind

It's tough to describe your state of mind when things are going well, because by definition when you're climbing well, you don't have a state of mind.

There's just emptiness, and that's what's so satisfying, because when all is said and done, you're like, "Wow, I just climbed so well, and nothing else was going on." No chatter. No distractions. I just performed. That is definitely what I experience when I'm climbing my best—emptiness and perfection.

But on a long solo I come in and out of that flow state, because when I'm on easy terrain I do think about other things. I totally relax. I'm not 100 percent focused. And if I start to solo something that's going to take 3 hours, for example, the first 20 minutes or so I'm not really in the zone. My footwork might be a little choppy. At first I don't feel as comfortable, then I start trusting my feet and get more relaxed. And if I have to do some really hard climbing, that really focuses me and from there I can relax and let my mind wander, and I never go back to the choppy footwork. I'll be calm for the rest of the route. It's interesting.

For instance, while soloing *El Sendero Luminoso* (12d) at El Potrero Chico in Mexico, the crux for me was the second pitch. It was hard 12c, really tenuous.

But even after I climbed that pitch, I didn't feel great quite yet, because I hadn't been climbing long enough. I was still tense. I mean, I

"When you live in Yosemite, where you don't have good cell service, you have to take advantage of times when you can get a signal."

climbed it fine. I was smooth. Once I got past that section, I began to relax, and the rest of the route was mellow. I even stopped twice to take my shoes off and eat a bit. I relaxed, and I trusted my feet more the higher I climbed.

Fear

How do I deal with fear? Oh man! I deal with fear the same way everybody else does. You just take a deep breath and you deal. You find a way to manage.

The difference is, I may be better than others in differentiating between *appropriate* fear—that is when you are *really* in danger and should heed the warning—and when fear is *irrational* and you should just ignore it.

I believe that I'm good at ignoring irrational fear. But when I'm truly in danger, when there's a solid reason to be fearful, I experience it the same way as anyone else. I have to decide whether or not I'm willing to face the danger, and if I decide that I am—I just go forward.

I have definitely reached points while soloing when I decided I wasn't into it, so I downclimbed. But that's never happened on the big solos, the climbs that make the news, because those are routes I prepare for. Psychologically and physically I'm totally prepared for those climbs, and I don't attempt something like that unless I'm fully committed.

But when I'm out casually soloing for myself, there have been all kinds of routes where I get to the base and look up and think, "Oh, that's not for me today." Then I walk home. And there are 500-meter-high walls where I've made it 10 or 20 meters off the ground, and I've thought, "I'm just not into this today," so I've gone down. You know, it just depends what kind of adventure I'm signed up for.

The preparation for hard solos is partially physical. It's rehearsing the route to make sure I can physically climb it. But hard solos are mostly a mental process. Thinking about the route. Thinking about all the consequences. Thinking about the whole situation.

Why do I want to do this? What is there to gain from it? What will happen if I fall off different sections? Where could I potentially fall? Why is this particular section hard for me?

I think it all through, and then I give it the proper time to marinate so that when I finally go to solo the route, I'm not suddenly blindsided by something that never occurred to me. I don't want to be halfway up and think, "Oh, maybe this pitch is going to feel different when I'm tired." I should have already thought through all those scenarios, so when I commit, I'm fully relaxed.

The physical preparation is rehearsing the route a few times. It may require some training so I can do the crux moves more easily. But it's the mental preparation that takes far more time and is more abstract. I never think, "Now I'm going to mentally prepare for a hard solo." I just fixate on some project, and then I think about it all the time. Eventually, when I've thought about it enough, it becomes doable.

When I soloed *Moonlight Buttress*, I had spent days mini-traxioning the route—basically toproping it—until I had it completely wired. I knew exactly what to do, and I knew all I had to do was physically execute. It felt totally solid.

With Half Dome, I'd climbed it several times over the years, but I hadn't really rehearsed it. I went up there with a friend 2 days before and free climbed the route, so I knew I could do it, but I didn't practice anything. I didn't rehearse.

Then I took a rest day and went back and soloed it. I was very much improvising sequences as I went. I knew I could climb the route, but I didn't know exactly *how* I should climb it. So I actually stalled out in some places, and I got kind of scared on moves I had done only 2 days earlier but that now I couldn't remember exactly.

"Oh, really? I have to use that foothold?"

"I don't really want to weight that foothold."

So it turned out be a full-on experience.

And since then, it just depends on the situation. Sometimes I rehearse until the climb feels casual, and sometimes I like to climb more spontaneously. What I would most like people to know about me is that I primarily climb with a rope, and that I probably climb a *lot more* than people think. That all the things I do come from this huge base of experience. Many people, but non-climbers especially, think I'm this guy who only climbs without a rope and that I just walk up to these walls and climb them.

No. No. No! I've climbed them all before. I know their histories. All my friends have climbed these routes. I am immersed in the climbing world. Soloing is just a tiny piece of that world that people get to see. What they don't see is that I've been climbing my entire life, that I train continually to climb at a high level, and soloing is one small part of what I do.

290 Pitches

So last year on my 29th birthday, I decided to climb 290 pitches in a day. Honestly, the only reason I did it was because I was climbing at Squamish with a friend who had just turned 30 and he was doing 30 days of horrific

The exit moves of *Wet Lycra Nightmare*, a flaring bombay chimney (13a) that Todd Skinner said badly tweaked his back during the first free ascent

challenges. Like trying to make 30 free throws in a row. He never made it past 18, but he was trying all these difficult challenges in honor of turning 30. So out of solidarity I said I would do just 1 day to join the fun. But 29 pitches sounded stupid. So how about 290? I did the math in my head, and I thought, *Oh, I definitely can do that. It's possible, but God, it's going to suck!* But you never know until you try so I just went out and climbed 290 pitches.

It was all solo and I've always counted downclimbing as well as up-climbing as a pitch—so I did 145 up and 145 down in 16 hours. That's a lot of climbing. It's funny, because I could have probably done 400 pitches if I had just kept going for 24 hours, but how horrible does that sound? When I got to 290, I did think that maybe I should go for 300, just because when am I ever going to climb that many pitches again? Then I thought—who cares? What's the difference between 290 and 300? I want to go to bed.

The Future

If I weren't a climber? Hmmm . . . well I started studying engineering in college, so I suppose if I weren't a climber, I might be an engineer—although that sounds very depressing. Right now I'm very glad I'm not a civil engineer. Even though I think building stuff is cool, climbing is just so much more fun. In 10 or 20 years I hope I'll be doing the same things I'm doing now—traveling and climbing—but perhaps I'll also be doing more nonprofit and environmental work. That's why I started the Honnold Foundation. In a lot of ways that feels more significant. It has a bigger impact. And at some point I can definitely see myself settling down and having a family. I can definitely see myself having a house . . . and a wife and kids . . . maybe.

Actually, I don't know about kids. I'll just see as I go. I definitely see myself retired as an old person. I remember my grandpa playing cards with all us grandkids and hanging out at the family cabin in Tahoe, and I definitely want to be a grandpa like that. Watching birds, playing cards, and hanging out around the picnic table. That's what everybody aspires to, but you might as well start practicing now and enjoy it for 50 years rather than waiting until you're old and can only do it for a few years.

And I think I will always climb. Maybe not at a super-high level, but I will always enjoy climbing. And I think I will always solo, because some of the easy soloing is just so fun. For example, I can't imagine not soloing something like Cathedral Peak (in Tuolumne)—something that I can easily do in my approach shoes, and it's almost part of the hike. I hike up there. I climb the peak. It's all part of a beautiful day in the mountains. I can't imagine not doing that. Even when I'm old, I will still enjoy going into the mountains and scrambling up peaks and enjoying the scenery. But I doubt if I'll be free soloing at an elite level forever, because it requires a ton of dedication. You have to be climbing *all* the time, and you have to be on your game to do that kind of thing. I'm sure that at some point real life will get in the way. I'll have a baby or there will be health problems or something.

Hopefully, I won't actually have to give birth to a baby. But we'll see. If that were to happen, it would probably tie in with the health problems.

And I definitely have a list of fantasy climbs, a whole list of things I would love to do. The hard part is trying to put them in the right order to maximize fitness, conditions, and so on. I definitely have things I'd like to do in Patagonia, and I'd love to go to the Himalaya—but I don't think I'll ever become a true alpinist. I can see doing one cool trip to the mountains a year and being totally happy with that.

CHRIS KALOUS

When I was compiling my dream list of people I wanted to talk with about why we climb, Chris Kalous, the distinctive voice of the world's first climbing podcast *The Enormocast* (www.enormocast.com), immediately sprang to mind. Not only is Kalous a talented climber who has made notable first ascents around the world, he has dedicated himself to getting normally reticent dirtbags to bare their soul before a microphone, including many of the athletes in this book as well as in *Women Who Dare*: Lynn Hill, Brittany Griffith, Tommy Caldwell, Angie Payne, Mayan Smith-Gobat, Alex Honnold, Peter Croft, Ines Papert, Kate Rutherford, and Madaleine Sorkin—to name but a few of the more than one hundred climbers Chris has interviewed.

It's possible no one has done more to explore and map the bewildering badlands of the climbing brain than Kalous. From the mainstream perspective, the people he interviews are a bunch of whack jobs, social misfits thumbing their nose at what the "1 percent" considers success. But Kalous and his guests make the alternative sound so appealing—so fun, cool, and attainable—that after listening to an episode, even an investment banker will want to run off to join the climbing circus. *The Enormocast* is pure undiluted climbing—scruffy, unwashed, unadorned, unkempt, and unapologetic.

As Chris told writer Brendan Leonard, "I'd like to be the climbing world's David Letterman . . . is he still on the air? I want to be a go-between for people who would never walk up to their climbing heroes and talk to them. I feel I can do that."

And that's because Kalous knows what he's talking about. He's one of the rare talents who can climb 5.13—both in Rifle and Indian Creek. As his tick list demonstrates, whether it's making first ascents in the desert, on remote big walls, or making ten ascents of El Cap, many of them solo, Kalous knows his shit. So if you'd like a regular dose of many of the same themes explored in *Why We Climb*, tune in to Kalous and his band of merry pranksters. It may not increase your grip strength, but it will definitely strengthen your smile.

Chris Kalous climbing his route *Ivory Tower* (13b) on Castleton Tower, Utah

Significant Ascents

1995 *World's End,* V 5.10 A5, The Titan, Fisher Towers, Utah; second ascent solo

1996 *Grendel,* VI 5.10 A4, Mt. Proboscis, Cirque of the Unclimbables, Canada; first ascent with Kevin Daniels, Chris Righter, and Greg Epperson

1997 *The Reticent Wall,* VI 5.11 A5, El Capitan; second ascent with Kevin Thaw and Mark Synnot

1999 All eight Bridger Jack Summits in a day, Indian Creek, Utah; First linkup with Ron Van Aernum

2003 *Cowboy Poetry,* IV 12c, and *Premonition* IV 12c, The Ghost River, Alberta, Canada; first ascents with Andy Genereux and Marco Cornachione

2007 *Dar al Salaam,* IV 13a, Wadi Rum, Jordan; first ascent with Heidi Wirtz, Aaron Black, and Ben Firth

2011 *Blow It Up on the Internet,* 12c, Sicily; first ascent with Jonathan Thesenga

2012 *Ivory Tower,* 13b, Castleton Tower, Utah; first ascent with Sam Lightner

2014 *Event Horizon,* 5.12, Black Canyon of the Gunnison, Colorado; first ascent with Josh Wharton and Stephanie Bergner

Roots

My name's Chris Kalous. I was born March 25, 1971, in Green Bay, Wisconsin. I grew up in Chicago, but I now live in Carbondale, Colorado. I started out as a trad climber, but now I split my time between big multipitch and sport climbing.

I'm unique in that I decided to become a climber many years before I actually had the opportunity to climb. When I was still in high school, I saw an article about John Bachar, this blonde California rock star climbing in tube socks and tiny shorts. I was athletic but I didn't fit into the high school team-sports mode. I saw these amazing photos of Bachar clinging to nothing, and I decided then and there I would become a climber. So I decided to start training. The only problem was I didn't have a clue what that meant.

So I signed up for a weight-lifting class taught by one of the football coaches. He was this big, thick-necked guy, and I was a bit sheepish sharing my little dream of becoming a climber. But it turned out the guy had actually

The crux dyno on *Ivory Tower.* "Everyone fantasizes about living close to the edge, but climbers do it," Kalous says.

tried climbing, during a NOLS course, so he said, "I don't know exactly what you need to do, but I'm guessing we want to make you stronger without bulking you up."

So that's what we did, and a few years later I was accepted at Colorado State in Fort Collins. On my very first day on campus, I went toproping at Horse Tooth Reservoir with some kids from the dorm. It was my dream come true, and my training actually helped. I was strong—probably as strong as I've ever been—and I did pretty well.

But even more important, I had brought my van with me from Illinois. Every weekend my new friends and I would pile in the van and drive to Lumpy Ridge or Eldorado Canyon. That's how it all started. Those first adventures were the most important thing that's ever happened to me. Climbing has been my path ever since. Sometimes when you've been fantasizing about something for years, the reality doesn't measure up—but climbing was everything and more than I imagined it would be.

Friendship

My first day in the dorm, I met Jonathan Thesenga. Twenty years later we're still climbing together. JT likes to tell a story about walking down the hall and seeing this guy (he says was me) with a mullet, camo pants, and a cutoff t-shirt standing in the open door of his dorm room rocking out on a guitar.

And I was, and still am, a guitar player—that much is true. But the rest is a combination of things that *might* have happened. I really doubt I had the balls to stand in an open doorway and shred in front of strangers passing by.

Not long ago JT and I were a few pitches from the top of a route in the Black Canyon. It was getting dark. Then it started to rain. I turned to him and said, "Hey man, thanks for ruining my life! I might have been a millionaire. I might have written the great American novel. I could have been successful in all sorts of ways if you hadn't gotten me involved in this stupid sport."

But seriously, the friendships I've made through climbing are the strongest I have. Sharing hardship, fear, triumph—they can all happen every time you go out, and the result is a deep understanding and trust. Even the mother of my child started out as my climbing partner.

Lessons

The most meaningful climbing accomplishments are the ones where I had to grow the most—and those were back in my big wall days. I'm a bit notorious, because I once posted a satirical video on YouTube that really gave aid climbers a hard time. It now has 75,000 views. But the truth is I was an avid aid climber. I did a bunch of hard walls in Yosemite, big long aid routes on El Cap, and I did many of them solo. One time I was up on the wall in winter for 9 days by myself.

Part of the appeal of roped soloing was that I didn't have to deal with a partner. I didn't have to make plans with someone who would inevitably bail at the last minute. Those ascents pushed me as hard as anything I've ever done.

I learned a lot about commitment and the depth of my reserves. Now, whenever there's anything stressful in my life—like when my son was born—I like to say, "Hey it's *no problem*! You know, I climbed El Cap. I've got this."

I've changed a fair bit since then. I've grown up and become more cautious. I always joke that if someone suddenly transported me now—the 45-year-old Kalous—back to the middle of one of those hard pitches where I'd been hooking, and I looked down and saw all those hooks dangling on tiny granite edges, I would completely lose my mind!

That guy is gone now, the person who could divorce himself from the realities of that kind of risk. It was a mental trick I could do. I could pretend it wasn't me, like I was watching someone else.

So maybe I'm no longer a fearless wall climber, but there's still a part of me that meets a challenge and thinks, "Hey, this isn't so bad. It was a lot colder on that winter ascent. There are no ice chunks flying my way, so everything's cool." Personally, I believe that climbing did forge me into someone who can deal with problems quicker, easier, and with less stress. It continues to change me for the better. I believe that being a climber allows me to see the big picture. You understand what consequences are. You understand what to stress over and what to let go.

"Are we going to die? Am I going to lose a limb? Are we going to have to carry a bleeding body out of the mountains?"

"No?" Well then, let's chill out. All the risk management in climbing—thinking about consequences and predicting what those consequences might be—teaches you to do that.

There are some negative lessons as well. A lot of young climbers get addicted to the rush, to the partying, to the antisocial behavior that comes with being a dirtbag. You're down off the wall, you still want the thrills, and you don't want an ounce of responsibility for anyone or anything.

But giving up other things in life that could have been fulfilling just to keep "feeding the rat" can be a big mistake. It's easy to think you have it all figured out when you're 20. I think that avoiding meaningful relationships or other pursuits because all you want to do is climb can stunt your humanity. I hate to say it, but there *really* is more to life than climbing!

Strengths

I believe I stand out as a climber because I'm an all-rounder—that is, I have a good skill set in a lot of disciplines. I really feel I have all the different climbing systems on lockdown. Having said that, I'll probably go out, forget to tie my knot, and get killed, and everyone will say, "Well, he shouldn't have been such a smart-ass."

I like predicting consequences on big routes; understanding how the gear works; understanding the logistics of getting from Point A to Point B. I have a good track record with climbing big objectives. Sometimes it's just dumb luck, but I believe we make our own luck by being prepared, patient, and, most important, climbing well.

I guided professionally for years, and after a class I would ask my students a trick question: "So, what's the primary thing you need to concentrate on to make sure you don't hit the ground?"

We had just spent all day talking about gear and rope work, so they would say, "The piece below you," or "Tying your knot," or "The anchors."

And I would say, "No. It's your *climbing ability*. It's your ability to climb without falling, because if you do that, all that other stuff is irrelevant."

The thing that's helped me most is building a solid foundation. In college we would be thrilled to climb a three-pitch 5.6. Then we would climb a 5.7 and a 5.8. My friends and I went years without taking a leader fall. In the gym era that may sound like an *old guy* approach, but those experiences built a solid foundation of understanding climbing systems in any situation.

The flip side of my *old guy* mentality is that there have been times when I've been held back by my preconceptions. I might have succeeded if I had seen myself differently. I've had breakthroughs, when other people forced me to see climbing in a way I couldn't see it for myself. They convinced me to push harder and dig deeper than I thought possible.

For instance, I'm still scared to fall. I don't care if it's on a bolt or not. Even after 26 years, I can still be scared. And that stems from those early days when we didn't know if that hex was placed correctly or not—because

"What's the soul of climbing? That's easy—it's *community*. It's a tribe whose core desire is to elevate life." Kalous and Brittany Griffith on *Six Star Crack* (13a), Indian Creek.

sometimes you climbed past it and "Zing!" out it came, sliding down the rope. So we learned not to fall, and that fear kept us alive. Of course, there are plenty of times when it's perfectly fine to fall. Watching really good sport climbers carelessly lob off steep routes helps me shake off the fear and go for it—but it's still hard to let go of the old conditioning.

The Enormocast

The other half of my climbing life is *The Enormocast*, which is a podcast I produce about the climbing lifestyle. It's part art project, part journalism, part storytelling. I got the idea from a hugely popular podcast called *WTF with Marc Maron*, in which he interviews fellow comedians in his garage.

Maron started by having his friends in the industry rap about what goes on inside the world of comedy, and I thought I could do that with climbing. Wouldn't it be interesting to talk with climbers, not just about what they're climbing, but who they are, how they got into the sport, and wherever that leads?

I have plenty of climbing friends who are semifamous. So the first guinea pigs were just friends from Carbondale. I brought them in, sat them down, and said, "Dude, we're going to do this."

"Do what?"

"Talk about climbing."

Getting a few beers in them helped, too.

Now I have over one hundred episodes posted, and from a historic perspective that's a huge body of work. It includes everyone from the really young to some of the oldest climbers around. I recorded Eric Bjornstad just before he passed away. So even if I were to stop now, that record exists. It's online for anyone to enjoy.

The thing that surprises me most about all the conversations I've had is the similarity of experiences. The deepest shows, the ones that resonate most with me and the audience, often reveal the level of doubt that even elite climbers have about themselves. Just like the rest of us, they get scared. They consider themselves failures for not accomplishing more than they do. That surprises me. But of course, they're just humans. We all have silly doubts and fears.

The audio format speaks to me. The tone of a person's voice when he or she is choked up or laughing, being serious or goofing off. That's something writing can't do. I love climbing literature. I read books and magazines, but podcasting is a different angle. For example, I do almost no editing. I believe podcasting is the most unfiltered format available if you really want to *know* a person. And the biggest compliment I get is when people say that listening to the show feels like hanging out with me and my friends. That's always been my intent. I wanted to create a virtual campfire, and if you just happen to walk by, I'd say, "Hey, man, sit and join us. Have a beer. This is my friend Tommy Caldwell."

The Soul of Climbing

What's the soul of climbing? That's easy—and my experience with *The Enormocast* has made me even more certain: The soul of climbing is *community*. It's the people you climb with. It's a tribe whose core desire is to elevate life, shake off modern comforts, and seek challenge.

I recently became a dad, and everybody says it's going to be challenging. Even my girlfriend says, "It's going to be sooo *challenging!* Aren't you worried?"

And I say, "No, I'm not worried, because that's what climbers do." When our life isn't challenging, we go to the mountains and challenge ourselves in serious ways. That makes us special. Sure, I'm an elitist. Climbers aren't the only people who do this, but the fact that we don't spend our lives looking for the easy way out is a big part of what makes us climbers in the first place.

Every time we rope up, we take responsibility for another person, and that strengthens our sense of community. Traveling the world is also a big part of the appeal. You go anywhere in the world and you automatically know the person climbing next to you has a few of the characteristics that are the basis for a deep relationship—even if you don't speak the same language.

It's such a supportive, fun community not based at all on the bullshit status symbols of normal life. "You climb?" That's good enough for me—rich or poor; black, brown, or white. I can't think of another tribe in which I'd like to be so deeply integrated. As I always say, "If golfers were climbers—I wouldn't be a climber."

Why We Climb

Recently I interviewed Stacey Bare, who went to Angola to rock climb, and the first thing he said was, "We understood that the people in Angola are just trying to survive, and the idea of going to risk our lives on purpose in a place like that probably seems senseless."

That's a common criticism of climbing, that it has no purpose—it's certainly not curing cancer. But the other side of the coin is the fact that when everything's comfy, humans need a challenge—even if it's frivolous. So many climbers I know do great things in other parts of their lives: volunteering, important research, great art. They will all tell you that climbing fuels the desire to challenge themselves in other ways. Even Stacey's trip to Angola. He was returning to a place where he'd spent years risking his life clearing land mines, and his group did a bunch of volunteer work as well as climbing.

The big mistake many people make is thinking that climbers are thrill seekers. Every climber I know rejects that perception. As they say, if you're full of adrenaline, then things have already gone haywire. Sure climbing is thrilling, but if that was all it was, it would be an amusement park ride not a lifelong pursuit.

Climbing can tear you down to your rawest emotions. It can be the most physically demanding thing you've ever done, while demanding problem-solving where a mistake can be catastrophic. It's all encompassing, and since humans have always strived to surpass their limitations, climbing gives us a means to test and better ourselves.

In any walk of life, the people who have mastered themselves are the most admired. I feel that every day I go climbing I'm becoming better. Not just a better climber—a better person.

I believe this is why *The Dawn Wall* appealed to so many, why the Meru film appeals, why Everest (which most real climbers dismiss as a circus) continues to appeal—because these are all stories about living mythically. They are stories about heroes who go out to the edge of the world. They suffer. They strive, and sometimes they don't come back. Everyone fantasizes about living close to the edge, but climbers do it. That's what we're really up to. We're living mythical lives.

Climber's Mind

After interviewing more than a hundred climbers, I can't tell you what's going on in their brains, but I can speak to similarities I see. For instance, climbers talk of feeling out of sync with normal life. When they were young, school wasn't their thing. Sports with coaches and rules weren't their thing. They felt disconnected. With boys, that disconnection is often expressed in dangerous activities—blowing things up, driving too fast, drugs. Our society doesn't give young people a constructive means of harnessing that energy. I believe a lot of climbers, both men and women, don't grow out of that phase like other people do. Instead they find climbing, and it saves them. In some cases they were on a path to a miserable life or early death—whether from risky relationships, drugs, alcohol, or some dumbass accident.

To be a really good climber you have to cultivate *high executive functioning*. You risk estrangement from family and society. Yes, it's possible to maintain loving relationships, but climbers understand there's always a gap between themselves and the rest of the world. This is especially true of expedition climbing. It's a bit like war. You're gone for months living these harrowing experiences, then you come home and it's Monday morning and you're surrounded by people without a clue.

Sport climbing and bouldering require something a bit different. The focus is more on physicality and training. It's more about developing an athlete's mind-set. But to be great, the pursuit still requires a dedication beyond the norm.

One of the things I hear people say on the podcast that they love about climbing is the clearing of the mind. You're in the moment. Everything else is gone. Like everyday worries. "Do I have enough money?" "Do I get to keep my job?" All those concerns disappear when you are pulling so hard the self is lost, even if only for a moment.

For me the optimum mental state is when I'm on a long route moving smoothly and efficiently. I'm not having to stop and think. My mind is going in many directions, but I'm not directing it. When I can achieve that on a big route in a committing place like the Black Canyon, it feels like a perfect day. Those are my happiest times.

Sustaining that flow is hard. There are always nagging concerns. Is it going to rain? Could we snag the rope? It's funny, because in other parts of our lives we're conditioned to avoid anxiety. We're supposed to make life comfortable. But in climbing, anxiety can be fun, even during those times when I would say, "No, this isn't great. Now I'm getting really concerned."

Some people would collapse in those situations, but climbers come alive. Afterward I think, "Yawn. What was that? I was just traveling through my emotions. No big deal. We're still alive, after all."

Spirit Matters

I'm not a religious person. Generally speaking, I'm an atheist. But I do believe in spiritualism in a weirdly scientific way. I think we're genetically wired to be spiritual. It helps us accomplish our goals and connect with one another. My attitude is that we're wired to be spiritual for a reason, so why not embrace it? In the end, I suppose I'm open to "spiritual" experiences because they feel good. I'm a spiritual hedonist.

I feel the spiritual in what I would call the *vision quest* aspect of big wall soloing. Those ascents were a crucible testing all my skills. They were a quest to see what I was made of. It's Day 6. Can I get up and keep going? Is that cloud the harbinger of an approaching storm? How will I deal with another day of exhaustion and anxiety? And when you reach the top, all those experiences flush everything else away, all the confusion of normal life.

The seeker calls that spirituality. Scientists call it chemical euphoria. The important thing is that it's not a momentary high from drugs. It's where deep and lasting satisfaction comes from. I don't care whether it's chemical or it comes from a higher power. It's the feeling I want. Like all climbers, I wish I could make it last.

Evolution

I like to throw out these drug analogies—and that's not to diminish what real addiction can do to you—but climbing can be similar. We're old junkies now, and we don't get the same rush from the same dosage. But I'm not going to give it up because of that. I can't. I'm going to learn how to evolve.

I'm much less ego driven than I was, which is important, because let's face it, otherwise my ego would be crushed. I can't climb the way I did when I was 20, and these days every kid in the gym is climbing harder than the previous generation. So I could grow old and bitter about how many people are climbing better than me—but if that's the way I feel, I probably have a bunch of problems unrelated to climbing.

I just have to find new challenges that are right for me. I'm lucky in that I've had few injuries. I always say that's because I don't try very hard. I let go before I hear my tendons snap. Which is a joke, but there's truth to it. Climbing is a sport where you can

Chris Kalous, the voice of *The Enormocast*

keep going and improving because there are so many different avenues to pursue. Still, it's not much of a revelation to say that you have to learn to be okay with growing weaker and more brittle.

Advice for the Next Generation

The obvious advice is not to worry about grades. But I won't say that, because it won't work. Grades and competition are fundamental to climbing, especially coming out of a gym background. So telling people not to be concerned with numbers is the right thing to say—but in my heart I don't even believe it myself.

So what I would say to a young climber? First, I'd say ask yourself why you are climbing. Is it because your friends do it? Because your dad wants you to? Because you want to be the best, and become famous? Or is it because you love it?

Because in 5 years everyone doing it for those other reasons will be gone—and those who love it will still be climbing at whatever grade they can.

And second, I would tell a young climber to pay attention to safety throughout your career, not just when you're learning. I've seen too much stupid tragedy kill people and destroy the lives of those left behind. There seems to be a phase after being a newbie where you think you know more than you do. People stop checking knots, using signals, and other basics. I tell people to watch out for that, go back to when you were a little scared.

A lot of people email me at *The Enormocast* asking about getting into climbing. A typical letter goes something like this: "I'm a good gym climber. I've climbed outside a little, and I know how to clip bolts. How do I get into trad?"

My answer is: "Be afraid! Take it slow! If you can find a mentor, that would be great. If not, hire a guide to show you the basics. But I know—you're young and you want to climb hard! You want to go *Aaargh!* Well, do that bouldering or on a well-protected sport route. When you go trad climbing, that's the day you're there to enjoy nature and have fun with your friends. Try to divorce yourself from the grades, from trying super hard. Work up to the harder routes incrementally. You'll be a lot safer and a lot happier in the long run."

Oh, and one last thing I tell every climber, young and old: be sure to subscribe to *The Enormocast* and continue with style! (Hah!)

Kalous jamming it up in Indian Creek. "I feel that every day I go climbing I'm becoming better. Not just a better climber, a better person," he says.

ADAM ONDRA

More than one hundred ascents of 14d or harder, including over thirty 5.15 sends. Boulder problems up to v16. World Cup gold medals. Two World Championships. Any one of Adam Ondra's successes would be a lifetime achievement for 99 percent of climbers—but he's just getting started. Ondra is the gleaming spear tip of climbing's future. He represents the amazing potential of a new generation born to climbing parents and raised in gyms. Adam's career is a case study in what happens when enormous talent and desire find their life's purpose at an early age.

When he was growing up in the Czech Republic, Ondra's parents, their friends, and the kids he knew were all climbers. Taken to the crag as a toddler, Adam doesn't even remember his first climbing experiences. His first reliable memory is when he came in third in his first comp at age 6. By the time he turned 7, Adam wanted to climb every day. Rather than make daily trips to the gym, his parents compromised by building a tiny wall in his bedroom so he could climb on "rest days."

Ondra went on to win the junior competition series in Europe every year from ages 11 through 16. He climbed his first 14d (9a) at 13, and at 15 he repeated *Action Directe*, Wolfgang Gullich's 14d test piece, a route that was once the hardest in the world.

Flash-forward to 2016 and Ondra is widely considered the best rock climber on the planet. Perhaps most remarkable in this era of increasing specialization—where most World Cup competitors climb and train primarily indoors—Ondra excels on both rock and plastic. To date, only two humans have climbed 15c (9b+)—Sharma and Ondra. But Adam is the only climber to have redpointed three routes at that grade: *Vasil Vasil* at Sloup in the Czech Republic; *La Dura Dura*, the world's first 15c, bolted and subsequently repeated by Sharma at Oliana, Spain; and *Change*, a route Ondra developed at Norway's Flatanger Cave.

Adam Ondra climbing *Les Tres Panes* 14b, Pelvoux, France

Ondra has been winning World Cup comps since he was 16. In 2014 he won the World Championships in both Lead and Bouldering, the only athlete to ever do so in a single year. In 2015 he won the overall World Cup title in Lead, and he has won these titles while pursuing a university degree in economics and business management.

The Reel Rock film *La Dura Dura*, which introduced Ondra to the world, dramatized the "competition" between Adam—at the time a gangly teenager living in a van with his parents—and Sharma, the sport's tan and muscular superstar. Both were vying to be the first to redpoint 15c. Ondra made it to the chains first, but Sharma was close behind, redpointing the route 2 weeks later.

Since then much has changed. Ondra still sports the same mop of curly hair, but he has filled out, and he now has his own van and a girlfriend. He's tall for a sport climber, wiry, powerful, and incredibly flexible. He's known for following a training regimen so fierce it would put most climbers on the disabled list. ·

In person, Ondra is refreshingly down-to-earth. There's no attitude. If you met him at the crag and didn't know who he was, he would seem like any other stoked, young climber. But once he touches rock, any similarities melt away. To watch Ondra climb is like watching a Michael Jordan play basketball or an Einstein do math. You realize you are witnessing a level of mastery that only two or three people on earth possess at any one time. As Ondra says in the pages that follow, he has a "lifetime" project at Flatanger that if climbed will be harder than *Change*. Which means that if Ondra succeeds, our concept of what is humanly possible on rock will advance one more remarkable notch into the future.

Roots

I'm Adam Ondra. I was born February 5, 1993, and I'm a sport climber, a boulderer, and competition climber. I was born into a climbing family. My parents have been climbing for 30 years, and when I was a baby, they brought me with them to the rocks. I can't remember the first time I climbed. I think it came gradually, starting with playing in the dirt under the crag, to hanging and swinging on the rope, to more serious climbing.

Ondra competing in the finals of the 2015 Briançon World Cup. "World Cup Lead is the ultimate fitness test," he says.

The first climbing I really remember was when I was 6, and that was the time I entered my first competition. I think that my attitude then was not that I loved climbing so much, but that everyone I knew—all my parents' friends and all their friends' children—was a climber. The fact is, when I was little, I didn't know anyone who *didn't* climb. I thought *everyone* in the world was a climber! So I would have felt strange if I hadn't been a climber too. But all that changed when I was 6 and I placed third in my first competition. I won my first medal, and I put it over my bed and thought, "I would like to get more of these!"

Then when I was in third grade and could read a little, a family friend gave me the book *Rock Stars: The World's Best Free Climbers* by Heinz Zak, and that inspired me so much! That's when I started thinking I only wanted to be a climber. Already at that time, I was enjoying traveling and discovering new crags, so that's when I decided I wanted to live exactly the way I'm living now—and that feels pretty good!

There are different roles in my life, and I enjoy them all. I'm primarily a climber, but at the same time I like my studies. I like having something else, because I don't think it's healthy to be occupied only by climbing.

At university I'm studying economics and business management. I just completed my second year (summer 2015), so there's one more year for my bachelor's degree and three more for my master's. So far I'm enjoying it. The main reason I decided to go to college now was because I wanted to compete in the World Cup. I wanted to train hard and potentially win World Championships. So I started studying, because I knew it would keep me home and there would be nothing else to do except go to school and train and I could be 100 percent prepared for the World Cup season.

In 2014 my main goal was to win the Lead World Championship, and I trained super hard for that. When the World Championships were held, I was very well prepared physically and mentally, and it was just enough for the victory in both Lead and Bouldering. That was one of the best moments of my climbing career, for sure.

To be honest, I was a bit surprised what a high level of satisfaction it brought me, because I had already won quite a few World Cups when I was 16 and 17 years old. But I suppose the difference was that I wasn't really training for competitions back then, just going to comps between climbing trips, so it wasn't as much of a priority. For sure winning both World Championships in a single year was an amazing moment, but it didn't compare to the feeling I had after succeeding on routes like *Change* or *La Dura Dura*.

Competition vs. Rock

Competition climbing on plastic is very different than rock climbing outdoors. For me competition climbing is just a sport. I enjoy it for the challenge. I like to train, and competitions are nice games that motivate me to get better.

For the World Cup, the first thing you need to do is train hard to be physically prepared, but it's not just about being strong, it's about climbing well on demand. Those are different things, and you have to be good at both. And every World Cup wall is different.

Climbing outside on rock, on the other hand, is more about the lifestyle. Sure, I like climbing hard routes, I like the challenge, but I also like all the other things that are connected. It's not only about movement on rock, it's also about the travel, driving to the crag, being in nature, meeting new people. This is something I understood when I was only 7; I have always loved climbing as a full package. Many climbers don't like the fact that sometimes they have to camp. They find it uncomfortable. But I love it all.

Today most World Cup climbers are quite specialized. They don't go rock climbing often, and then only in the off-season. And I think the reason is because the style of competition is changing so quickly. It's very different from rock climbing—especially bouldering, but also in lead.

In order to go from the rock straight to a comp you would need to be a really complete and universal climber. You need to adapt to this highly specialized style very quickly, and I think that ability is quite rare.

World Cup Lead is the ultimate fitness test, because the climbing is so continuous. It's hard to find rest points, whereas on rock it's all about doing hard moves with little rests in between, sometimes even knee bars and similar techniques. In that I'm quite good. If I can get a knee bar and release my hands for only a few seconds, I can recover. But I need to train *super hard* to be able to rest on a bad hold, which is a necessary skill for World Cup, because the routes are so long—too long to climb "with only one breath," as we say. So you start climbing and try to sprint as fast as possible. In that way you can make perhaps thirty moves, but a World Cup Lead route requires forty to fifty moves. To climb that far you really have to find little bits of rest, shake out, then continue.

And modern World Cup Bouldering is now almost *Parkour* style. The problems themselves are not so hard in terms of grade. For sure you need power, but it's more about coordination and skill. How to quickly decipher the solution! And sometimes that's a lot about luck! There may be five different ways to attempt the boulder, but in 4 minutes there's not enough time to try them all.

Mind Power

During a World Cup competition we come out to make the *observation* (pre-view the route), and I try to remember the route as much as possible. Usually I can memorize every handhold, every foothold, and every clip during the 6-minute observation period. Then it's very important when I go back into Isolation to go over the route several times in my mind to be assured I will remember it when my turn comes—which can be 2 hours later. It's really important to visualize the climb in my mind until I feel like I'm actually on the route so that it doesn't feel like an on-sight, that it feels like a redpoint.

If you think about it, the difference between a redpoint and on-sight is not so big. The only difference is the information you have. When redpointing, you know the route. When on-sighting, you don't know the route. But in either case the route's the same. The holds are the same. The amount of power you have is the same. So the more information you can obtain during the observation period, the closer you'll be to a redpoint. So you get as much information as you can, and you remember it as best you can.

Sometimes, of course, you visualize the sequence incorrectly. Then you have to be flexible. On-sighting is all about making quick decisions. So okay, I've got my beta, then I go up, and I see that the sequence demands a different way. At that moment I need to look around as fast as possible. Get new information and process it to make a new decision. This is difficult to explain in a few words, because it happens like the flip of a switch. For example, I get a crimp, look around, and in a split second I make a decision. Maybe it's more than a second, but certainly no more than two!

And after I make that decision, I don't change it. I have to go for it and hope for the best. Maybe it's not the easiest or the most efficient movement possible, but trying to find an easier way might take another 10 seconds, and after 10 seconds holding on to a small crimp, I would be finished.

Because I've done a lot of bouldering, if I do a hard move even on lead, it won't necessarily tire me out, and I have the confidence that there are not going to be that many hard moves on the route. So even if I have come up with a harder sequence, I have a good chance the next moves will not be as demanding.

"I would say having flexible hips is my biggest strength."

But just passively waiting—trying to hold on to a bad hold without moving—that's when I get *so pumped*. There are climbers who don't get that pumped while being passive, but for me it's important to keep moving so that one hand can relax while the other is holding—again and again. For me holding on for 3 seconds with both hands—that kills me. This might sound strange, but it's the way it is.

In Isolation I do the visualization process a few times, but the rest of the waiting period I try to simply relax and not think about climbing too much, because when you think about climbing it's like you're subconsciously using your muscles, and that makes things harder when it's time to compete. At least that's the way I feel.

Achievements & Strengths
I've accomplished quite good things in sport climbing, in bouldering, as well as in competitions, which is quite rare. I would say my biggest climbing skill

is being an all-rounder. Then in a comp I don't mind if the route is short and bouldery or if it's a long endurance piece.

But between becoming a double World Champion to climbing 15c or on-sighting 14d, I can't really tell what has more value. Every experience, every route, and every competition is different and special.

And my biggest climbing strength is making strange moves, like drop knees, high heel hooks and rocking up over my feet. I can rest in totally different positions than other climbers because my hips are quite flexible. As long as I have a high foot and I can rock up on to it, I can release the weight on my hands and recover, even if I'm holding onto bad holds. So I would say that having flexible hips is probably my biggest strength.

In contrast, my weakness would be raw power and campus moves. I've gotten better at that, but I would still consider it a weakness.

Injuries

In terms of injury, I've been lucky. I've never had an injury for more than 5 to 7 days. And I think the reason is that when something hurts, I try not to push it. I just take a couple days off and see how it's going to turn out, and that usually helps. I believe the worst thing you can do if something hurts, is to keep climbing and training. That's when small problems become serious.

When I was 7 and 8, people on the Internet who didn't even know me were forecasting I would be forced to stop climbing in a few years because my fingers would be ruined. And for sure that could have happened, but I actually think that starting so young helped me avoid injuries, because my level was gradually increased. It took many years for me to climb harder routes, so my tendons and knuckles got well adapted to the stress. It really depends on the way you climb when you're a kid. For example, I never did any campus or special training until I was 15 or 16, it was all just climbing and bouldering.

Training

I've always been an individualist. I hated being told what I should do by my parents. So my parents were never coaches for me. In my opinion, it's dangerous if your parents are also your coaches. It can create tensions I see in many kids that are not positive.

So from the age of 7, I would not listen to my parents about what I should climb. Instead, before we went on a trip, I would study the guidebooks. I committed the guidebook to memory, and I had all the routes I wanted to do in my mind. Then when we reached the crag, I didn't need a book or anyone's advice.

The same was true of training. Even when I was only 8, I would experiment with the way I would train for routes or boulder problems to see what worked best. And until I reached 20, this was the way I trained. I think it has worked quite well. After all, I was able to climb *Change* at 15c by training in this way.

But last year I contacted Patxi Usobiaga (a former Spanish World Cup competitor now a climbing coach) to help me train specifically for the World Cup, because that's a different game, especially if there's one important comp during the season. It's difficult to train in a way that you are sure to be strong and well prepared for a single day, and I've failed to do that in the past.

So I began training in accordance to Patxi, because he's the only person I could trust. He's famous for saying that he was never a talented climber and that he earned everything through hard work. I knew I could trust him, because he has gone through the same process, and he can understand how I feel and judge how my training is going.

According to Patxi, I divide my training into different periods when I train *really* hard and go through enormous fatigue. This means training three times a day, 6 days a week. I do some campusing, some bouldering, and some endurance training every day. It doesn't really matter whether I'm training for boulder or lead, because if you're lead climbing you still need bouldering power. And in the bouldering comps, it's also a power endurance challenge, because you're allowed six tries on each problem in 4 minutes—and that's going to wear you down if you don't have endurance.

So at the beginning of the season, I train a lot for 2 to 3 months. Then when the World Cup starts, I train less but focus more on quality. During that period I do a little campusing in order to work on raw power, and then I concentrate on trying to climb World Cup-style routes. I know that during a comp

I will need to climb two routes a day, so I warm up and then I give a route two good burns—which I take as seriously as if I were actually competing.

Then during the season, if there's a 2- or 3-week break between events, I can train for a week but still have time to rest. In this way, I can stay fit the entire year. But you also have to decide which comps are most important and when it's time just to have fun. For example, right now after the Briançon (France) event, I know I would probably be in better shape if I went home to the Czech Republic and trained really hard for 5 days ahead of the next comp.

But I just want to have some fun, so I'm going to Ceuse (where Ondra made the second ascent of Sharma's route *Three Degrees of Separation*, 14d, a route Ondra thinks may be as hard as 15a). Maybe that won't work as well for the next comp, but there's still time left in the season, and if I only train in the gym the whole year, it's too hard for my head, and the head is very important in competition climbing. Regardless of how strong you are, the more relaxed and happy you are, the better your results will be.

Diet & Nutrition

Diet is important. I don't feel like my diet is very special, but I suppose some people would think it is. The most important thing is how I eat during the time I'm training hard. Right now I'm climbing outdoors, and in comparison I don't climb as much so diet's important, but less so.

I definitely try to eat as much natural food as possible. For breakfast I have porridge or a smoothie. Throughout the day I eat only fruit, nuts, and seeds, as well as some carbohydrates with vegetables and good spices like turmeric, curry, and cumin mixed with rice, buckwheat, or millet. In the evening I have some protein. It can be meat, eggs, lentils, or legumes. I don't eat that much meat. I find that if I eat too much meat, I'm not as strong. But at the same time, if I go 2 weeks without meat, I also feel weak. So I eat meat once or twice a week.

Why I Climb

There are many reasons why I climb. Climbing is beautiful. There are moments when I'm high on the rock, and I'm enjoying every move, every handhold, every foothold! That feeling is hard to find! I believe it's a feeling you can only find if you bring to an activity the kind of passion I have for climbing.

I don't know if I want to use the word *freedom*. Many people describe climbing as a kind of freedom. I don't think *freedom* is precise enough, but I've never found a better word. How do you describe the feeling you get when you wake up in the van in the morning, then you go to the crag all day, and come back to camp in the evening, and have a nice dinner? It just feels great! It feels like I'm doing what I was born to do.

Then there's the challenge. If I only climb easy routes, I get bored. Besides I usually find the harder routes more impressive. For example, at Flatanger I've been working on a 15d (9c) line for some time. It's become my lifetime goal.

It's more impressive than any other line in the cave, and that motivates me to train harder, because I want to do that route! I want to get better. I want the satisfaction that I'm climbing better than last year. Because it's fun to climb these beautiful lines!

Projecting

There's no limit to how long I will try a route. As long as I enjoy it, I will keep trying. It doesn't make sense to set a schedule. Every route is different. Working a route is an interesting process, because for the first few weeks you always make some progress. That's because for 1 or 2 weeks you don't lose that much power. And you are getting to know the route better, which allows you to climb higher and higher. But after that, it's much more precarious. You may start falling lower than before, and it becomes really hard to motivate yourself.

So the moment comes when you say, "Okay, I'm done. I need to go home, train, and come back with fresh motivation, more strength, and perhaps better conditions, so I can get a new chance." That's the approach I've used for many routes, but especially for *La Dura Dura*. I went to Spain for that route five different times. And on every trip I was stronger. But then I got back on the route and said to myself, "Okay, you're stronger, but you're still not strong enough!"

During the "Observation Period" at Briançon, Ondra, Jakob Shubert, and Sean McColl discuss the finals lead route. Ondra says that during the 6-minute period he can memorize every handhold, foothold, and clip.

It wasn't until the last trip. I tried *La Dura Dura* on the first day, and I knew, "Okay, on this trip I'm going to send." And I succeeded 1 week later.

Finding Balance

When I was in high school, at times it was really tough. I didn't want to make excuses. I was attending normal school like my peers, but I was missing a lot of days because of climbing, and it was my responsibility to learn the lessons on my own.

It was really hectic. I was traveling a lot, sometimes going straight to school after spending the whole night in the car. But I still believed it was important to keep up. I believe the knowledge you get in school is priceless.

But after I finished high school, I really wanted to enjoy some freedom just traveling around for a year. That's when I spent a lot of time in Flatanger, bolting new routes, eventually sending some, and it was great. But even living this great lifestyle, I felt a bit bored. As I said, I believe you need different things to occupy yourself, and that you enjoy the process of climbing even more if you can't go every day. What happens if you get injured and all you have is climbing? There's nothing else? You would definitely get much more depressed! So sure, there are times now when I would like to have more free time, but I'm happy with my current situation. I'm studying, and things are going well with the competitions. For sure, I will soon be free again and spending a lot more time out climbing rock.

Life Lessons

I don't know exactly what climbing has taught me. It has definitely shaped me, but since I've spent my entire life doing it, it's hard to say what I would be like without it. I do know that when I was a kid I was really shy, not very talkative, afraid, and not very self-confident. Climbing has taught me to be better in all these areas. I think it has also taught me to be strict with myself and work hard to attain my goals. And thanks to climbing, I've met so many people around the world who have shaped my point of view. It's kind of strange to say that climbing is responsible for everything about me—who I am, who I'm with, what I do. It may sound dumb, but when I think about it, that's the way it is. And I might be naïve, but I definitely believe that when you meet climbers there's a higher probability that these people are going to be more honest and friendly than the average person. That's a good society to be in!

Climbing is strange. You drive 12 hours to the crag. You sleep in the dirt. You get on the rock, and it's cold. The holds are painful, and you wonder, "Why am I doing this? Why is it that so many hobbyist climbers are doing this in their free time? They are not forced to!" It's like we are some strange and rare species! It's definitely not for everyone. I like to think that we climbers are different somehow.

Spirit Matters

Yes, climbing can be a spiritual practice, but it doesn't have to be spiritual for everyone. It all depends on your personality, and what you want from climbing.

Climbing is such a wide activity. You may climb only in the gym. You may only boulder. You can do so many things, but it's still called climbing—it's still based on getting from the bottom to the top. That's nice, that this one little activity can be so many things for so many people. For most gym climbers it's just fitness. They want to look good, get some muscle, and be fit.

I definitely think climbing is healthy, but for me there's no other activity that takes me so deep within myself. Because when I'm climbing well on a hard route, it's like my mind is somewhere totally different than my body. I can't really say I'm focused, because I think of focus as a conscious experience when I know I'm concentrating. This is different, because when I'm succeeding on a hard route, it's more like my movements are driven subconsciously, driven by my intuition and experience. That's when I climb my best.

And that's hard to achieve. What I enjoy most about it is not necessarily the moment I'm climbing in that state but the moment just after. It's like I entered a different world or different dimension. It's certainly something I've never experienced anywhere else. And I think it can only happen if you do something very well.

It might sound strange to call it a kind of mental ritual to get into that different dimension, but that's what it feels like. Sometimes when I get down from a climb, I don't remember certain moves because I was so fully in the moment.

I think if you don't have this intuitive ability, you haven't climbed enough. You are not a complete climber, because your intuition is not strong enough to tell your body what to do.

I find it very interesting to do an activity so much that you can enter this state. I would like to try different things. I would be psyched to snowboard or to paraglide for instance, but at the same time, I know it would take so much time to get good. Not good because my ego demands it, but good enough to be able to enjoy the same intuitive state of mind I feel when I climb.

Fear

While sport climbing I experience fear very rarely, and that's kind of sad. I feel like I've lost something. It doesn't have to be fear, it can just be the thrill, even though you're relatively safe. Most climbers experience fear, but for me sport climbing is so routine I have to be pretty high above the bolt to experience fear, or I need to do some trad climbing—that's where situations can get potentially dangerous.

Sometimes in sport climbing there are big runouts, but it's usually overhanging, so you can safely take a big fall. The truth is I like situations where I know it's safe, but at the same time it's exciting to be 5 meters above the bolt.

I try to avoid situations that are objectively dangerous. I know I can trust my own abilities. I can always try to gauge the level of risk. But in some situations in the mountains, there are factors you can't measure. That's why I don't like free soloing. For sure, I see why people do it, but it's not something I want to do.

Creativity

I'm not sure I would call putting up new routes creative, but it's very exciting. I don't think it's true creativity, because it's more like you are following what nature has offered. You're not creating holds. But you do need to recognize the line and the nature of the rock, and that's interesting and exciting. If I rappel down and touch the holds and imagine the way I will climb them—that's one of the best things in climbing! So it's more like exploration than creativity. Even though it's sport climbing, it's adventurous. You're discovering something new. It's like exploring a white spot on the map, a place nobody has been before.

But then perhaps it becomes more creative, because now you've got a certain line you need to follow, and perhaps there are more holds than you need, so you must choose the right ones in order to make the climbing as efficient as possible. Once the route is clean and chalked up, it's probably quite easy to choose the correct holds. But in the beginning, when the rock is dirty and chossy, it's up to you to find the way.

The Future

For sure I will be climbing in the future, but beyond that I don't really know. Right now I'm really psyched for sport climbing, to open new routes, to complete my projects, and to try different crags around the world. But maybe some seasons I will exclusively boulder, I don't know. I decide quite spontaneously

what's going to make me feel the most excited. In 2015 it was World Cup competition, but right now I'm not psyched for comps anymore. I want to take advantage of all the training I've done and apply it to climbing outdoors on hard sport climbs.

The Next Grade

It's a really hard question: When will we see 5.16 (10a)? Nobody knows what 5.16 should look like, and how much harder it should be than 15c (9b+). It's purely subjective. But in my opinion there should be big jumps between the specific grades, otherwise it's impossible to judge a new level of difficulty. Because the higher you go up the scale, the more subjective it all becomes. It can be more height dependent, more dependent on conditions, more dependent on finger size, and so on. So if we don't make big jumps, we can't really say *why* it should be a new grade. Therefore, in my opinion, we will have to wait quite a while to see 16a. And I don't think I will ever climb it. Certainly I'm capable of climbing 15d, and I can imagine what 16a might look like, but someone stronger and younger than me will come along, and hopefully he or she will succeed on a 16a. We will see.

Advice for the Next Generation

I think there are now so many people focusing on being good at just one thing, but to me the most important thing, especially when you are young, is to try to be as universal as possible, to know how to climb different kinds of rock and to try to on-sight as many routes as possible, to develop the kind of intuition that allows you to climb efficiently and well. Wait until you are 16 to really start working on power. In the long run, this approach is going to allow young climbers to accomplish much more than only training hard and focusing on their achievements.

As Ondra says, "In order to go from the rock straight to a comp you would need to be a really complete and universal climber."

INES PAPERT

I've been a fan of German climber Ines Papert ever since I began reading about her decades ago. One of the best things about this book has been the opportunity to meet some of my heroes, so I was delighted to learn that Ines would be passing through Utah on her way to Patagonia with Mayan Smith-Gobat.

Few climbers dominate their chosen specialty the way Papert has dominated modern ice and mixed climbing. By any measure, she's one of the world's best ice climbers—male or female. During her competitive career she won four World Championships in mixed climbing, as well as most of the individual World Cup events. In 2005 she not only beat all the women at the Ouray Ice Festival—she beat all the male competitors as well.

And when you hear Papert's life story, her accomplishments seem even more incredible. Growing up behind the Iron Curtain, the most physical thing she did as a child was sing in a choir. It wasn't until the Berlin Wall fell and she could move to the West that she had the opportunity to participate in sports. By the time she started climbing seriously, she was a single mom caring for a newborn son. But Papert has a knack for transforming obstacles into opportunity. As she tells it, she began competing *because* she was a single mom and her limited free time forced her to be more efficient in her training than her fellow competitors.

Hungry for new challenges, in 2006 Papert took her legendary fitness and laser-like focus to the mountains, seeking out new routes that could be climbed in the finest style. The results are bold new lines like *Finnmannen* (M9+) in Norway, a route that before Papert's success many had tried and since her ascent no one has repeated.

In 2012, Papert and Thomas Senf made a first ascent of the North Face of Nepal's Likhu Chuli 1. Only 20 feet from the end of the technical difficulties, they encountered a cornice of unconsolidated snow that repulsed their

Former World Mixed champion Ines Papert attempting an unclimbed project in Provo Canyon, Utah

efforts. Rather than summiting, as they had hoped, they were forced to make an open bivouac on an ice ledge, their only shelter a tent fly. Sometime in the night their body heat melted the ice upon which they were sitting. Suddenly they were free falling through space to the end of their safety line. Shaken and nearly frozen, they climbed hand-over-hand up the rope in the darkness to begin chopping out a new ledge and wait for dawn.

On February 22, 2015, Papert made what may be one of the most remarkable mixed climbing ascents in the history of the sport, the first female ascent of *The Hurting* (Scottish Grade XI, 11). The name of the route says it all. First climbed by Dave Macleod, a climber legendary for his boldness, in Scotland where bolts are seen as sacrilege, *The Hurting* has been hailed as the hardest mixed route in the world, protected only by traditional gear—and that's on a good day. Ines sent *The Hurting* in a blinding Scottish gale with wind and snow gusting to 80 miles an hour.

Simon Yearsley, who belayed her, wrote:

I've been climbing for over 35 years and this was the most impressive lead I've ever witnessed: sketchy moves from the start; a couple of bits of poor gear until a secure and comforting sling; then a tenuous traverse before a dubious hex. Up a few more meters until suddenly the wind was so powerful it blew the good sling clean off. Ines continued. As she pulled over the roof the wind was increasing in strength, physically pushing her from side to side, easily gusting 80 mph, if not more.

I thought about closing my eyes as she linked the off-balance moves on the steep headwall, at one point losing a placement and dropping straight-armed onto her one remaining tool. It held. I kept my eyes open. She continued. A seemingly endless series of loooong powerful reaches, flagging feet, and skittery tools. Several times she completely disappeared in the maelstrom. Then the whoop. The very loud and joyous whoop. It was over.

But as exciting as Papert's mountain adventures are, she is most excited when talking about the times she shares climbing and traveling with her son

Emanuel. No parent will be surprised to learn that climbing a runout and poorly protected mixed climb is not nearly as scary as watching your son make his first trad lead. When it comes to finding a balance between the intensity of alpinism and the more quiet matters of the heart, most fail. By her example, Papert teaches us all that chasing the extreme means little if it is not grounded in the love and companionship of family and friends, in stories, laughter, good food, wine, and all the other grace notes of a life well lived.

First Ascents
2007 *Finnmannen*, M9+, trad, Senja Island, Norway
2008 *Into the Wild*, M12, Icefall Brook Canyon, Canada
2009 *Power of Silence*, 13a, Cirque of the Unclimbables, Canada; *Cobra Norte*, WI5, M8, ED+, Kwangde Shar, Nepal
2011 *Quantum of Solace*, WI7+, M7, A0, Kyrgyzstan
2012 *Sensory Overload*, 5.11+, Mount Asgard, Baffin Island, Canada; *Black Madonna*, 8a, Untersberg, Germany; *Azazar*, 8a, Taghia Gorge, Morocco; Likhu Chuli 1, Khumbu Himal, Nepal
2015 Southwest Buttress of Mt. Waddington, 5.11+, ED1, M4, WI3, Canada

Roots
My name's Ines Papert. I was born April 5, 1974, so now I am 41 years *young*. (Laughs.) I'm best known as an ice climber, but I do all kinds of climbing. I love big alpine faces, the bigger the better. I grew up behind the Iron Curtain in East Germany. My parents had a hard time accepting life under Soviet rule, so every week we went to meetings pushing the revolution forward. When the Berlin Wall fell, it was an emotional time, because travel was impossible under the Communists, and we all wanted to explore the world. So at 19 I moved to Bavaria. I worked as a physical therapist in Berchtesgaden, and I still live there.

As a child, teachers encouraged me to participate in sports. But my parents would not allow it, because if you became involved in sports in Communist Germany, you became part of the state system and your childhood was over. It was like China is now—all they care about is winning—not the well-being of the kids. So instead, my parents introduced me to music. I played the piano and the saxophone, and I sang in a choir.

By modern standards I started climbing quite late, when I was 21. My first experience was in a gym, and I was annoyed by how *terrible* climbing seemed. I thought, "Holy shit, this is climbing?" I need fresh air to be a good person. I need to move my body outside. I like gyms more now but I still use them only for training. After that first experience, for several years I explored the mountains by hiking.

But it didn't take me long to get bored. For some reason, I thought it would be nicer to go straight up a mountain rather than walking around it. So I started climbing near my home in Bavaria. It's not the center of the Alps, but we have great possibilities. And I wanted to explore, so I organized a trip to Peru. But I thought before I climbed in the Andes, I should try ice climbing closer to home.

And once again, my first experience was horrible! We were a party of three. The strongest went first, with the second and myself following on the same rope. Stupidly, I tied in only a meter behind the second, almost touching his heels. So when he dropped chunks of ice, they fell straight in my face. I had a huge cut on my nose, and it was so cold I couldn't feel my fingers.

But I'm not the kind of person who gives up. I tried ice climbing again, and I noticed that the faster I climbed, the better I was and the more fun I had. This was in the early 2000s; steep mixed climbing and the first mixed competitions were just starting. Only a handful of people were doing it, so I thought, "Why not try a competition for fun? Why not meet some interesting people from all over the world?"

And through those early competitive experiences, by hearing everyone's stories, I got *really* psyched. I found a group of friends who were also highly motivated, and we began training. We competed together, and we attempted hard mixed routes in the mountains. After 6 very intense years of competing, I retired. I missed climbing outside with friends. That was when I started traveling specifically to establish new routes.

"I like to feel my body and spirit working as one," Papert says, here moving into a "Figure 4."

Why Ice?

I'm not sure if I chose ice climbing. I feel like the ice chose me. For one thing I prefer colder temperatures over summer heat. Perhaps that's something that makes ice nicer for me than for many women. But it's a tough business. It's definitely scary, yet the fear is also one of the most interesting parts.

It's not just about technique. It's knowing how to place your tools. It's so much more than simply recognizing the line—where to climb—you also have to pay attention to the risks. You have to decide whether you're comfortable trying, or if there's too much danger and it's time to retreat. I think the depth of experience I have is the reason I can do harder climbs and survive. I like exposure, but I never want to push too far. I always stay focused on the last piece of protection and ask, "What would happen if I fall?" I've never been badly hurt ice climbing, and I don't want to be.

It's a delicate balance. If you're too scared, you will never move away from the last screw. If you're not scared at all—you won't live long. I've been able to find a balance. I'm not too scared and at the same time I'm very focused on risk management. This is ice climbing. Everyone who has tried it knows this to be true. You become super attuned to the color, the sound, and the structure of the ice; to the air temperature; to changes in the weather. That sensitivity to your environment is something very special.

Because let's face it—the rock is always there. Sure, sometimes it's wet. Sometimes it's dry. But with ice you can climb the same line ten times, and every time it will be different. Each time you have to feel it, read it, interpret it, as though for the first time—and that's fun.

Finally, I trust myself and my partners. I don't climb with people I don't know. All these different threads have come together, and I have become quite comfortable climbing ice.

You could say that mixed climbing and I grew up together. I was a new climber when mixed climbing was born, so I've evolved along with the tools, the techniques, the comps, and the training. I was part of a young international community and that was really fun. We're still like one big family, visiting each other, climbing together, going on trips.

It's been almost 16 years now doing this kind of climbing, so I've climbed many *many* meters. When I touch ice, even after a summer off, it feels completely natural. I'm not worried or tense. I like the powerful movement. After being outside all day climbing in the cold, you feel your body, you feel your strength, you feel your mind—because mentally this kind of climbing is intense. You come home tired and hungry. That's one of the best things about it. You can eat so *much* after ice climbing, and the food tastes so *good!* I love eating!

Strengths & Weaknesses

Climbing makes me incredibly focused. If I'm in the middle of a hard pitch on a big climb, I don't notice what's going on around me. Once in Canada, my partner said, "You know a storm's coming." And when I looked around, the storm was there. I hadn't even noticed the "Boom Boom" of the thunder. I get so into the climbing I let it take over my mind. I'm totally in the here and now.

For example, I did a first ascent of a route in Norway called *Finnmannen* that many Norwegians had wanted to do, but only if they could do it in traditional style without placing bolts. Without bolts it was obvious the climb would have one section that was very difficult to protect. The first time I tried it, I failed. I couldn't do the crux. It's a runout slab, and I couldn't reach the ice. But we returned the next day and I tried again, and for some reason the second time I climbed right through the crux without any fear—and it would have been a *really* big fall! It's a very difficult climb. It's never been repeated, although several people have tried. And I've always wondered: What happened in my mind that day that allowed me to do that climb?

In fact, I don't think I would ever repeat *Finnmannen*. When I think about the crux, it's still scary. So I came home thinking, "Wow, I'm super strong in my mind." Then a few days later I went out sport climbing, and I was scared to fall above a bolt. In a matter of days, I go from one situation where falling is not an option to rock with good protection, yet I'm afraid. What changes?

In Norway, I climbed that route in the last 10 hours of our trip. We finished the route, went straight to the airport, and flew home still wearing our climbing clothes—which makes me think that perhaps I need the pressure of a deadline to overcome the fear. Otherwise, if you always have one more day—you find plenty of excuses not to go.

I had a similar experience in Scotland last year. I was working on *The Hurting* and had a slide show to present 2 days before I had to leave. I had tried the climb, and conditions weren't great. I wasn't sure if I was strong enough in body or mind to do it. So I did the slide show and then had one more day before my departure, and it turned out to be the worst weather of the entire trip. But I thought, "Why not try? The last day has often been the best."

When we got to the base, it was blowing a full Scottish gale, complete with high wind and hail. It was obvious I had only one chance. After 30 minutes on the climb, I wouldn't be able to feel my fingers or toes, and I could not ask my partner to belay twice in those conditions. I still have no idea how I did it. Maybe because it was my last chance. I don't know.

I've always been weird in that way. After I won my first World Cup, there were always expectations—from sponsors, spectators, other competitors, and myself. And many people struggle with that kind of pressure. Often when they start climbing in a comp, they fail because they are too nervous. I too was always super nervous before a competition started, but once I did the first move, I would become focused on what I needed to do. And the crowd helped me do that.

I have a lot of weaknesses, but as soon as I notice one, I start working on it. For example, right now I'm on my way to Patagonia, so I stopped in Utah to work on my crack climbing. Same thing with slabs. I like slightly overhanging terrain—both for mixed and rock climbing. Slabs aren't something I'm good at. And if I don't have a goal, I'm weak. I have a hard time pushing myself. I know people who love training, but I only train when I have a reason.

Finally, I'm not super patient. Climbing with slow people—that's probably my biggest weakness! I would be a terrible guide.

Intuition

Once we climbed a new route on a hanging dagger of ice, and right after we climbed it, the sun hit the face, which was black rock. And I realized that we should go down very quickly, that the whole dagger was going to fall. We rappelled off, walked a short distance, and *BOOM!* tons of ice released and fell down the climb.

That experience left me with mixed feelings. I was glad we had been lucky, but at the same time you don't want to push your luck too far. In the end, it was a good lesson to see clearly what the risks in ice climbing really are, to be reminded how dangerous this activity can be.

But I also think that intuition isn't trustworthy. You always have to ask yourself, "Is this really intuition speaking or am I just listening to my weaknesses? Am I feeling tired, so my mind is creating excuses to back down?" You always have to ask yourself whether there's actual danger, or if irrational fear is posing as intuition. And that's when you have to rely on your friends. If someone pushes it all the time and ignores the risk, I don't want to climb with him. And, on the other hand, those people who are always looking for any sign of danger, always finding reasons to quit—that pulls me down as well. So there's a perfect mixture that's found in just a few friends. There are maybe five really good partners I know I can listen to and who will listen to me. I never make the decision by myself. We talk to each other, we weigh the pluses and minuses, then we find agreement. It's always a team decision.

"If you're unhappy with your life, if you always have the feeling you're missing something, you'll end up an unhappy person—and that's not who I want raising my son," Papert says.

Motherhood & Mixed Climbing

For difficult climbs the motivation for all team members has to be high.

In a few days I'm going to Patagonia with Mayan Smith-Gobat, and she is a super-motivated person. She's always psyched, and she takes climbing *very*

seriously. And I take climbing seriously too, but I have other responsibilities in my life. I have a 15-year-old son to think about. I spent last summer in Canada with my son Emanuel, and Mayan was there too. It was hard, because part of me wished I could go off climbing with Mayan, but at the same time I felt so happy climbing with Manu.

We tried to make it work, but it didn't work very well. I realized I needed to go climbing either with my partner, or with my son. When I'm with my partners, we can push ourselves. We can focus on achieving our goals. But when I'm with my son, that's the most important thing in my life and I'm very glad I have it.

The truth is I couldn't have become such a focused climber if I had not been a single mom. Manu was only a year old when I started competing, so I couldn't be gone for more than a few days. At home I only had 2 to 3 hours a day to train, so I used this small amount of time to train really hard and really well. Most of my friends had far more time, but in the end they trained less efficiently.

This is another reason I pursued competitive climbing. I realized, "Hey, I'm doing well. I can actually do this with a baby." I can take Manu along to competitions, and I can breathe some of the same air as the professional climbing community. I feel very lucky to have had that.

Now I give slide shows and women come up and say, "You're my role model. I would love to climb as much as you do, and be as strong . . ."

And I always wait for what comes next: "But I can't. I don't have those possibilities."

Yes, I've been lucky. I have the support of family and friends. I make my living from climbing, so I don't have to go to an office from 9 to 5. But believe me, it hasn't been easy. I get homesick. I don't want to leave on trips. But if I stayed home all the time, only taking care of a child, I wouldn't be the person I am. Climbing gives me balance in all areas of my life.

When you have kids, there are always problems. Children go through all kinds of phases and difficulties, and many parents end up stressed all the time. But I've tried to compare the challenges of normal life with the situations I've encountered in the mountains. And that makes me realize, "Well,

Ice climbing is a delicate balance, Papert says. "If you're too scared, you will never move away from the last screw. If you're not scared at all—you won't live long."

this is just a small thing. You've dealt with far more serious problems while climbing. You will solve this one as well."

Maybe it's a bit selfish to continue climbing once you're a mom, but if you're unhappy with your life, if you always have the feeling you are missing something, you will end up being an unhappy person—and that's not who I want raising my son. So I always tell women, "Having having a child doesn't have to end your climbing. You can deal with both."

Emanuel is older now. He likes to climb, so that's a whole new challenge. If I climb with my friends, we're responsible for ourselves. But last summer, climbing with Manu, I realized that I have all the responsibility! That really brought me down. "Do I really want this?"

And at the same time, we enjoy being together so much. Yes, it's hard to watch. Emanuel is always doing crazy stuff on his bike, but I trust him. He's not the kind of person who pushes so hard he ends up in an accident. But at the same time, as a mom it's hard to watch knowing what might happen. I have to remember that when I started climbing I had to go through all these same experiences in order to become a safe climber.

When Manu was 5, I was packing for a trip and for the first time he asked me not to go. But I was so excited, I didn't listen. It's a route in the Dolomites up the south face of the Marmolada. It's called *La Via Pesca (The Way of the Fish)*. It's known for technical runout climbing with tricky gear. When I was climbing the seventh pitch, which is only grade 4, almost walking terrain, I came to a huge flake. It was at least 5 meters wide and it looked solid. I placed some protection and started traversing to the right, but when I touched the flake, the whole thing came off. I fell and all the gear blew. We were very lucky the belay anchors held. I survived, but my leg was badly broken. That was the only time Manu ever asked me to stay home. After that, he was scared about climbing for a long time.

Partners

For a difficult project, everyone on the team has to have the same motivation. And you need to be clear about everyone's strengths and weaknesses. For example, Mayan is a much better crack climber than I am, but I'm a better ice climber, so in Torres del Paine, when we reach the ice, it's my turn, and if we come to a big off-width, for sure it's Mayan's turn!

That's what makes a team interesting. It's not about making everyone follow one person's rules. It's about having fun—not getting so serious that we forget how much we love climbing. For example, my friend Thomas Senf will be with us in Patagonia. He's a really good climber, an extremely talented photographer, and also very funny. He makes me laugh all the time, and that's essential when you're attempting big climbs. When the weather turns bad for 10 days, it's so hard to keep motivation high, but with Thomas it's no problem. We just laugh while we're waiting.

Why I Climb

I like to feel my body and spirit working as one. And I like to explore—I love using climbing as a means to visit new places. Climbing's not just a sport, it's far more. It's moving against gravity, being in exposed places, getting over your fears, surprising yourself with what you're capable of. When you run, you might run fast or slow, but when you climb, you either make it to the top or you don't. There's nothing in between. Climbing makes life clear.

And there's a creativity component. I've always had a hard time going to the same places, repeating routes. So creating new routes is a big adventure, because you never know if you'll succeed. The possibility of failure is high. When you top out, you feel elated. That's something missing in sport climbing. Usually you don't reach a summit.

The thing I hate about climbing is when bad weather comes. Being on an exposed climb and being surprised by a thunderstorm—that's when I get really scared. But again, it's all part of the game. I don't hate bad weather generally, it's just something to deal with, but thunderstorms are something I really hate.

Accomplishments

I've tried not to create big goals in my mind, because I feel that if I accomplish them then I might feel lost. So every trip is important, even if it's not successful. For example, my second trip to Kyrgyzstan was special because Emanuel came with us to base camp. He and I had a really great time traveling together.

So when it was time to climb and he had to leave, it was heartbreaking. It was much worse than any time I've had to leave him in Germany. I couldn't shift gears from being a mom back to being a climber, and I transferred some of those feelings from Manu to the expedition team and I tried to be a "good mom" to them—and that did not work at all! They were all young climbers super psyched to be there, but not serious enough for what we were attempting. They all got sick, and then they all worried about being so far from civilization. I was the only person who didn't get sick, because I couldn't, then everyone would have been sick. That was pretty much the end of that expedition. We didn't succeed at all.

Lessons

There are problems in life—with your child, with his friends, even dealing with his father (which has not always been easy), and I'm not the kind of person who likes conflict. Because once you're fighting often things don't come to a helpful end. Some people like arguing, but I hate it. I don't want to argue with my son. We talk with each other, and even if I don't agree, I listen and take him seriously. I believe that talking with one another and trying to find a way that works for all is one of the most important lessons I've learned from climbing.

The lessons we learn in the mountains can cross over to normal life, but they are also separate. The situations are very different, but how to deal with problems is the same. You can always say, "This is too hard for me. It's too scary." You can bail. In life and in climbing, you can always stop trying when things get hard—or you can deal with it. So dealing with difficulties, that's what I've learned from climbing and brought into my normal life.

Ethics & Tradition

Through traveling I've learned about the different ethics and climbing traditions of the countries I've visited. For instance, local climbers like Ian Parnell in Scotland taught me not only how to deal with Scottish winter climbing, but also how to appreciate its tradition. And the same in Norway. Once I learned the local ethic, I realized the route I wanted to do was possible without bolts,

Concerning her chosen specialty, Papert says, "I'm not sure if I chose ice climbing. I feel like the ice chose me."

so that's how I did it. But in Norway bolting is not as clear-cut as in Scotland. I would *never* consider placing a bolt in Scotland.

Seriously, the locals *would* kill you! But then you go climbing in Morocco, which is well-known for bolted routes, so I bring my power drill. You have to understand why climbers in certain regions are strict about their ethics. During my slide show in Scotland I had a clip from a movie about climbing in Morocco's Taghia Gorge, and in the movie we were placing bolts. You could hear the *rrrrrrr* of the drill, and the Scots in the audience had never seen or heard anything like it. They were literally shrinking from the sound of the drill! To them it was painful, and it took me a minute to understand. I had to explain that climbing in Morocco is completely different, in a totally different part of the world, and that the ethics are different there as well.

Training

When I was younger, I was really into the quantity of the climbing, and now I'm more into the quality. I'm listening more to my inner voice, which can say, "No, this is enough." I couldn't do that when I was younger. And I train differently. I've always trained specifically for my goal at the moment. For instance a World Cup Final only lasts 12 minutes. So we never trained endurance for more than 12 minutes. We kept moving fast and hard but for 12 minutes and no more. But in the mountains 12 minutes is pretty short. So what I'm doing now requires a different kind of training. You have a long approach with a heavy pack just to get to the climbing.

Now I'm going to Patagonia, and the route we are attempting, *Riders on the Storm*, is really long. So before I left home, I tried to climb not less than ten pitches a day. I would start with 7a, 7b, 7c, then 8a, and so on, until at the end of the day I would have climbed ten pitches. But if I weren't going to Patagonia, after the fourth or fifth pitch I would have said, "Okay, now I'm ready for a coffee!" (Laughs.)

So I train very differently now, but I don't train any less. I climb 5 days a week. I climb 2 days on, 1 day off, then 2 more. Sometimes 3 days on, 1 day off.

Advice for the Next Generation

My son and I don't talk too much about climbing, because climbing is the life he's grown up with. When he was a baby, he slept in a hammock at the base of the crag while his parents climbed. He grew up breathing fresh air, and now he likes the gym, but he's *super* psyched to climb outside, which is different from most kids his age. Many young climbers today prefer climbing indoors. So it bothers him, because many of his friends are better than he is inside or in comps. And he's better on rock.

He's very motivated. He probably has a bit of my genetics, because he's super psyched when he succeeds. But he hates coming in fourth or fifth, which I understand. I would have stopped competing if I had no chance to win. So I try my best to teach him that competitions are just competitions. They are far removed from real climbing. I take him outside, and we climb together as much as possible.

When we were in Squamish last summer, there was a 5.10 that was easy to protect, so I asked Manu if he wanted to lead it. And he said, "Well, okay." So Manu started and he was doing well. But with experience one learns that you need to place gear *before* it gets hard, and he just kept climbing, and suddenly it got harder and harder. I had to remind him it was time to get some protection, because he was already 6 meters above the ground.

So I was getting worried. Then he got worried. "Oh, oh, oh! Wow! I don't know if I can get something in!" And I'm thinking, "Holy shit!"

But then he got the first piece in, and after that he did really well. It was a good lesson—for both of us. You can't just toprope. You have to learn by doing.

DOUG ROBINSON

Doug Robinson has been a hero of mine for 40 years. Like many climbers of my generation, I responded to Robinson's writing in the early 1970s—particularly his treatise on clean climbing in the 1972 Chouinard Equipment Catalog—which gave voice to the youthful, visionary, environmentally based spirit of American climbing at the time.

"When cracks that will accept nuts peter out, long unprotected runouts can result, and the leader of commitment must be prepared to accept the consequences that are only too clearly defined," Robinson wrote. "Personal qualities—like judgment, concentration, boldness, the ordeal by fire—take precedence, as they should, over mere hardware."

His words epitomized the zeitgeist of the free-climbing revolution that was just beginning and that climbers like Caldwell and Honnold continue to this day. On the surface Robinson was trumpeting the shift away from the use of pitons which damaged the rock to the embrace of nuts and other passive protection, which left no trace of a climber's passage. But in a broader sense, he was espousing a deeper philosophy—one that elevates skill and boldness above safety and security and voluntarily gives up some of the advantages of technology in order to live cleanly and sustainably.

Robinson is a true *soul* climber, someone for whom climbing is a side effect of his lifelong love affair with mountains. As he once said, "If you are more at home in mountains than anywhere, you are a mountaineer. To be a mountaineer is to love mountains. Then to climb them."

Robinson's life and aesthetic marry the nature-based spiritualism of John Muir with the Buddhist/Taoist thinking of Gary Snyder and the counterculture free-thinking of the 1960s. His ideas like his actions, are grounded in the white granite flowing clouds and water of his beloved Sierras.

In 2010 Robinson was the recipient of the American Alpine Club's Literary Award. In 2015 his collection of essays, *A Night on the Ground, A Day in*

Doug Robinson, age 70, bouldering in the Buttermilks

the *Open* (which includes "The Whole Natural Art of Protection" from the 1972 Chouinard Catalog) was listed as one of *Climbing* magazine's thirty-three must-read climbing books of all time. In 2013 Robinson published *The Alchemy of Action*, a book that combines the latest research of modern neuroscience with a lifetime of personal experimentation in the ways action sports affect human consciousness. Like this book, *Alchemy* asks the question "Why do we climb?" but from a scientific perspective I've barely had time to touch on.

Robinson has been called the father of clean climbing, not only for his writing on the subject, but because in 1973 he, Galen Rowell, and Dennis Hennek made the first "hammer-less" ascent of the *Northwest Face* of Half Dome, the first big wall to be climbed without placing pitons. Robinson also made the first ascent of the longest alpine rock climb in the Sierras, *Dark Star* on Temple Crag. He helped develop and popularize bouldering in the Buttermilks, and during first ascents with Yvon Chouinard and others, of ice climbs such as *V-Notch*, *Lee Vining Icefall*, and *Ice Nine*, was integral to the testing and evolution of modern ice tools. In 1979 he was part of a team that made the second ascent of Nepal's Ama Dablam. A mountain guide with 50 years of experience, Robinson served as the first president of the American Mountain Guides Association.

Roots

My name's Doug Robinson. I was born in Washington, DC, in 1945. My father was an aeronautical engineer who worked for what would become NASA. When I was 5 we moved to California. I grew up in Silicon Valley when it used to be called the "Valley of Heart's Delight," and it was. When we arrived the shoulder-high wildflowers that John Muir walked through when he visited were gone, but there were still plenty of farms and orchards. Right away my parents took me camping in Yosemite. That was my introduction to mountains. Welcome to the West! Welcome to mountain walking around Tenaya Lake!

In those days you could camp right on the shore of Tenaya and we did. On the old Tioga Road you could barely drive 10 miles per hour most of the way up from the Valley. By the end, you were driving over granite slabs connected by sections of pavement. So Tuolumne was my first wilderness experience, and I loved it from the start. My younger brothers and I would make rafts and set sail for islands in the lake. That was a grand adventure.

We went back every summer, and as I got stronger, the wilderness began to expand. I joined the Boy Scouts and learned how to backpack, and I taught my family. We began going on trips deeper into the Sierra. I discovered the John Muir Trail. I began taking longer hikes, scrambling up peaks—and naturally scrambling led to climbing. When I was 13, I climbed Pywiack Dome and got stuck. I spent an entire afternoon standing on my tiptoes, palms flat on the rock because I couldn't climb up or down. I needed a rescue. Getting delivered back to my parents' camp in a ranger car was not exactly my idea of how that adventure was supposed to end—but I was plenty happy to be alive.

At first my parents grounded me, but after a couple months they let me attend climbing classes offered by the Sierra Club. Having a rope on was great! I loved it right away. I was learning from these geeky guys—Silicon Valley engineers out playing in their Army surplus pants and high-top leather boots. But they all had the spirit. I noticed that right away. And they were very good technicians, really safe climbers. Thank you Sierra Club! And thank you for everything you've done to save the planet! I was still involved with the Scouts. I began teaching hiking, backpacking, and camping. By the time I was 15, I was leading weeklong trips in the Sierra. That led directly to my career as a guide, and I'm thankful for that because it's been a rich, wonderful life turning people on to the mountains.

Mountain Life

I was lucky to learn to love mountains first and then discover climbing as part of that lifestyle. I've noticed that people who start as urban climbers go to places just to climb. Yes, they can climb very hard, but after a time they often quit. It's a sport to them and nothing more. But to me climbing was always part of living in mountains, a life I could never get enough of and still can't. So climbing is just a side effect. That's the way I came to it, and now that I'm getting older I still love climbing, but I'm also happy wandering in meadows and sitting by creeks. And as a guide I love turning people on to the lifestyle.

Hey, this isn't just car-to-car and back to the bar! It's total immersion in wild country, and that includes immersion in your own wild self. You're out there pushing. You've been climbing all day and you're getting tired. It's getting dark, maybe stormy, and you've still got a long way to go to get down. Some of your wilder self comes out in response to experiences like that.

The mountains and your unconscious push against each other, and they both get evoked. As a writer, part of what I do is evoke the wilderness, which is outside of us, but I'm equally interested in bringing out what comes from the inside as well, the insights pulled out by terrain and difficulty—the joy and wonder.

Guiding

I like to say that my function as a guide is to make myself useless. When people come to me, they are expecting to have a safety net placed around them as they experience mountains. And my job is to gradually remove that net, while at the same time pushing them ahead into their own experience. Okay, I've taught you how to make a good anchor, so we don't have to do that anymore. And maybe I've helped you learn how to lead, so you can do that on your own too. Pretty soon, what do you need me for? We've had a good time. But if you'd like, you can come back and I'll take you up harder stuff. Maybe we'll do an 18-hour day and not get back until 2 a.m.

I can push and they can respond because they know I'll get them down. One step at a time. You don't *conquer* mountains you know, you slip through their defenses.

The people who do freak out, or who don't like the process, drop out, and I never see them again. But I have other clients who come back twice a year for 20 years. We get to be friends, companions, and climbing buddies.

Writing

While I was still in college I wrote a story about climbing Mount Lyell called "Tuesday Morning on the Lyell Fork with Eliot's Shadow," and I sent it to *Ascent* magazine, which was brand-new at the time. I got lucky, because they liked it and printed it. And that launched my writing career.

Robinson writing in his Rock Creek cabin. "Part of what I do," he says, "is evoke the wilderness, but I'm equally interested in the insights pulled out by terrain and difficulty—the joy and wonder."

"Climbing is a *practice*," Robinson says, "because you've got to grapple with all the deepest emotions. The alchemy of fear and desire, prudence and aspiration—that's so rich."

I was a kid without a lot of self-confidence. Climbing helped me with that, and so did having *Ascent* and other publications accept my writing. So I ended up with this dual career as mountain guide and writer. And I've always been grateful I didn't need to depend on one or the other, because I noticed long ago that all the old guides have bad knees, and all the writers drink and smoke too much. I like to split the difference.

John Muir and Hanshan and Gary Snyder have been heroes of mine ever since I first discovered them. Climbing and living in the Sierra high country, the spirit of John Muir is everywhere. And Gary Snyder worked on a backcountry trail crew in Yosemite in 1955 and wrote about it in his first book of poems, *Riprap and Cold Mountain Poems*, and that book included his translations of Hanshan. So I got turned on to all those guys, and they posed questions and made statements that were wonderful and deep, and you know—I'm still working to get to the bottom of some of the statements they made about wilderness and about being alive on this planet. It was very natural for me to be influenced by the way they saw the world, and that has seeped into the way I see and think and express myself. I'm eternally grateful to have had them as my guides.

So I was climbing full-time and writing by the time I went to work for Yvon Chouinard at Chouinard Equipment (which became Black Diamond) as an assistant bong bender. I sat barefoot in the courtyard where we made the gear, and while I worked, I thought about clean climbing, because that was what was in the air at the time—pushing ourselves on the rock in a free-climbing way, but also in terms of protection. So in a sense my essay on clean climbing for the '72 catalog was the culmination of all those things: days out on the rock, building gear, and the perspective of those early wild men of the mountains.

Climbing's Yin & Yang

Climbing has so many facets. We're never even going to be able to name them all. But to me the two obvious ones are *spirituality* on the one hand and *competition* on the other. I saw competition all the way back in the Golden Age of Yosemite, the clearest example being between Royal Robbins and Warren Harding. But the spiritual side of climbing is a little subtler. I believe I was lucky to have a visionary turn of mind. Right away as a kid the mountains appealed to me as this shining experience, and I was fortunate I wasn't raised in an organized religion so I could see that as pure spirituality, rather than calling it Jesus or something else. I guess I've spent the rest of my life exploring the spiritual aspects of climbing, while trying out all of its other facets as well.

The spiritual dimensions are endless. They're wonderful and deep, and resonate with how I see nature and consciousness. Maybe I'm just getting older, but I like to see my function now as evoking the spiritual in my own and other climbers' experiences, gently nudging people's way of seeing the world a little away from competition, and a little more toward wild nature, Mother Earth, and the bounty of this planet. Are we lucky or what?

One trend in modern climbing accentuates its intensity. Car-to-car climbing in the Sierra is popular now. No need to carry camping gear. And hats off to those who are able to pull it off. A young friend just did three big routes on Temple Crag—sixty pitches—in a day—and I happened to see him walking out well before sunset. But I was up there on a slower wavelength, camped for days, rambling around, climbing some, writing in my notebook, whistling up the trail with no particular goal in mind except just being there. Immersion in wilderness. For me, a lot of the spiritual value only reveals itself gradually and over time.

For instance, I've had the interesting experience on several occasions of having a vivid dream on my third night out. In one I recall, I found myself in a shopping mall in Atlanta—a place I've never been. I was wandering around lost. I think that metaphorically I was spiritually lost, because I was in this consumer place where I don't belong. One of the big disadvantages of modern society is that there is no way to decompress. I had to feel the tension and noise of that dream and let it go before I could reach the calm of wilderness, where I could absorb and feel more deeply.

In civilization, information itself is so fragmented and comes at us so fast these days that the pace of life itself becomes *anti-spiritual*. The way we've structured things, it will probably all implode because we've gotten it wrong. Then our civilization might be rewritten in a slower, more meditative and appreciative way.

Spirit Matters

For me, climbing is overwhelmingly a spiritual practice. It's a lot of other things for a lot of other people, and even for me at times. For instance, I've earned a good living as a guide. I've written about climbing, and I've designed equipment. But climbing has never been a sport for me. It's far more, starting with the fact you don't step onto a measured playing field with a rule book or a scorekeeper to tell you who's won or lost. It's much deeper. At its best it reverberates within your whole being. It gets you in touch with parts of yourself you didn't know were there, but that maybe you're curious about—like fear. So climbing is a *practice*, because you've got to grapple with all the deepest

Speaking of his dual career as writer and guide, Robinson says, "I noticed long ago that all the old guides have bad knees, and all the writers drink too much. I like to split the difference."

emotions. It's close to meditation. And it's also physical because it all starts with grasping holds on rock. Worrying about the drop. The alchemy between fear and desire, prudence and aspiration—that's so rich.

After roaming through the world's religions, I got closer to Zen Buddhism than any of the others, but finally I just decided that *everything* is sacred. Pantheism is as close as I can come to what's behind all this. All I can do is see and feel for myself—and I feel the earth is sacred.

I feel that life has gained more freedom through evolution. After all, I'm not a tree rooted in place. I'm not a monkey swinging through the trees. I've got consciousness. So it looks to me like the most exciting thing to explore is spirituality. And climbing is my vehicle to do that, because it arises out of my physical being expressing itself in nature. Because suddenly—what's this? Joy. Acuity. Emotional sensitivity. They all come out of that interaction.

We start by looking for hand- and footholds, and we end up with higher consciousness. To me those things cannot be separated. I go out climbing and I come back *high*. So I see climbers ultimately as alchemists who brew spirituality out of physical practice.

What does that mean? To me spirituality is a higher form of consciousness. I'm more physically aware. My body tingles. I have a heightened emotional response. I get these intense ideas. I get excited. The excitement is part of whatever is flowing out of me. I'm very, very alive. Therefore, spirituality to me is being *very* alive.

Climbers aren't alone in clamming up when talking about spirituality. Many people do that. Everybody starts wiggling in their chair. Why is that? Maybe it's because spirituality asks the big questions, and the big questions remind people of death. Personally I don't think there's anything beyond that curtain, so I'm trying to make the most of what happens in the here and now.

The Alchemy of Action

I wish I could remember the quote—it's something like Zen experience is experience that's all burned up. There's nothing left but ashes. I interpret that to mean that if you are really in the present, it seems like you have less memory of an event. Memory doesn't form as clearly as it does at other times. That's one aspect of the intensity of climbing. That intrigued me, and it started me studying brain hormones.

I'll give you five brain hormones that help regulate consciousness. First off, it ain't adrenaline. That's a huge red herring. I could explain why, but we don't have time. Let's just move on to noradrenaline. That's your wake-up juice. When you open your eyes in the morning, your noradrenaline bumps up a bit at the base of your brain. Drink a cup of coffee—it bumps up again. Take a walk around the block—another bump. But if you go climbing, you bump it up a lot, because it takes a lot of attention to climb. So being awake, aware, and alive is noradrenaline.

Second is dopamine, our pleasure hormone. It feels good to be awake, alive, and climbing, and all those things ramp up our dopamine.

Third is serotonin, which is our *roll with it* hormone, our own internal anti-depressant. When you're feeling low and the world's pulling you down, it's because your serotonin has dropped off. If you took Prozac, it would amp your serotonin back up. But it turns out that if you're out there pushing it, being confident and forward thinking, serotonin increases as well.

Those are the big three substances that run your brain. Take them away? End of story.

The last two are a bit controversial. The first is anandamide. Most have never heard of it. It's the hormonal equivalent of marijuana. And it gets elevated by exercise. Put somebody on a treadmill and 50 minutes later his or her anandamide starts ramping up. The scientist who first isolated it, Raphael Mechoulam, said that everything marijuana does, anandamide does too. It even gives you the munchies. He named it after the Sanskrit word for *bliss*, and bliss is one of the best ways of describing this elusive state of consciousness we feel when climbing.

And the last hormone in our mental cocktail is DMT, dimethyltryptamine, arguably the strongest psychedelic compound known to man. It's the active ingredient in ayahuasca, which people travel all the way to the Amazon to experience. It cures depression. It cures alcoholism. Magic stuff! And right at this moment your pineal gland is pumping out just a trickle of DMT, which goes right to the emotional heart of your brain. It affects the tone of our

Working a problem in the Buttermilks. One of Robinson's early jobs was assistant bong bender at the early Chouinard Equipment Company.

consciousness in such tiny quantities, that the best way I can express its effect is to say it might be why we see life in Technicolor. Visions anyone?

I've run all this by the scientists I've worked with, and they concur. Yes, these things are all operative in our brains right now, but especially when we're climbing, when we're out at the edge of our physical abilities and pushed by fear—when we're most alive.

So religious experience is based on brain chemistry, but there's a lot more to it than that. The chemistry is there to buoy up your mood, to sharpen your perceptions, to encourage your visionary response to reality. That's your appreciation, the vividness of what you're experiencing. In other words, your brain chemistry is necessary, but by itself it's not enough to explain your response. I've done enough research to know this is a human response, not just something I've gotten into. Our response as climbers to the intensity of what we do can only be described as spiritual experience. I don't know any other way to describe it.

We could say the brain hormones are necessary to make us receptive to that experience. *Receptive* is a good word, but consciousness is a huge mystery. In fact, maybe it's the ultimate mystery in the universe, I don't know.

Physics is pretty good at explaining the physical universe, where it came from and how it works. And out of physics comes chemistry. And out of chemistry comes biology, which is life. And out of life, leaps consciousness. Consciousness is the most recent of all these processes, which makes it new and fascinating. It has its own rules and its own results, which have nothing to do with organic evolution. So we're privileged. We're really lucky to be on the cusp of exploring what this new thing really is. And explaining it is not the same as exploring or enjoying it. Reveling in our consciousness is actually a big part of its value. I like to think that we climbers are doing our little bit to revel in what consciousness is, and to explore it more deeply.

Addiction

So yes, climbing is addictive. Try not doing it for a few days, and you will go through some form of withdrawal. But it's a positive addiction. It's the healthiest addiction I know. As my mentor Smoke Blanchard said one day in the Buttermilks, "I've never seen so many healthy addicts." That's really true. Our bodies are healthy. Our minds . . . well, yes, people can say we're all torqued up, that we're weird. But we're probably weird in a direction that will determine the future of human evolution.

Lessons

The most important lesson I've learned from climbing is to just keep doing it. If I stop, I get depressed, and I'm less of a *human* being. If I keep climbing, I get to be more alive. Any questions?

Even so, it's tricky to try to apply the lessons we learn from climbing to our flat-land lives, because the addicted misfits who love climbing don't fare well in the ordinary *make-a-living-from-9-to-5* world.

But the lessons learned on the cliff sure seem to give us a glimpse of our better selves. They give us a better understanding of the sharing that comes from partnerships and a close community, in contrast to the competition of day-to-day life. Maybe climbing gives us a glimpse of a larger view that leads us to become environmentalists; to protect our planet; to look out for our fellow man; to be kinder, gentler, more proactive people. At least I like to think so.

In Yosemite in the 1960s we quickly came to love the rock and love the Valley. And at the same time . . . oops! We were also destroying it by using those crude Iron Age tools called pitons in order to keep ourselves alive as we ascended. So the clean climbing revolution was a wonderful opportunity to transcend those early tools with new ones that required more finesse and partook more of art than brute force. Maybe that's exactly what we need to solve the environmental problems hammering us today, the destruction of our planet by gouging out all the minerals . . . filling the air with carbon dioxide, and so on. Clean climbing succeeded not because it was the right thing to do, not because of a moral imperative, but because it was fun, it was a challenge. It was play, a kind of deep play because your life was on the line, and you were forced to solve problems with more finesse and less force, in an aesthetic way.

Climbing helps me connect with my soul and the soul of the earth. It taps me on the shoulder with beauty, wonder, and transcendence—and that's some of the greatest stuff in life. I'm over 70 now, and I'm not climbing as hard as I used to, but every time I go out, I seek flow. I can try for finesse even on 5.4. Especially on 5.4! I can move well and with grace. And I don't need much pro on a 5.4 so I can keep moving, literally get in a physical flow, which leads to the flow of my spirit—the soaring you feel when climbing is going well.

Why I Climb

I love climbing for the states of body and mind it evokes. Body first: I love the motion. I love the challenge. Then I begin to notice the mind states that flow out of that action of the body. And I love being turned on by the mind states created by the action.

So here's my body pushed toward its limit. I find a kind of love in that. I'm fulfilled in motion in ways we moderns have forgotten. Forty percent of us now have jobs as information handlers. We sit at keyboards. We forget our bodies, and our bodies are nudging us, like a dog asking for a walk. The lucky ones find physicality. And the luckiest of all don't find it on the tennis court or the football field, but in wild nature. Climbing is wonderful that way. You and the natural environment are working on each other, and what comes out of that are these exciting states of consciousness. You're more aware. You're more connected to your emotions. Thoughts come tumbling out. All of that is self-fulfilling.

An Accident

When I turned 40, I treated myself to a climbing trip of several months, and I got in the best shape of my life. Near the end of it I was in Joshua Tree and

I hung out a bit with John Bachar. I interviewed him, and I watched him solo *Leave It to Beaver*, which at 12a was one of the hardest solos anyone had done.

And I think I got a little over-inspired by being with this world-class athlete—which I certainly am not. I came back to Bishop, and I had a 19-year-old client who wanted to learn crag climbing. So I took him to the Buttermilks, where there are a bunch of cracks on one wall. I was climbing really well. I was leading 5.9 cracks one after the other without any problem, just to put the rope up and belay my client. Then at the end of the day we were walking back to the car when I noticed a crack I hadn't seen before. I laid the gear down and started checking it out. I climbed 30 feet of easy—although overhanging—terrain, and I reached a headwall with a nice crack in it. I was a ways up that crack when it started getting hard. It might have been in the hard .10, maybe low .11,

"I see climbers ultimately as alchemists who brew spirituality out of physical practice," Robinson says.

range. I don't know. I could never force myself to go back and see.

So I got up on this headwall, and like many Buttermilk climbs near the top, it rolled over into what Blanchard called *shaggy rock*, which is loose and scaly. I couldn't go any farther, and I couldn't reverse the moves below me either. I was stuck.

I could only take one hand off the rock at a time, for just a few seconds to shake, then I had to put it right back in the crack. My client ran up the back of the formation and dropped the rope down to me, but by then I was getting pumped. I couldn't tie the rope around me. Neither of us thought of the obvious—which was to tie a loop in the rope so I could put an arm and shoulder through.

After about 5 minutes of struggle I was completely burned out, and I could see where I was going to land—40 feet below on a granite slab. The last thing I remember were my hands as they left the rock, then I blacked out because I didn't want to experience what was about to happen.

I came to the moment I stopped bouncing. My legs still worked. My arms worked. My skull wasn't broken. And I immediately started worrying about my client. So I started yelling—"I'm all right!"

Well, I wasn't quite *all right*. My back was broken, and there was a lot of blood coming out the back of my pants. I was only a quarter of a mile from the road, so I decided to crawl out. By that time it was twilight in late December and the temperature was dropping. My young client behaved brilliantly. He threw his jacket over me, and he ran to get his car, which was parked farther up the road. Then he realized the keys were in his jacket. He actually broke the window of his own car before remembering the steering lock, so he had to run back to get his keys.

By then I was tired of crawling, so I stood up and realized I was numb from my shoulders down to the back of my knees. I walked the rest of the way to the car. *Very slowly.* I was seeing stars. Then I sat in the glass from the broken window on the way to the emergency room.

When I walked into the hospital, the receptionist said, "Okay, sit down and fill out these forms." I said, "I think I'll just go in and see the doctor."

I pushed through the swinging doors, and there was Peter Hackett (a mountaineering doctor famous for his research on altitude sickness). Then I knew I was in good hands and could let go, and the shock overwhelmed me. I lay down on a steel table and it started banging because I was shaking so hard. My blood pressure was 60 over nothing. Then it was 50 over nothing and Hackett was shaking his head asking, "How did you walk in here?"

All I could say was, "It seemed like a good idea at the time."

The emotional reverberations of that fall lasted for at least a year. I remember 9 months later I was in the Needles. I was leading a 5.8 that was bolted—and well bolted at that. And suddenly I started freaking out. I just went all to pieces. *I'm outta here.* I backed down and rapped off. Things like that would come over me at random. I never knew when or where. But gradually, over months, they faded. My practice to heal was simply to keep climbing. And if it bit me in the ass occasionally, I would go down and try again the next day. I never thought of quitting.

Home

I now realize I could spend several lifetimes in the eastern Sierra and not exhaust my responses to it. Can we talk about all the first ascent possibilities here on all those sunny days when maybe you'd rather dive in a lake and lean back against a warm rock instead of climb? It's all part of the Sierra experience, and that's been very rich. I've been all over the world, but increasingly I can't be bothered to leave the Sierra. So sometimes people ask me what was my favorite climb, and I always say it's the one I did yesterday. It doesn't really matter whether it was a first ascent on Temple Crag, a big wall, or a day spent on boulders that I've climbed before and was fondly revisiting. Climbing is so rich. There's so much to choose from. I can solo an ice field with my ice ax. That's not particularly hard, but it takes me to the top of a peak where I get a view I've never seen before. Those experiences are infinite.

Advice for the Future

I love talking with young climbers. They're so alive. They're leaning into the experience. They're hungry. And maybe I can remind them it's not all about climbing harder—but climbing with more joy. Save your tendons and maybe you'll reach transcendence. Hah! And may I humbly suggest you occasionally peek outside the gym? Go outside! There's a whole planet out there waiting. People have asked me if there is a way to learn to climb outside a gym. Yes, we used to do that all the time!

CHRIS SHARMA

How's this for a fantasy? Close your eyes, and just for a moment imagine that unlike 99.9 percent of the other climbers in this part of the galaxy, when you travel and visit different crags, there aren't any routes hard enough to challenge you. Imagine what it would be like if you could show up at Rifle, the Red, Boux, or Ceuse and climb every route there without much effort.

It may sound like science fiction, but that's the reality Chris Sharma has lived for the past 19 years. It's a world where all the 12s, 13s, and 14s on Earth aren't all that hard.

Well, there was one route at Ceuse that at age 20 Sharma found interesting. It was bolted by Jean-Christophe LaFaille but never completely freed. LaFaille named it *Biographie*. In order to climb it, Sharma had to invent a whole new grade of climbing difficulty. When he eventually clipped the chains, he had taken technical rock climbing a major step forward in its evolution. He renamed the route *Realization*—the world's first 15a.

On a planet with seven billion and growing being the best at anything—even for an afternoon—is amazing, which makes the fact that Sharma has been the best rock climber in the world for the past *2 decades* all the more mind-blowing. Nineteen years at the pinnacle of any sport is rare, but it verges on the superhuman in elite climbing, which takes a tremendous toll on the body and has seen monumental growth during the same period. To put Sharma's importance in perspective, consider that in 2016 it's possible to be a fully sponsored climber—simply by repeating Sharma routes. No need to discover, bolt, and send new routes of equal or greater difficulty. If you want to make headlines and get sponsored, simply do what Chris has already done, in some cases years ago.

In fact, as of 2016, there are only two climbers at Sharma's level—Adam Ondra and Alex Megos. Ondra's achievements have been discussed in the previous pages. In 2015, Megos raised eyebrows and made headlines

Chris Sharma climbing his route *Bon Combat* (15b/c), Cova de Ocell, Spain

worldwide by redpointing *Realization* in a day. Megos has bouldered v15 and is making a name for himself by dispatching cutting-edge routes and problems in a matter of hours—rather than months. But as impressive as Ondra and Megos are, they are still young, and only time will tell how lasting their contributions will be. In comparison, modern rock climbing has been shaped by Sharma's vision. Whatever Sharma thought was cool, we followed. Bouldering. Projecting hard sport routes. Deep-water soloing. All were popularized by Sharma, and he's done it with a singular grace and humility, driven by an unflagging love of the sport.

Not only did Sharma have the *guns* to become the first human to climb 5.15—he had the *genius* to see that it was possible, coupled with the commitment to spend months and years proving it. Starting as a teenager, traveling the world, Sharma has sought out, bolted, and redpointed the world's hardest routes and problems—*Necessary Evil, The Mandala, Realization, Witness the Fitness, Three Degrees of Separation, Es Pontas, Jumbo Love, La Dura Dura, Bon Combat*. It's a legacy of influence that may not be matched for generations.

To me Sharma is the most interesting climber in this book. Not only because he is so uniquely talented but because he's an enigma, possibly even to himself. Sharma has cultivated a mellow, laid-back Southern California persona—but underneath he's intensely competitive, focused, and driven. As he points out, high-end climbing isn't touchy-feely. To climb the hardest routes in the world, you've got to get your *grrrr* on big time, often for months at a time.

I interviewed Sharma at a pivotal time. As he told me, "For the past 20 years I've been told I'm the best climber in the world and now that's coming to an end. I have to find a new way to define myself."

And for such a natural athlete, that may prove even harder than climbing 5.15. Two months after I spent time with him in Barcelona, Sharma married Venezuelan model and television personality Jimena Alarcon. They welcomed their first child, a daughter named Alana, in the summer of 2016. After years living in rural Spain near Oliana, Sharma has moved to a high-rise apartment in the heart of the big city of Barcelona near where he and a group of investors opened a state-of-the-art climbing gym in the fall of 2015.

"When I did *La Dura Dura*," Sharma said, "I thought, 'I can climb harder than this.' But since then, I've wondered whether that is really the best use of my time and talents. Should I devote more years of my life to putting up another line 40 feet left of *La Dura Dura*, or should I try new things?"

Sharma is a rock star, but not just in the sense of someone who gets our blood pumping in climbing videos. He's also like those other rock stars, the kind who live in a rarefied atmosphere of travel, celebrity, money, and influence. Jeff Leads, the former athlete manager for Prana, remembers that when he set up team poster signings at trade shows and climbing festivals, the other pro climbers would be done signing in 30 or 40 minutes—but the line for Sharma went on for hours.

"He's definitely in a league all his own," Leads says.

Sharma is arguably the best-compensated pro climber in the world with an annual income well into six figures provided by international brands such as Red Bull, Prana, Evolv, Sanuk, Sterling, and Petzl. He's continually offered endorsement packages by corporations like Ford, and he's paid handsomely for stunt work in motion pictures such as the recent remake of *Point Break*. He's even been paid to take billionaires bouldering for a weekend. But Sharma knows the days of being paid simply to climb won't last forever. He's working hard to reinvent himself as a husband, father, and businessman. He's part owner of Evolv, and he has a business relationship with several gym companies, including Sender One, Momentum, and his own signature franchise in Barcelona.

In the 5 weeks before we met, Sharma flew back and forth between Europe and the United States four times (a number even he admits is excessive). The previous week he was in the redwood forest of California climbing a giant sequoia for Red Bull. The next week he met with city officials, architects, and construction bosses to discuss the Barcelona gym, then he flew to Iceland for a photo shoot. This was all while planning his August wedding in a five-star Barcelona hotel, which brought in climbing glitterati from around the world for an all-night bash. And between these and hundreds of other events, responsibilities, and engagements, he climbs. But not like the rest of us.

Sharma on the beach near his Barcelona home

Sharma is the most naturally gifted climber I've ever seen. With all his responsibilities, he may actually climb less than the average recreational climber, and by his own admission he's never done much specific training. Yet he can easily hold his own at a Psico-block event against World Cup competitors like Sean McColl or Daniel Woods, for whom training is the air they breathe. And when Sharma does climb, he goes all out, pedal to the metal, pulling down with every fiber of his being. He does a quick warm-up on a horizontal 13b, then he jumps on his 15b/c test piece *Bon Combat* and suddenly it's the Sharma we've all seen in hundreds of videos—shouting, exploding from hold to hold, feet flying. Face contorted with effort, climbing as though his very life depended on it, climbing as though he were Chris Sharma—and no one else in the world can do what he does.

Roots

My name's Chris Sharma. I was born April 23, 1981, and I'm a rock climber. I spend most of my time sport climbing, but in general I love all kinds of rock. I grew up in Santa Cruz, California. It's not a climbing town. It's better for surfing and mountain biking. But when I was a kid, I was always climbing trees so my mother took me to a climbing gym when I was 11, and that's how I got my start.

Climbing was love at first sight. Before that, any sport I tried—whether it had a board or a ball—I was pretty clumsy. I always knew I was athletically gifted, but before climbing, I'd never found the one thing I did well. I didn't need anyone telling me to go to a gym to train, and that's been my approach ever since. I love climbing so much I want to do it all the time. The discipline to become a good climber comes naturally when it's something you love.

My mom and dad separated when I was young, but I alternated between them—a week on and a week off—with each. And they both had their spiritual sides. I grew up going to a school founded by Yogi Baba Hari Dass. It's not a religious school, but it has a background of spirituality. For example, we would do yoga in gym class. In the same way many families go to church on Sunday, in my family things revolved around yoga and Eastern philosophies. For me that was normal.

I went through a tough period when I was 16. I'd been climbing since I was 12. I was already a professional, and I'd made a lot of sacrifices. Those are pivotal years. You're trying to process a lot of things and figure out who you are. I injured my knee bouldering, and all of a sudden I couldn't climb for nearly a year. For a while it seemed like all my dreams were shattered. That prompted a lot of self-reflection. And I did that by returning to the traditions I'd been brought up with. So I did a lot of soul searching by learning more about meditation and Buddhism. And that definitely gave me tools to deal with difficult moments.

The world's strongest fingers? Sharma has not been seriously injured since his teens.

Lessons

Getting injured at 16 taught me that life has its ups, its downs, and its difficulties. You can apply this to climbing or anything else. Often we make a situation more difficult or painful simply by our resistance to what's happening. Life can be challenging, but acceptance of the situation goes a long way toward learning to live with it. An injury like I had can be physically painful, but obviously the psychological hardship we put ourselves through can be accentuated by the way we respond. So the ability to relax in the present moment, to accept what's happened and know everything changes, everything is always coming and going, that as painful as this moment is—it too will pass. You learn to be patient, sit tight, and not add more mental strife to an already difficult situation.

Getting injured was tough, but what it taught me has affected my entire approach to climbing and life. Because when I got hurt, I was winning World Cups. I was traveling the world. I believed the world was my oyster. I was probably a little cocky and a bit of a punk, so it was a huge reality check for me to have all that suddenly taken away. It taught me humility, to realize that as great as those experiences were, they could be gone in an instant.

And it also made me realize how much it sucks to get injured. So I learned to be more careful and stay safe, because I found out how hard it is not to be able to climb. I haven't had any serious injuries since.

Now I feel very fortunate that I had that experience. Those were my first few years of being in the limelight. I still saw climbing in this two-dimensional way—it was only about doing hard climbs. For example, as a kid I hated hiking. I would only hike to climb. I didn't have much appreciation for nature. I was hungry and ambitious, and then all of a sudden I couldn't climb at all. So I had to take a step back and learn to enjoy being in nature, and to learn how to be happy without climbing. Those were big lessons, difficult to learn, but super valuable. It's so common and normal that we wrap our contentment with the results of our external life. Then if it doesn't work out, we're not happy. I was forced to find peace with it all. I saw the hollowness of pursuing sports-related goals and fame. Suddenly it all seemed shortsighted, and it forced me to contemplate the things in life that could provide lasting happiness. Through that process I developed a whole new connection to climbing, one that was very personal and very spiritual.

For example, I would do my knee therapy by riding my bike up the coast from Santa Cruz, and there was this little bouldering spot called Panther Beach. I would go there every day. I think during one period I went 45 days in a row.

It was just this tiny wall by the ocean where I would climb barefoot and make up little eliminates. By no means world-class! But it was very special for me. Those were pure climbing experiences. They touched on what it means to have a deep connection to moving on rock, learning that climbing is a way of connecting with yourself and your body, being alert and present, both with yourself and your surroundings. It cut through all the externals—sponsorship, grades, publicity, and competitions—and got right to the basics of climbing for the pure joy of movement. That was huge. It changed everything.

As for other climbing lessons? Well, working difficult projects has taught me the value of hard work, being patient, not giving up, not taking myself too seriously, and enjoying the moment. I try to apply that to the rest of my life. I'm not always successful, but life is always a work in progress, right?

And projects have taught me a lot about failure. You've got to find ways to measure incremental progress. Celebrate small successes. That's key. For instance, noticing that I found a new way to grab a hold. Maybe I didn't make it any higher, but I had a really good sensation, and I climbed more efficiently.

Transitions

Climbing has been the focus of my life since I started traveling at 16. That's when I took my first trip to Europe. Tommy Caldwell and I hitchhiked around France by ourselves. Those experiences were enriching and educational. And today climbing remains my main passion, but everything I do is a way of getting in touch with who I am. You can't define yourself with one thing. For instance, what if you're a climber, that's all you are, then suddenly you can't climb. What then?

I've never wanted to put a box around myself. I've always tried to embrace whatever comes, and somehow that's always been connected to climbing.

Climbing is the window through which I've seen the world. But this is an interesting time. I'm 35 (in 2016). I'm still a pro athlete. I still feel at the height of my power and my ability. But I'm also aware that being a pro is not something I can do my entire life. So I'm interested in building gyms, because I started climbing in one, and it's neat to see how much the sport has evolved, to see it becoming mainstream, and to be involved in that process. And I'm in a unique situation because I'm recognized internationally, so I'm involved in a California gym called Sender One, and now my business partners and I are opening Sharma Climbing BCN in Barcelona.

Obviously I have a lot to learn about business, but I like the challenge in the same way I like working a hard route. It's a struggle for sure, but you have a vision of something you want to create, and that passion is a precious thing. For me the bottom line is having a project, whether it's in the garden, school, or on the rock. The important thing is to stay busy, keep growing and evolving.

I've always tried to create circumstances so that whenever I go climbing, I do it for pure enjoyment, not for some other reason. And that's tricky. I've seen lots of people struggle with being a pro, trying to find the right balance between business and passion. Most people go climbing because it's an *escape* from everyday life. They take the time to just be themselves and get away from everything. But when climbing *is* your life, that changes. Suddenly the pressures of your career are all mixed with your passion. And I've seen those pressures affect both my own and other people's climbing experiences. So I've always tried to keep my climbing pure. And I've been fortunate to be supported in that by these amazing companies who've allowed me to follow my dreams.

So I'm at a point now where I'm starting my own company, and that's an interesting transition. I'm still a sponsored climber, and at the same time I'm dabbling in other ventures, splitting my time between Europe and the United States. I'm traveling back and forth, dealing with different sponsors and projects and trying to immerse myself in this other world that's totally foreign to me, learning about spreadsheets and all that stuff. So yeah, life is hectic, but I'm happy, and I'm as psyched as ever. Whenever I go climbing I feel as giddy as when I started.

"When you stop questioning and embrace the life you've been given," Sharma says, "that's when you discover meaning." The *Warm Up* (13b) at Cova de Ocell.

But here in Barcelona I've been able to develop a routine where I usually climb 1 day on, and 1 day off. I'll do business in the morning, then go climbing in the afternoon. Living in a place like Spain, where you have so much rock climbing and basically a 10-month season, it's not a problem getting enough. In fact, you have to pace yourself, find the sweet spot where you don't climb so much that you burn out. I was leery at first of living in the big city, but it's been enriching to combine an urban lifestyle with a half-hour drive to the middle of nowhere to climb beautiful walls. It feels very complete.

When I was 20, I actually considered quitting climbing. I'd just climbed *Realization*. I'd won World Cups. I'd done the hardest routes in the world. I'd done a lot of the things I'd set out to do. And I had the awareness that there's more to life than climbing. I knew there were a lot of things to experience, and I thought maybe this is the time to change gears and try something else—because at that moment I didn't know where I wanted to take my climbing. I was doing a lot of soul searching. I traveled to a variety of meditation centers. It was a chance for me to hone my mind in a way I hadn't done before, to discover who I was without climbing.

Then I went to Majorca and discovered deep-water soloing, and that was what made me fall in love with climbing all over again. I realized I could free solo over water and do these amazingly difficult things in a super-pure style.

That was pivotal. It took all the existential stuff—the questions about what does climbing really mean—out of the picture. For example, I had friends who were working construction jobs just to get by, and I realized, "Man, I'm really lucky!" I realized that climbing is my gift, my way of inspiring people, my way of contributing. No matter what we do, we have to find a way to give back and stay connected. It's easy to think the grass is always greener on the other side, that I'd be happier doing *this* or *that*. But I had this moment of realization that I don't need to change who I am to have a meaningful life. I just need to embrace what I've got.

When you stop questioning and embrace the life you've been given, that's when you discover meaning. Meaning to go climbing, to have all these projects, to make films, to do slide shows and events to share climbing with others. It's so rewarding when people come up and say, "Man, I started climbing because I saw a video of you."

You don't need to look for something outside yourself. Just be yourself to the best of your ability, and everything you do will be that much more meaningful and rewarding.

And the second part of the equation was finding a place I could call home, where I could do what I love. That's something I've always struggled with. Growing up in Santa Cruz, I was always traveling to climb. It wasn't until I came to Spain that I found a place that could provide a well-rounded way of life that includes climbing.

Sharma working a new project that could be a 5.15 traverse. "Projects have taught me a lot about failure," he says. "You've got to find ways to measure incremental progress. Celebrate small successes."

Deep-Water Soloing

My friends at Big UP Productions had filmed the boulderer Klem Loskot deep-water soloing in Majorca. And Klem had heard about it from a local climber, Miquel Riera, who invented *psicobloc*, as they call it in Spain. So when Big UP wanted to go back for more footage, I went with them, and I met Miquel. Coming from Santa Cruz, I grew up in the ocean, but once I discovered climbing I was always running to the mountains. So finding a way of climbing above the sea brought my two worlds together once more.

To me deep-water soloing offers all the things I like most about climbing. On one hand it's similar to bouldering. There's pure freedom of movement and no gear, but at the same time you always have to be aware of how you fall. You don't want to land on your back, just like you don't want to fall on your back from even 10 feet on a boulder problem.

And at the same time it's a lot like sport climbing, in that you're climbing long sections of overhanging limestone.

It also shares elements of trad climbing, because you are always attempting a ground-up on-sight. You're climbing up and down. You might be on the wall for an hour trying to figure out a sequence, then climb back down to rest, because you don't want to fall.

Finally, it's similar to free soloing, too. Just you and the rock. But instead of climbing above the ground, you're over water, so you can attempt moves at your limit. Climbing at your limit is out of the question with normal free soloing, because the consequences of falling are too great. I could never do that.

And finally you're interacting with the ocean, knowing how to deal with the sea. For all these reasons, deep-water soloing embodies for me the perfect form of climbing. Take *Las Pontas* for instance. It's a route I put up in Majorca. It's 5.15, but I can solo it. For me, that's as good as it gets.

Starting a Family

I'm super excited about this next step with Jimena. We're starting a family, and that's something I've always wanted. (Chris and Jimena's daughter, Alana, was born in June 2016.) It's something I've looked forward to. And at the same time, I'm still hoping to do all the things I like to do. I want to keep climbing. I still have a lot of things I'd like to do. And it's interesting to get involved building climbing gyms and starting my own company, to keep evolving, finding new ways to stay relevant, to continue being an ambassador and help the sport. I feel I'm in a unique position to be able to help guide the sport in a positive way. I think as climbing becomes more mainstream, it could easily get distorted. For instance, I'd like to instill in people a healthy approach that's connected to nature and a more spiritual side of climbing—aspects people might miss climbing in a gym. I want to remind people that climbing is much more than a sport. It's a way of life—a way of discovering who you really are.

Motivation

I believe one of the reasons I've been able to stay psyched on climbing for so many years is because I listen to my heart and follow my motivation. I don't want to sound lazy, but I like to keep climbing fun. People beat themselves up because they don't feel psyched to climb. They'll force themselves to do ten laps on a route because their training regimen says so, or so many feet of climbing per day, or whatever. But I think that what we do has to come from the heart. Otherwise it can backfire. I've seen many people burn out by forcing the situation. It's really natural, you know. I've been climbing for over 20 years, and it's impossible to be 100 percent motivated all the time. Motivation goes in waves. I've always trusted that my motivation will come back. And when it does, it comes back tenfold. Then you have the experience of falling in love all over again! You can't force yourself to climb hard. It has to be something you really want.

After ascending something like *La Dura Dura, Realization,* or *Jumbo Love,* it's normal to take time to step back and reassess. I try to live in a spontaneous free-flowing way. So much so that people often think I don't train. But it's a natural flow. When I find a project I'm passionate about, that inspiration motivates me to work really hard. And if the inspiration and the motivation are there, the discipline comes. It doesn't even feel like discipline, because it's what I want to do.

So working on a big goal naturally organizes all my time. That's one of the coolest things about having a project. I can put my whole life into it. Your whole life becomes focused in this crystal-clear way, so you know exactly where you want to be and what you want to do. That's one of the greatest things in life—to have a purpose.

Projects

Well of course looking for a project is about pushing limits and trying really difficult things, but it's more than that. If it were only about seeing how strong I am, I can do that on a hang board or by seeing how may pull-ups I can do. Climbing is about difficulty, but it's also about aesthetics. It's very creative to find these beautiful forms and features, discover stunning positions and amazing movement. There's an entire adventure based on seeking out those elements. And I've always loved that adventure because it's so personal. It's not about comparing yourself to anyone. You're just going out doing your thing. This is where art and climbing intersect. You find this amazing line that just barely goes. It's been created by nature but it almost seems designed to climb. It's so perfect, but it's just beyond reach, so it makes you want to get better. You want to get stronger so you can do the climb. It's all connected. The discipline and hard work necessary to be a high-level athlete comes from the inspiration of nature, seeing these beautiful possibilities and wanting to bring them into reality.

The term *King Line* was originally coined by Klem Loscot, but something that's always appealed to me is the search for really spectacular beautiful lines. It's not enough to do something hard, it needs to be in an amazing, position, a route that asks you to pour your heart and soul into climbing it. I have so many routes I want to try. It's beyond my capacity to do them all. You have to pick and choose your battles, because there's only so much time and energy. You have to choose what's most important. It's classic scenario. Often when you bolt, you're hanging there in your harness and you feel the holds and you think, "Oh, that feels good. That'll go." Then you try the route and, "Whoa! This is way harder than I thought."

I always say my eyes are stronger than my fingers. So you need to be realistic, you need to get focused and pick a route that makes the most sense for you in that moment.

Training

If I'm really busy, I'll do some hang boarding or I'll go climbing in the gym to keep my fitness up. As I get older, I have to maintain a bit more, whereas in the past I could take 2 months off, go straight to a comp and win. Now I have to work harder. But, my basic approach to training is to get inspired by a line, for instance most recently *Bon Combat* (15b/c), then work it over and over. You can call it training if you like, or you can just call it climbing your project. But the reality is that if you want to achieve something at your limit you're going to have to work *really* hard. And everyone has their own way to do that. You have climbers who spend a year training in a gym, then they go out and send their route second go. I like to work the actual project until I can do it. You might say the first climber sent the route in two tries, while the other guy took a year. But the reality is both climbers required a year of solid effort. I've always needed the objective in my face, telling me I need to work harder. Everyone needs to assess his or her personal situation and find the approach that works best. Even if you don't have the luxury of spending a year on one route, you can still approach climbing in a holistic way. Don't think, "Now I'm training," and "Now I'm climbing." Just go climbing and find enjoyment in the entire process. To me, that's success. We should even embrace the suffering involved in training, because the entire experience we call "climbing" is a struggle. It's frustrating to fall over and over again on the same move, but that's what makes the route so rewarding when we succeed.

This is the paradox of hard climbing: That to climb our best we have to be able to free ourselves of attachment to the outcome. Attachment can cloud our ability to be in the moment and climb well.

But at the same time, if we're not attached, how are we going to try so hard? The answer is learning to enjoy trying, working hard, and learning to make these amazing moves. The answer is to have fun.

Mind Games

For sure we all have our tricks and different ways of getting into the proper mind-set. It's important not to be too attached to the final outcome, but it's also important to get to the top. Otherwise what's the point? But it's really difficult to walk up to a climb you've been working literally for years and have an open mind. There's so much baggage.

The psychological side of redpointing can be even more difficult than the physical side. You know you're capable of doing something, but the mind sabotages you. That's happened to me many times. So, I'll try to trick myself in order to take some of the pressure off. For example, on *La Dura Dura* my first burn would often be my best attempt of the day. I'd feel super strong and fresh. But at the same time I would be a bundle of nerves—all these expectations creating a knot in my stomach.

But on the second try, I would relax, because I felt I'd already done my *serious* effort. I would say, "So now let's just have fun." You have to find a way to convince yourself not to take the process so seriously.

In competitions I used to tell myself, "Well you know, you're not really in very good shape right now." I would find a way to accept the *possibility* of defeat before I even started. "It's probably not going to go very well today, so let's just accept that and deal with it." And once I'd accepted it, I'd be free to be myself however things turned out. That worked for me, but I've heard other people say, "No, you really need to believe in yourself and be confident."

But it's a fine line between confidence and having expectations that create extra pressure. That pressure, creates nervousness, which can lead to not living up to your expectations.

So I always strive to find ways to take the edge off, to return to the mindset I had years ago at Panther Beach, just climbing by myself, when there were no goals other than trying hard moves. Just getting back to having fun is crucial, because those are the moments we are really in our flow. I probably did some of the hardest moves I've ever done on that beach. But who cares, right? It was for the sake of enjoying climbing, tapping into kinesthetic awareness, being in tune with my body and my mind with no expectation whatsoever. And sometimes I have to try over and over to attain that, until finally I get lucky and fall into the right headspace and everything clicks. It's funny, I can come across as easygoing and just going with the flow. But climbing is interesting, because it's not like snowboarding or surfing where you're going with gravity, flowing down a mountain or wave. Climbing is more like

Sharma and wife Jimena on the balcony of their Barcelona apartment

fighting. There's a real struggle involved, and you have to embrace it. In high-end climbing it's only when you try 100 percent that you feel any flow. When you first work a project, everything feels super hard and awkward. You're trying over and over, you're training for it, and you crimp on these holds as hard as you possibly can. Then suddenly it starts to flow. But that's a funny kind of flow!

I suppose that can be a metaphor for life. Life requires hard work and frustration, making mistakes, failing again and again. So, yes, learning how to enjoy the process and flow with it, hard as it may be—that describes what I try to do.

Someone might ask, "Wouldn't it be more fun just to go and do a bunch of 5.13s—just flow up the rock all day?" But for me it's more interesting to try things that are beyond my limit, routes I'm not sure I can do. And that becomes this super-involved, dramatic process. It requires that you put everything in, and only then do you get so much back, when you actually achieve your goal.

Strengths

I feel fortunate to be genetically gifted. I'm sure if my dad had climbed when he was a kid, he would have climbed 5.15. But being strong is only half the equation. The mental side is just as important. And, again, the climbing mind-set suits me well. I'm stubborn. I'm not willing to let go. I will work something until I get it.

Weaknesses

And I've got plenty of weaknesses, but some of my main climbing weaknesses are tricky slab climbing and mantels, stuff like that. I don't enjoy that kind of climbing. I'm not sure if I don't enjoy it because I'm not good at it, or I'm not good at it because I don't enjoy it. It's hard to say. Obviously I have a lot to learn about crack climbing as well. I've done a fair amount of cracks, but it's not my strength. I like climbing moderate 5.12 cracks, but once it gets harder than that, I'm not that into it.

But that said, I'd love to do *The Salathé Headwall* (13b). Out of all cracks I can think of, that's the one I'd really like to do.

Injury

To avoid injury it's important to start young and have all your physical growth and development oriented around rock climbing. It's a difficult balance to get better, to get stronger. You have to push yourself to the edge of injury—but no further. To do that, you have to listen to your body. People get injured when there's a disconnect between body and mind. If your body's telling you it's not psyched, and you're not listening, that's when things go wrong. If body and mind work together, you'll stop before you do something you shouldn't.

Why I Climb

Well, we've got to do something, right? (Laughs.) We can't just watch TV all day. I believe we need passion. We need something that motivates us that we can put our heart into, something that allows us to express who we are. Climbing does all that for me, and more. It allows me to tap into a deeper side of who I am. As I said, I've done meditation retreats, but the fact is, when I go climbing,

I can tap into a meditative state of mind so much easier than I can sitting in a room with crossed legs. That state of mind is super alert, super present in your body, where you are functioning at a really high level—all your pistons firing. It's like mastering a martial art or learning classical music or studying ballet—all require a level of focus where one is functioning at a higher level. That's what it takes for us to realize our full potential.

That's why I like climbing hard things, because it forces me to master myself. It brings out the best in me. It allows me to work toward perfection.

We could try to make the reasons we climb seem deep, but in the end it's simple. Climbing's fun.

"The climbing mind-set suits me well," Sharma says. "I'm stubborn. I'm not willing to let go. I will work something till I get it."

Climbing's an amazing activity, an amazing community, and an amazing way to see the world. In fact, I can't think of any reason *not* to do it!

Climbing is my way of being in the world. It's changed my life in countless positive ways. Take away all my achievements and my career and I would still be an ambassador for the sport, because I believe it has a lot to offer anyone who tries it. It changes you. You develop an appreciation for nature, and in general climbers are down-to-earth, cool people.

Evolution

When will we see the first 5.16? Who knows? It was a huge leap for me to climb 15a, then 15b, and finally 15c. And there are routes I've tried that I believe could be 15d—but I believe that 5.16 should be a leap to a whole new level.

It will require another *really* big step in the evolution of climbing. So right now is an interesting time. You have guys like Ondra and Megos and kids like Ashima (Shiraishi) blowing everyone's minds. So it will be interesting to see what they can do, and how far they can take the sport.

I got to a pretty high level in bouldering—where I could climb v15—and it seemed to me that boulder problems were just getting longer, not necessarily more difficult. It felt like there was a natural limit to the maximum technical difficulty and a limit on how many of those moves one could make in a row.

But the interesting thing about sport climbing is that there's a lot of room for doing harder routes if you break things down into individual sequences. For example *Bon Combat* is a v11 on top of a v11 on top of a v11. And if you look at climbing from that perspective, there's a lot of room to do harder routes. I believe sport climbing has huge potential in the sense it's mixing cutting-edge bouldering with endurance. That makes me think there's a lot of room to push it further.

Advice for the Next Generation

Keep climbing! Kids are starting early now, but there's a make or break time, when they become teenagers and their social circles become a big influence, when they have to decide if they will continue. And I encourage them to stay with it at whatever level, because I know that I need climbing to feel happy and sane. It's a place I can go to connect with myself and to nature, and my past. I can return to a boulder I climbed 25 years ago and have an instant connection to who I was back then as a kid working that problem.

Then there's the community. Climbing is filled with so many great characters, all of them connected by a strong lineage. Climbing is both global and local. You can go climbing in Spain, then go climbing in California a month later and run into the same people.

And finally, it's not like gymnastics, where you train, go to the Olympics, then move on with your life. These days people can climb from the age of 3 into their 90s. So I would encourage kids to make it a lifelong pursuit, because it's amazing!

Sharma competing in the 2015 Psicoblock Masters, a competition he founded and helps produce.

RAPHAEL SLAWINSKI

What is acceptable risk? This is the existential question facing climbers every time they grab the rope and leave the house. For most, the question amounts to little more than, "How far apart are the bolts on my proj?" But what if the risks weighed included not only the considerable dangers of attempting an unclimbed Himalayan peak, but the possibility of being murdered by the Taliban?

This was the riddle facing Raphael Slawinski and Ian Welsted in 2013, when they attempted Pakistan's K6 West, a mountain that had previously shut down several of the world's best alpinists.

Slawinski and Welsted were traveling up the Karakoram Highway when they heard that militants at the nearby Nanga Parbat base camp had just killed ten foreign climbers and a cook. As Slawinski describes, that was a uniquely troubling situation, and whether or not to continue was a uniquely difficult decision. Normally climbers don't have to choose between the risk of death by avalanche and AK-47. But as Slawinski says, the ability to weigh risks and think analytically in stressful situations is probably the single most important skill a mountaineer can have.

Canadian climber Dave Cheesmond once said, "If you can climb (in the Canadian Rockies), you can climb anywhere," and Slawinski embodies the truth of that statement. A late bloomer who didn't start technical climbing until college, he's one of those gifted souls who climbs hard on any medium—rock, ice, plastic, and mixed. The result is a long list of new technical routes throughout the Canadian Rockies and the Karakoram; single push ascents combined with new lines on Denali; and first place victories in mixed climbing competitions.

Reasoning that their objective was removed from Nanga Parbat in a part of the Karakoram without a history of violence, Slawinski and Welsted decided to continue their expedition. Their gamble paid off. The pair went on to make

Raphael Slawinski on his route *French Roast* WI5, M6,
Stanley Headwall, Canadian Rockies

a remarkable first ascent of K6 West via the *Northwest Face* (M6+ WI4+) for which they were awarded the most prestigious honor in mountaineering, the Piolet d'Or (Golden Ice Axe) Award.

When he's not climbing the world's hardest alpine routes, Slawinski poses as a mild-mannered physics professor at Mount Royal University in Calgary, Canada. I had the pleasure of accompanying Slawinski up *French Roast* (WI5, M6), one of several routes he's pioneered on the Stanley Headwall. Watching him dance up ice so hollow and brittle—I was afraid to watch—was an education in the climbing arts. A few days later, watching the blood drain from the faces of some of his physics students as their midterm exams were returned, was an education in another kind of fear—one I was very grateful I no longer have to confront.

Significant Ascents
Mixed Climbing
1997 *The Day After Les Vacances de Monsieur Hulot* (M7, WI6), Stanley Headwall, on-sight first ascent with Matt Collins

1999 *Rocketman* (M7, WI5), Mt. Patterson, Canada, first ascent

2000 *Animal Farm Direct* (M11-), Gulag Cave, Canada, first ascent

2003 *Rocky Mountain Horror Picture Show* (M11+), first on-sight flash ascent; *Musashi* (M12), fourth redpoint ascent—both in the Cineplex Cave, Canadian Rockies

2006 *DTCB* (Grade V, M7), Mt. Andromeda, Canada, first ascent with Scott Semple

First Winter Ascents
2004 *Sphinx Face* (Grade V, M6), Mt. Temple, Canada, with Valery Babanov

2004 *Greenwood-Locke Route* (Grade V, M6), Mt. Temple, with Ben Firth

2005 *Japanese Route* on Mt. Alberta, Canada, with Scott Semple and Eamonn Walsh

2009 Direct Start to *The Wild Things* (VI, M7, WI5), Mt. Chephren, with Dana Ruddy and Eamonn Walsh. This was the first single push ascent of a Canadian Rockies Grade VI done in winter.

Mountaineering

2005 *Infinity Direct*, (M4/5) Denali, Alaska, first ascent with Valery Babanov

2011 *Common Knowledge* (WI6+) and the *Cassin Ridge*, Denali, Alaska; single push ascent with Joshua Lavigne

2013 K6 West (7,040 meters), Charakusa Glacier, Karakoram, with Ian Welsted; first ascent of the Northwest Face (M6+, WI4+)

2014 Recipient of the Piolet d'Or Award for alpinism

Rock Climbing

2012 Yamabushi (8 pitches 12d), Yamnuska, Canada

Competition Climbing

1999 ESPN Winter X Games, second place

2000 Festiglace du Quebec, first place

2000, 2002, and 2003 Ouray Ice Craft Invitational Competition winner

Roots

My name's Raphael Slawinski. I was born March 4, 1967, in Warsaw, Poland, but now I live in Calgary. I do all kinds of climbing, including bouldering indoors on plastic, but if I had to choose one style that is the most meaningful, that I remember most strongly, it would be alpine climbing, because that's how I learned. Even though I wasn't all that interested, my dad needed someone to go mountaineering with, so he would drag me along. We would climb moderate peaks in the Canadian Rockies. Sort of half scrambling, half glacial travel, but the emphasis was always on reaching a summit. So to this day, even though I really like technical climbing, getting to the summit still matters.

Is that old-fashioned? I don't know. My friend Kelly Cordes pointed out that these days a lot of people stop at the end of the technical difficulties, where the climb turns from vertical to 50 degrees, and yes, the remaining ground to the summit is not as sexy, but in many ways that's where the real effort and commitment come in. You don't just start rappelling. You commit to going all the way. I believe that's where the real rewards lie.

Love at First Sight

For me climbing wasn't love at first sight. I had been going out for years pursuing mountaineering objectives, but a love of climbing didn't grab me until I moved far away from the mountains. During school my main focus was on physics, and the University of Chicago had a very good graduate program. When I was filling out application forms, the fact that Chicago is in the middle of cornfields thousands of miles from the Rockies somehow didn't seem terribly important.

That is until I got there, and all of a sudden I realized I *really* missed the mountains. But I was stuck. So I took up rock climbing at Devil's Lake, and in winter I started ice climbing at Starved Rock, 2 hours west of Chicago, a place that in a good season has maybe 2 months of climbable ice. So I had to actually move to the American Midwest away from what is arguably the best ice climbing in the world to discover my love for climbing.

And it was never my intention to return to Calgary. At that time I was extremely committed to physics. I always pictured myself going wherever my career would take me. But you could say that my physics began to suffer as climbing began conquering my affections, and suddenly the number of places that were acceptable to live in narrowed dramatically.

I've chosen to live near the Canadian Rockies because it's an incredible mountain arena. Even though I don't always have time to go to the big mountains, it would be hard to live without them. When I want to do something big, the mountains are there. And what I like doing best are climbs that combine adventure, exploration, and technical challenge, and the Rockies excel in those possibilities.

The Physics of Climbing

I'm not sure to what extent physics informs my climbing, but one of my heroes has always been George Lowe, because, like him, I'm a climber and a PhD physicist. Early in my career, I remember reading an interview with Lowe, where he said that you should always try to separate your position on the mountain from your hopes and fears. That's always stuck with me—the fact that you should try to think objectively about what's going on, where you are, and not let either your fears or your desires distort your vision of the situation.

The challenge with alpine mixed climbing, Slawinski says, "is feeling enough fear that you are not casual or foolish, but at the same time you aren't paralyzed."

"I think the soul of climbing is risk," Slawinski says. "In the end, if we remove all risk from climbing, we would find the soul of the activity has been lost."

What does that mean? Climbing is very much about passion. In fact, without passion it would be totally pointless. Yet at the same time, when we get into big mountains, if we rely solely on passion, climbing can be very dangerous. Especially in the big ranges, it's essential to step back and objectively assess a situation. On one hand, "Yes, I really want to go for the summit." But on the other, "Conditions are bad and the weather's getting worse." Therefore, the objective reality is that we should go down.

Or there's the inverse. "I'm really uncomfortable and I don't want to be here any longer." But when I think things through rationally, I realize there's no reason to turn around. So I suck it up and go for it.

A good example of this was in 2013 during a trip to Pakistan to attempt K6 West. We'd been in the country 4 days when the Taliban walked into Nanga Parbat base camp and executed ten climbers and a local cook. As you might imagine, our first reaction was, "What are we even doing here? We should get out of this country as soon as possible." But then I started thinking, and I realized the region where we were going was far from where the attack took place. So once we got over the horror of what had happened, I felt that objectively there was no reason to go home.

So I would say that it's the more general rationality of physics and science that colors my approach to climbing, rather than details such as figuring out the forces involved in setting up an anchor.

Strengths

Obviously it's hard to judge oneself, but I think my biggest strengths are perseverance and stubbornness.

I'm definitely not the physically strongest climber around. Every time I go to the gym, that's made painfully clear. A lot of my partners are quite a bit stronger than I am. But once I put my mind to something, I'm stubborn, and that, combined with a decent level of fitness, sometimes allows me to succeed where others might fail. Take on-sighting for example. I'll hold on as long as I can, even when my forearms are bursting. I've definitely backed off routes, but once I commit, I find it *very* hard to quit.

That perseverance has helped me succeed on some hard routes. I'm not saying I'm the most successful climber around, but I do believe that the most successful climbers are not necessarily the strongest. Climbing is a funny sport, especially alpinism, where desire and mental strength count for a great deal.

And of course, your greatest strength can also be your greatest weakness. So persevering to the point of stupidity has gotten me into trouble. Almost 20 years ago I took a gigantic fall on the Stanley Headwall, when a free-hanging ice dagger collapsed. Maybe it was stubbornness. Maybe it was ignorance. Even now decades later, I remember thinking when I got to the dagger it didn't seem unreasonable. The ice was bad, but after the overhanging rock I'd just climbed, I found it almost restful. And somehow the fact that I wasn't getting in any gear that would hold a fall didn't strike me as a good reason to back off. Obviously, in retrospect, it was a bad idea, but at the time I wasn't feeling any fear. All that changed the instant I placed a tool and with a crack the entire dagger crashed down. In the end I walked away—although with a nearly paralyzed arm that took months to recover.

Another time I was climbing an alpine route at the Columbia Icefield and it was too warm. Instead of being thin ice, the crux pitch was slush. But I kept going anyway. Again, it wasn't like I was pushing through fear, it just didn't occur to me to back down. So I started hooking the rock beneath the slush. And the next thing I knew I was flying past the belay and knocking my teeth out. That was a bad show.

So I've taken some lessons from those hard knocks. I have to watch to make sure I'm not overly comfortable. I have to ask, "should I be worried here? Should I be backing off?" You have to have a healthy level of fear to keep you safe.

A Feel for Ice

Except for very loose rock (and there's no shortage of that in the Canadian Rockies), ice is the most ephemeral and unpredictable climbing medium. I think that if you believe you know exactly what's going on, and that you know exactly what's going to happen, you're fooling yourself. And with that in mind, I think it's good to always keep a margin of safety, because there's a great deal beyond our control. For example, given my experience on the Stanley Headwall, I'm a lot warier of freestanding pillars. Today I look at a feature like that and think, "Well, I could probably climb it and most likely nothing would happen, but what would be the consequences if I am wrong?"

Yet there remain those times when you take calculated risks. You know things could go wrong, yet you take a deep breath and continue. A memorable example of that for me was on one of the crux pitches of the new route Ian and I climbed on K6 West. It wasn't the technical crux of the entire route, but it was definitely the mental crux. I was on thin ice with marginal gear, and I looked up and saw a lot more to come. And I realized it was one of those *make it or break it* moments, when either we abandoned the route or I committed to leading through. So I committed, and very slowly, move by move, tapped my way up this thin detached ice.

On one hand, fear can be distracting. But on the other, it can help you focus. So the challenge is feeling enough fear that you are not casual or foolish, but at the same time you aren't paralyzed. On that particular occasion I managed to get into the zone, where the fear focused rather than destroying me.

Looking back now, K6 West is my most memorable climb. In some ways that's an easy answer, because it's also the highest mountain I've climbed. It's the biggest virgin peak I've climbed, and it's the climb for which Ian and I received the Piolet d'Or. So it's the obvious answer, but even laying externalities aside, it was an extremely meaningful experience. For one thing it was

"I'll hold on as long as I can, even when my forearms are bursting," says Slawinski. "Once I commit, I find it very hard to quit."

my fourth trip to Pakistan, and on the previous trips we never got up our main objective. And K6 West was a beautiful line. It was a route that suited Ian and me well, because it was largely ice and mixed climbing up a big face leading to the summit of an unclimbed 7,000-meter peak. And from beginning to end, the entire endeavor was surrounded by uncertainty. Even before the trip, I was explicit about my doubts whether we should even get on the mountain, because the objective hazards might be too high. In the end we managed to find a path minimizing the risks, but it was cool that there was this uncertainty hanging over the whole affair, which only resolved itself in the final days. And of course, when you add in the unexpected shock of the Nanga Parbat massacre, it made the trip something impossible to forget.

Commitment

I think there's a bit more rolling of the dice on big expeditions for several reasons. First, you spend a lot of time and money and put your life on hold to go on an expedition, and you don't let go of that investment easily. It's definitely much easier to back off something on a weekend climb near home than halfway around the globe. And in the Himalaya there might simply be no way of getting up your route without going through an ice fall, crossing under seracs, or climbing up an avalanche path. Big mountains are inherently more dangerous than small ones, because there's so much more terrain, and as a result things are less predictable. But you're forced to find a way through. When you compound that with the fact that you're in a place where rescue is basically not an option, these become very serious situations.

Why I Climb

First there's the variety. The fact that I can go bouldering on plastic 5 minutes from my house or I can go off on an expedition halfway around the globe—and as different as those two experiences are, they're still climbing. And I love the adventure. There are times when I immerse myself in sport climbing—projecting routes, working redpoints. But after a couple of months, I start feeling antsy, like something's missing. So I will return to a place like the Stanley Headwall. You're way up there above the valley floor, topping out after dark, then rappelling down

Slawinski training for an Everest expedition near his Calgary home

in the moonlight, and skiing back to the road through the trees. Even though I've climbed there tens, if not hundreds of times, it always feels like an adventure.

And there's the physicality. For example, on the crux pitch on K6 West, I found myself on an overhanging mixed pitch 6,000 meters above sea level—throwing kneedrops! Maybe there are other activities that offer that combination of adventure and physicality, but I'm not sure what they are.

In a way climbing can be whatever you make it. So for a lot of people, instead of going to the gym to lift weights, they go to the climbing gym. And then there are people who take climbing to an extreme like free soloing, and obviously that goes far beyond the realm of mere sport. You can call that a game, but if it is a game, then as the British climber Paul Pritchard says, it's *Deep Play*—a kind of game where the rewards are not necessarily commensurate with the potential losses. So the really cool thing about climbing is that on any given day, or at a given time in your life, you can make climbing whatever you want it to be.

And finally, a huge reward I get from climbing is simply having something I'm passionate about. If I didn't have that, I would feel something was missing from my life. If all I did was work, come home, and hang out on weekends, there would be a certain depth and intensity missing.

If I were not a climber, I'd probably be a much better physicist! At times I do feel that trying to do my job as a professor and at the same time trying to climb at a reasonably high standard means I'm not living up to my potential in either domain. But I enjoy the richness that combining the two gives my life.

Lessons

I often say that, ultimately, climbing is pointless. For one thing it's very selfish. In the end I don't think anyone really gets anything out of it—other than the participants. So I think the lessons I bring back from climbing are primarily lessons that matter to me, not something I can teach others. For one, I come back with a fresh perspective. I've noticed this during committee meetings at my university. As everyone knows, academics love committees because they love to talk. I see how intense people get about a topic, how they become adversarial, and sometimes downright nasty about something that if you just take a step back, doesn't really matter at all.

And at the risk of sounding melodramatic, the previous day I was out climbing, making what could be life-or-death decisions. Can I safely run under those seracs? Will this slope avalanche? You have just been in a place where decisions have real consequences, and that grants you a bit of perspective on everyday life. I feel it allows me to get through life with less stress—if nothing else it allows me to laugh at myself and the human condition.

I feel that one can go too far when talking about applying lessons from climbing to life. I think one runs the risk of sounding like an inspirational speaker. You know, "It's all about teamwork and leadership and finding your own personal Everest!" Just so much hot air—when to a large extent we use climbing as an escape.

And at the same time, even my wife, who is not a climber, has told me I come back from these big trips more relaxed. Not relaxed like someone sedated—relaxed like someone emerging from meditation.

Spirit Matters

I'm wary of the word *spiritual*, because as a scientist I'm very much grounded in the physical world. Until there's evidence of something's existence, I don't believe in it. But if we divorce spirituality from any supernatural associations, I think we can say that climbing, at least in some people, does satisfy some deep need that's not easily defined. A good day in the mountains gives one a satisfaction that's more than intellectual or physical. It's a response to the wonder of the environment and to the deep connection you share with partners during intense experiences. So I think you can have what could be described as spiritual experiences when you're climbing, when you enter a state of flow where your conscious mind stops getting in the way, and when you come back down it almost feels like waking up.

To me the ideal climbing state of mind is when you're hyperaware. You don't want to be so immersed in the activity that you're no longer aware of your surroundings. That can be extremely dangerous. And at the same time, you don't want to be overthinking—thoughts getting in the way of what you're doing. Let's say you're climbing a pillar of ice. You want to be very aware of the effect your tools are having on the medium. You need to be sensitive to the vibration, the sounds the pillar is making, but at the same time, in order to climb your best, you cannot be consciously directing every move. So there's this fascinating balance between being detached and totally present.

Fear

There are all kinds of fear. For example, there is fear of failure, which I often experience when I'm working hard redpoints, routes that have taken a lot of time and effort. It's so hard to walk up to the route for the umpteenth time and believe that somehow this time will be different, that this time I will stick the crux.

But a bigger fear is of physical injury or death in the mountains, and here I can be quite paranoid. For example, I often find it hard to sleep the night before a big climb. I remember walking up the glacier to the start of K6 and wondering if I would ever be walking back down that way again. Maybe I was being morbid. Maybe I was being realistic. I don't know.

Slawinski poses as a mild-mannered physics professor when he's not climbing.

And these days I also sometimes experience the fear of effort. Maybe I'm just getting lazier, or maybe it's the accumulated effect of experience. Now I have a better idea of what a given climb will demand of me. For example, I've done some single-push climbing in Alaska, where we climbed a route like the *Cassin* in under 24 hours round-trip. Waking up before a day like that, I find it hard to get out of the sleeping bag, not so much because I'm afraid of the climb, but because I know the huge physical effort that will be required.

Barry Blanchard has many good sayings, but one of his best is that you shouldn't make any important decisions before dawn. That's the time we're the weakest. We're cold. We're stiff. We're not quite awake, and the last thing we want to do is embark on a big adventure. But that's also the time to push through and continue. That's one of the hardest things about alpinism: when the alarm goes off, to unzip the sleeping bag, get the stove going, and put your boots on. That's a big part of the commitment, right there. If you can get past that, you're a good part of the way to the summit.

Heart & Soul

Before I got into climbing, I was into tennis. And at the risk of offending tennis players, I'm not sure I could say that tennis has a soul. You could say that tennis players have heart—for instance, if a player is two sets down, and he or she rallies and manages to win. But I believe that soul is something beyond sheer physical effort.

And I think the soul of climbing is risk. I think that in the end, if we remove all risk from climbing, we would find that the soul of the activity has been lost. That's not to say I want to get hurt, much less die, while climbing. But I do think that to go out into environments that present real risks—and then use my judgment and abilities to mitigate those dangers—is a big part of the appeal.

Aging

I never feel like I have quite enough time to climb, and sometimes I think that having a hunger that is never satisfied is one of the things that has kept me interested. I've been climbing now intensively for a quarter of a century, and perhaps I'm not quite as gung-ho as I once was. But a few weeks ago I got up at 3 in the morning to go climbing, and I returned home at 2 a.m. the following day. So I'm still motivated enough to do that kind of thing, and it's possible that if I could have satisfied that hunger early in my life I wouldn't have stuck with it.

I'm in my late 40s now, and at this point (let's not fool ourselves) I've probably lived more than half my life, so maybe the term *middle age* no longer strictly applies. In climbing terms, given enough effort, I think I can still be in the best shape of my life. But there will come a point within the next decade or so, when I'll inevitably start down the other side of the hill. And that will be a hard process, because a good part of the appeal of climbing for me is the fact that I can push myself and get better.

MAYAN SMITH-GOBAT

Okay, I admit *badass* is the most overused term in all of climbing, but it describes Mayan Smith-Gobat so well I'm going to use it anyway. Born at the foot of New Zealand's Mount Cook to a mountain guide dad and a German mom, it seems Mayan's destiny from birth was climbing. However, Mayan is so ridiculously good at everything she tries, it took 9 years of competitive horse riding and several years of professional skiing, culminating in an aerial crash, to make her realize that climbing is her soul's true purpose.

Still limping from her ski injuries, Mayan entered and won the national bouldering series of New Zealand. As she says, when you can't use your feet, your upper body gets much stronger! And if you're a natural-born, all-round athlete trying to limit yourself to just one sport, climbing's an excellent choice, because it's so many sports in one. Soon Mayan was traveling the world trying her hand at bouldering, sport, and trad. One result was the first female ascent of the world's first 14, *Punks in the Gym*, another was a send of *L'Arcademician* at Ceuse, making her the only Kiwi woman to have climbed 14b. While traveling full-time climbing 14s would be many climbers' dream come true, for Mayan these routes were just appetizers. From her youth she had dreamed of climbing El Capitan. The only problem was she didn't have the faintest idea how to climb cracks. In 2009 Mayan flew to Yosemite to learn how to jam. Three weeks later she on-sighted *Astroman* (11c), one of the world's greatest crack climbs.

Hooked on Yosemite, a year later she returned, determined to realize her lifelong dream of free climbing El Cap. Instead of the easier *Free Rider* (12d), Mayan set her sights on the *Salathé Wall,* which culminates with the 13b *Salathé Headwall.* After rehearsing the upper pitches, she succeeded in leading every pitch from the ground up, and a few days later, just for good measure, she free climbed *Free Rider* as well—in 14 hours.

As she says, resting has never been her strong suit, and when only a day or two later she discovered the woman's speed record for *The Nose* (at that

Mayan Smith-Gobat dances up the 5.11 headwall of Shune's Buttress, Zion.

time) was a measly 12 hours, it launched her on a multiyear infatuation with speed climbing. In 2013 Mayan and Chantel Astorga set the women's record for a linkup of *The Nose* and Half Dome at 20 hours 9 minutes. Then in 2014 Mayan and Libby Sauter set the female speed record for *The Nose*—at 4 hours 43 minutes.

As I was putting the finishing touches on this book, Mayan and Ines Papert returned from Patagonia after summiting one of the world's most notorious alpine routes, *Riders on the Storm*. Below Mayan describes how that experience turned out to be the culmination of her career, bringing her full circle back to her mountaineering roots and opening a whole new chapter in a remarkably adventurous life.

Roots

I'm Mayan Smith-Gobat. I was born in New Zealand on October 3, 1979. My dad's Kiwi and my mother was German. I started alpine climbing at 16, then quickly turned to bouldering and sport climbing. Now my specialty's big wall and trad, but I like mixing it up. My name comes from a German children's story about a bee whose name was Maya. My mother suggested calling me Maya, but my dad found it too harsh, so they decided to put an "N" on the end and I became "Mayan." It's the same name as the Indians from South America—but there's no connection.

Climbing's in my blood. My dad was an alpine guide, and I was born at the base of Mount Cook—the highest mountain in New Zealand. When I'm in mountains, I feel at home. When I was only 3, my family and I went for a hike to a place with a beautiful view of Mount Cook. After a few hours everyone else wanted to go home but, I said, in my 3-year-old voice, "No. I want to stay and watch the mountains." And I did. They left, and I walked home alone. Even at that early age, I had a deep affinity for mountains and a very strong independent nature.

But the sport I took to as a kid was horse riding. From 7 through 16, I pursued competitive horse riding in every form. During those years riding was my life. Then I got a summer job at Mount Cook. I took my first mountaineering course and absolutely loved it. The next summer, friends introduced me to rock climbing, and I had this instant fascination with the gymnastic movement, the mental and physical challenges. During my last year of school, I pursued climbing as much as possible.

After leaving school, my focus switched to skiing. I had learned to ski before I could walk, so I basically grew up on skis. For the next few years I pursued professional skiing—competing in free skiing competitions and big mountain events around the world. That phase of my life ended with a big crash. I flew off a cat track and hit a tree. I broke both feet and my jaw.

Being young and impatient, I found sitting still impossible even when I was injured, so I began training my upper body, and returned to climbing with one foot still in a cast. And I got *a lot stronger,* because for nearly a year I couldn't use my feet very well. A year after the ski accident, I entered my first bouldering competition—in New Zealand—and I won. That was the first indication I might be good at climbing. It fueled my motivation. After that, I've never looked back—climbing has been my focus. I'm extremely self-motivated. I love the challenge. Climbing fits my personality perfectly.

Mind Control

Riding competitions are stressful both for the rider and the horse. Horses are remarkably sensitive; they pick up on their rider's emotions. Because I grew up without much money, I often rode the young horses that had potential but weren't well trained. And if I was at all nervous, my horse would sense it and go crazy. This taught me a lot. I needed to stay relaxed, even when I felt nervous. I had to control my emotions. To keep the horse calm, I had to calm my body and slow my breath. I learned how to tense specific muscles while relaxing others. This training has been hugely helpful in climbing. I have the ability to pull back and ask myself, "Am I really in danger, or do I just feel like I'm in danger?" If you can't control your emotions, climbing (and riding) become much more difficult.

My Path

How did I get here? I wholeheartedly followed my passions. From riding to skiing to climbing, I've given total focus to everything I do. Early in my climbing career, I lived in Christchurch and spent much of my time exploring the boulders at Castle Hill. The style of climbing there is like Fontainebleau but with less friction. The round shapes forced me to smear, apply pressure in a very precise way, and move my body to make the holds more effective. Simply pulling down was not an option. Those lessons established an amazing technical foundation. But I soon realized how limited New Zealand climbing is, so I began exploring sport climbing in Australia and Europe. And I'd always been fascinated by Yosemite. Since I was quite young, I'd dreamed of free climbing El Cap. So in 2009 I decided it was time to go to Yosemite to learn crack climbing.

I remember walking up to my first crack and thinking, "What the hell do I do?" I didn't know how to jam at all! However, my experience at Castle Hill helped me adjust, both to the slickness and by positioning my body to make the holds work. After 3 weeks in the Valley, my partner and I climbed *Free Rider* over 3 days. Considering the limited amount of experience I had, I did reasonably well, leading and hauling every pitch. At the top I was utterly destroyed; my hands were swollen to twice their normal size, and I was bruised everywhere. But I loved it!

Yet having seen the *Salathé Headwall* as we traversed below, I was disappointed not to have been able to try it. From that moment all I wanted to do was return to Yosemite and attempt *The Salathé*.

So when I came back a year later and achieved my lifelong dream of free climbing El Cap via *The Salathé*, it became one of my most important accomplishments. *The Salathé* forced me to step a long way beyond my comfort zone. To prepare, I worked the route alone, rappelling down from the top and climbing *The Headwall* on a mini traxion. I'll never forget walking to the top of El Cap at 3 a.m., dropping over the edge, then working the route until midday. That was a special time and it taught me a lot about myself!

Until my experience in 2016 on *Riders on the Storm*, *The Salathé* was my proudest achievement. It changed my direction to big walls. Eventually it led to Patagonia and the next step in my evolution as a climber.

The other achievement that stands out is *Punks in the Gym* at Arapiles in Australia. *Punks* was the world's first 5.14, and it was right on my own Southern

Mayan and Ben Rueck road-tripping in Utah. "Climbing gives me an amazing excuse to go to some of the wildest, craziest places, then focus on trying something at the edge of my ability," she says.

Hemisphere doorstep. I remember walking by the route every day on my first climbing trip to Arapiles, thinking it looked impossible. In fact just making myself believe I was capable of climbing *Punks* was a huge mental leap. The route is more difficult for shorter people, and it hadn't been climbed by a woman.

Redpointing

Punks was probably my most frustrating project. I came extremely close to sending it early on, but it took *another 2 years* to actually do it! I fell off that route at least 300 times! I wanted it too much, and I put far too much pressure on myself, resulting in a serious case of *redpoint angst*! There were several occasions when I wanted to quit. Then I would ask myself, "Are you going to be happy if you walk away now?" The answer was always no.

Punks forced me to look deep inside and ask, "What does this route mean? Was I doing it for myself or only because I wanted the first female ascent? Eventually, I realized the route really was special and that I genuinely wanted to climb it. In the end I succeeded when I was tired and thought there was no chance. It was the third or fourth burn of the day and I had dropped all expectations. That lesson has helped me redpoint ever since. Now I try to reduce the pressure. I try not to want the route so much that desire holds me back.

But everyone's different. I know people who function really well under pressure. If they know it's their last shot, they give it everything. I need to be relaxed but confident. If I don't believe I can do a move, I won't give it everything. Visualizing myself as really strong and completing the sequence helps me relax and allows my body to execute the moves.

Redpointing is definitely one of the most frustrating aspects of climbing, but it lets me know when I'm climbing at my limit. I've always been drawn to find my boundaries and see what's possible. So, even though redpointing can be frustrating as hell, I love the process.

Strengths & Weaknesses

Mentally my biggest strength is my ability to make rational decisions, then shut off internal chatter. "This is what I'm going to do. Now stop thinking and go!" I'm pretty good at making decisions then blocking out residual fear. That strength runs through everything I do.

Physically I excel at technical endurance. I can keep going for a *long* time. In contrast, I have to work hard to develop power and explosive movement. That probably comes from learning to climb outdoors. Outdoor climbing doesn't lend itself to developing dynamic power, and it was a long time before I started training inside. And women in general have a harder time building power, because we have less fast-twitch muscle. So when training, I always focus on power rather than endurance.

Setbacks

I've grown more patient over time—but patience remains my biggest challenge. I've had several injuries, probably resulting from being impatient, pushing too hard, not resting enough. For example, at one point my left forearm became *perma-pumped*! I was living in Australia's Blue Mountains and the climbing there is quite repetitive—big pulls on reasonably good crimps. I was climbing constantly, and my fingers never got a break. The end result was an overuse syndrome, possibly tendinosis. Eventually I couldn't even ride a bike, because my forearm would get too pumped. I went to see a lot of doctors, and several wanted to operate, but no one could give me a definitive diagnosis, so I decided against it.

Another major setback came on my first trip to China. I was bitten by an insect and got streptococcal cellulitis. My whole leg swelled up with a big red streak running up it. I was sure I would either lose my leg or get blood poisoning and die. The infection destroyed all the lymph glands and minor blood vessels in my foot. I had to spend 2 months with my leg elevated, because if the blood rushed to my foot, it caused intense pain.

Most recently I had surgery on my left shoulder. I'd been struggling with pain for a long time and eventually had to have the bicep tendon and labrum repaired. I could climb up to the low 13s, but above that the shoulder didn't really work. But because I could still climb reasonably well, deciding to have surgery was one of the hardest decisions I've ever had to make. I had to choose whether to accept a weak shoulder for the rest of my life or 12 months of inactivity. In the end I choose the surgery, and it's the best decision I've ever made. That shoulder now feels stronger than the other, and the time off gave me a new fire.

What I've learned, and it's taken me a long time to learn it, is the importance of patience—to step back and look at the big picture. I now have more confidence that, yes, things do come back. A setback is not forever if you put in the work and take it slow. I went into the shoulder rehabilitation with the attitude I was not going to rush. I would be patient, listen to my body, and let things heal. It's been nice to see good results.

Training

Before *Punks* I never trained in a specific way. I didn't know anyone with enough experience to help me create a structured program. When I met Ben

"The single most important lesson climbing has taught me is to believe in myself," Mayan says.

Rueck and Rob Pizem in Grand Junction, Colorado, I did a short training program with them before I went to try *Punks* for the last time. It was only 3 weeks, but I definitely noticed a difference. I felt stronger, and moves I could barely do before, felt easier. That was a turning point. It made me want to learn as much as possible about training. Climbing's so varied, each climber reacts differently to various techniques. Recently I've been training at Café Kraft in Germany with Alex Megos's trainers—Patrick Matros and Dicki Korb. So far, I like their approach best. They view training as a long-term process, not something you engage in for a single route. They take a holistic approach, assessing you as a whole person and attempting to maintain your overall balance and health.

The way I train depends on whether I'm going for a sport project or a multipitch route. Right now I'm still trying to rebuild my strength after surgery. So I do a circuit that combines campusing with core exercises, then upper-body work on the rings—exercises that target what's lacking and balance my body. I'm working on strengthening my shoulders, while working my back, and opening my front to maintain proper positioning.

If training for a long project, I add interval training, mileage days, long trail runs, and occasionally sprints. I find that sprints aid climbing by teaching my body to recover quickly from short, intense anaerobic bursts. During a training cycle, I do some form of exercise nearly every day—usually only taking 1 full day off a week.

These days I'm attempting to feel how my body is adapting to training and structure my schedule around this, rather than simply committing to a rigid program. For instance, if my shoulder's hurting, I'll do more stretching and less climbing. Most importantly I try to keep training fun!

Speed Ascents

There was a time when being able to climb 3,000 feet in less than 3 hours was inconceivable. I couldn't see how it was possible, and that made it intriguing. What I found out was that speed climbing a route like *The Nose* is fascinating, but it's also dangerous. The risk of death is lower than free soloing, but the risk of injury is higher. After freeing *The Salathé* I was lounging in El Cap meadow with my girlfriends when someone mentioned the women's speed record on *The Nose* was 12 hours. Twelve hours! We all agreed that if men could climb it in 2.5, then 12 was not a record, it was simply doing it in a day. I immediately started planning. I'd never climbed *The Nose* before, but the first time I did we climbed it in 11 hours.

Speed climbing is addictive, because you feel you can always go faster. Every time I've climbed *The Nose,* a few minor things have gone wrong and you realize that fixing those errors can shave minutes off your time. But the faster you go, the more dangerous it gets. Pushing for under 2.5 hours is where I see it getting really dangerous. The first time I climbed *The Nose* with Sean Leary, we summited in 4.5 hours—simply by being well matched, fit, and both of us feeling comfortable on the terrain. That was a huge eye-opener.

The technique itself is complicated, but to summarize, both climbers simul-climb the entire route—which means never stopping to belay. Both climbers move together all the way to the top. One climber leads the first half, then the climbers switch the lead for the second block. They climb using a mixture of free climbing and *French Free*, which means using cams as handholds. There are only three pitches where I use direct aid, because it's too slow. The key is getting your systems dialed so that everything flows. For example, when you're seconding, figuring out the perfect spacing. Libby Sauter and I used a 50-meter rope and we were generally 20 to 30 meters apart. The hardest free move we did was probably 5.11.

There's no faltering. Place gear properly, pay attention, climb quickly, but don't sprint—falls are *not a good idea*. People ask me if other kinds of climbing feel slow after speed climbing. Yes and no. There's definitely a beauty to simul-climbing. Being able to start up *The Nose* at 7 in the morning, knowing you'll be at the top before noon—that's awesome! So when I'm free climbing and moving reasonably quickly, that doesn't feel slow. But waiting at belays? Yes, that always feels slow.

Why I Climb

Climbing is my life! I can't imagine doing anything else. Occasionally it can be frustrating having your job and passion linked, but I wouldn't trade it for

Trail running in Colorado. "How did I get here? I wholeheartedly followed my passions. I've given total focus to everything I do."

anything. The freedom is incredible! Climbing is an activity where I get to define my role. I pursue projects that are inspiring, and hopefully I motivate others by doing what I love—which is pushing my limits. I don't know where else I could have found personal development like this—mental and physical challenge combined with freedom. I can go alpine climbing, bouldering, put up first ascents, or go big wall climbing. The choice is mine!

Climbing takes me to the most beautiful places on the planet. I love traveling, but I don't want to travel without an objective. Climbing gives me an amazing excuse to go to some of the wildest, craziest places, then focus on trying something at the edge of my ability. And I love the friendships. Some of the strongest and most trusting relationships are between climbing partners.

Lessons

The single most important lesson climbing has taught me is to believe in myself. As a child I was super shy. In a group, I was the quiet one who never said anything. Climbing helped me realize my strength, value myself, and begin to see I have something to offer. Through climbing I've learned to set long-term goals but also to celebrate the small steps necessary to succeed. I may have some natural ability, but I've only gotten where I am through hard work. Climbing has taught me to deal with failure and not give up. I spend 90 percent of my time (make that 99 percent) failing—in order to reach those few moments when I succeed.

Everything I've learned from climbing can be applied to life. It has definitely helped me deal with challenges. I believe climbing is a sport with a lot to offer society in general—particularly people who don't fit into the norm. When I first got involved in climbing, my closest friend had just dropped out of high school and was doing drugs. I was living in a small New Zealand town where there wasn't much to do. People were hanging out taking drugs. I was getting sucked into that scene. But my mom got me a job at Mount Cook, and that brought me back to the mountains and changed my life.

Spirit Matters

Whether or not climbing can be spiritual depends on the type of climbing you're doing. For example, competition climbing? No. That's pure sport, but at the same time you could say that to become really good at it, you need to develop spiritually—because you must find the inner peace necessary to concentrate, excel, and deal with failure.

But when you go outdoors, climbing takes you to places where the beauty and wildness evoke feelings I would call spiritual—where you find peace within yourself simply by being there. So alpine climbing seems spiritual to me. When I'm in the alpine, I have a connection to nature—a world bigger than myself. Having said that, I don't really believe in any particular religion. If I had to choose a religion, it would be climbing because that's how I've developed most. When I'm climbing, I feel happy and at peace.

Climber's Mind

For me the best climbing state of mind is when I'm totally focused and not thinking about anything else. No space to think about issues in my life. I'm right here, relaxed, and attuned—but not blasé. Drive and fire are important—but no anxiety. For a redpoint my body knows the route, so I'm focused on each move as it occurs. I don't need to think ahead. When climbing multipitch, or on-sight, there are more thoughts. Since my body doesn't know the moves, I need to be assessing, planning, and thinking ahead.

I used to be extremely self-critical. If I messed up I would focus on the negative and mentally abuse myself. "You're so bad at this and that, and that!"

I still do that occasionally, but I've tried hard to change and focus on positives instead. "Okay bummer. You messed up, but you were tired. Look how well you did!" I work hard to keep a lighthearted attitude, because I tend to take everything too seriously.

Partnerships

I enjoy supporting good friends in their efforts as much as climbing for myself. Seeing someone else succeed can be as good, if not better, as doing it myself, especially if I have a deep connection to that person. And it helps me a lot when I know the person I'm climbing with is 100 percent supporting me. That connection allows me to give my all. Climbing partners mean the world to me. I used to go climbing with pretty much anyone, but now I prefer partners I know and trust. Personal relationships can make or break a cragging day, but especially an expedition. Why go climbing with someone you don't get on with?

Relationships

I haven't dated a civilian in forever. In fact, I can't remember ever dating someone who wasn't involved in my current sport—whether skiing or climbing. There are pros and cons to any approach. It's hard climbing with the person you love, because then you worry about them. But climbing is my life, so I would find it difficult to have a deep connection with someone who didn't get

it. The most important thing to me is the ability to have a full understanding with my partner. I've always been involved in all-or-nothing relationships that perhaps don't last long, but while they do, are super intense. Maybe that's not the best way to make things last—but it's sure a lot of fun while they do.

Riders on the Storm

(Three months after my interview with Mayan, she and Ines Papert, accompanied by photographer Thomas Senf, traveled to Patagonia, and from January 16 to February 20, 2016, made the fifth ascent of Riders on the Storm *[originally rated Grade VI, 5.12d, A3] a 38-pitch climb on the East Face of Torre Central in Torres del Paine National Park, Chile. Ines and Mayan were able to free several pitches that had previously been aided, but didn't have enough time or good weather to free the entire route.)*

I was intimidated by *Riders on the Storm* because it's such a big route with a big reputation. Some of the best climbers in the world have tried it and failed. But it was also appealing because 2016 was 25 years since the first ascent, and it's only had four ascents in all the intervening time. No one has been able to free climb the entire route. So that's what attracted Ines and I—the history, the reputation, the opportunity for hard free climbing, and the fact it had never been attempted by two women. And when we arrived—it *was super* intimidating. The wall was much bigger than we anticipated and fully alpine. For me, the alpine nature of the climb alone was a huge learning curve. I have plenty of experience on big walls, but El Cap felt like sport climbing compared to Torre Central.

Ines is really strong in the alpine. And I'm really strong climbing big wall cracks. So we meshed well, but we had to use all our skills and then some, to make the summit. We climbed the route in siege style. We fixed ropes about 600 meters up to a portaledge camp, then another 250 meters above that. Then when it looked like we had good weather, we pulled half the lower ropes and refixed them above. By then we were fixed high on the wall, but we couldn't retreat all the way to the ground. We decided not to worry about freeing the difficult lower pitches until we had tagged the summit. That turned

Mayan attempting *The Incredible Huck* (14a/b), The Cathedral, Utah. "Even though redpointing can be frustrating as hell, I love the process," she says.

Mayan training at Grand Valley Climbing, Grand Junction, Colorado

out to be a really good decision. We got lucky and summited on the last day of good weather.

Two of the pitches that had not been freed were near the top, so we climbed them during our summit push. These steep cracks were 13a and 12b respectively, overhanging 10 to 20 degrees and partially iced up. While climbing the upper pitch, I was jamming against ice and running water! They received barely an hour of sun first thing in the morning, so we rose at 2 a.m. and jugged 600 meters in order to reach them at first light. Then it was game on! As the sun rose, you had to be ready to give 100 percent in subfreezing conditions—because by 8 a.m. the cracks were running with water and the risk of falling ice became too great!

Some of the lower sections challenged us in different ways. There were a couple pitches where Ines was climbing with a rock shoe on one foot and a cramponed boot on the other—half smearing and half ice climbing. That was something neither of us had ever done. We protected those sections with . . . well, not much at all! (Laughs.) On one off-width I had to drive in an ice ax and clip to it for protection. It was purely psychological. I definitely didn't want to test it!

We experienced a lot of rock and ice fall. For me this was a different level of risk than I'd previously encountered—the kind you can't manage. One night a rock ripped our portaledge open, landing right next to Ines as she slept.

That's the kind of uncontrollable risk that you can do nothing about. All you can do is curl up tighter in a ball and hope.

Because of those kinds of dangers, Ines doesn't want to return and I don't blame her. She has a son to think of, and I totally understand and respect her for that decision. But I'm keen to go back. This experience opened my eyes to what's possible. I needed all the skills I've developed through 20 years of climbing to pull this one off. From the jamming I learned on *The Salathé,* to the mind control I learned working *Punks,* it felt like a wonderful symmetry, bringing my entire life full circle,

from my roots growing up below Mount Cook through my bouldering and big wall experiences—all coming together to perform extreme rock climbing in an alpine environment. So I'm excited! Since *The Salathé* and *Punks* I haven't had a strong focus, and I found that again in Patagonia. *Riders* is definitely not the end; it's a new beginning.

LEARNING TO DOWNCLIMB

Not long ago I was in a climbing gym with a friend a few years older than myself. We were bouldering, and a young kid came up to my companion and said, "Wow, you're a way honed geezer!"

There was a long silence—then my friend and I burst into laughter.

"Well thanks . . . I think," my friend said. "I'll take that as a compliment."

No one owns climbing. No matter how many routes you've sent, how many first ascents you've made—the river continues to flow. Today's crusher will fade into tomorrow's "way honed geezer." As the British mountaineer Don Whillans said, we must all learn to "downclimb" gracefully. In the end, perhaps that's the most we can hope for.

Climbing will continue to evolve separate from the actions of any one individual no matter how gifted. In fact, it will evolve faster than other more established sports, because climbing is so young. People have been running competitively for thousands of years, so increases in performance are incremental, but at this very moment in climbing gyms around the globe thousands of kids are starting climbing at an early age. At this very moment the next Sharma, Ondra, and Smith-Gobat are discovering their souls' true purpose. The gene pool is swelling into an ocean. Thirty years ago we were lucky to find a crusty mentor to show us the ropes, today there are long lists of children waiting to be coached by World Cup competitors. Older climbers already groan as 10-year-olds warm up on their "project," but we aint seen nothin' yet.

So in order to become a lifer we must each find something more durable than numbers and grades to hang on to. As the late great Alex Lowe once said, "The best climber is the one having the most fun." Lowe was paraphrasing Hawaiian Duke Kahanamoku, but the sentiment applies to climbing as well as it did originally to surfing. Lynn Hill agrees. "One summit or one competition doesn't matter," she said. "It's what you learn along the way and that learning is endless. It's always the process, not anything you accomplish."

The late great climber Alex Lowe living the dream in the Ak-Su Mountains of Kyrgyzstan

Jim Donini still
Chasin' Skirt (10+)
at age 72, Long
Canyon, Utah

Guide and graphic artist Tracy Martin enjoying *Spring Break* (11d) in Red Rocks

Each new generation will create new games with new rules, but hopefully certain aspects will always remain—challenge, risk, personal growth, adventure, friendship, community, travel, and a deep and abiding love for the wild places where people climb.

There is a magic in climbing that is like a dream, an epiphany that can be glimpsed yet never grasped, a thirst that can never be fully quenched. And therein lies the beauty. At the heart of all human striving there lies a great mystery. Why do we do this? The answer is not nearly as important as the quest to find out. The answer is out there waiting for each of us to discover for ourselves.

I have a recurring dream. I'm living in a cabin at the edge of looming peaks. The air is full of the scent of pine and the song

Jim Donini is the epitome of a "lifer," someone who even after a lifetime still embodies all the joy of the climbing lifestyle.

of flowing water. It's a life as simple and clean as the mountains themselves. The world of getting and spending, of never having enough, is far away.

I fall asleep to the sound of the river, and in the mornings I sit on the porch as steam from my mug rises to join the mist moving through the trees. As Rébuffat said, we must always marry action with contemplation. We should never have one without the other. The age-old dance of the fully realized life—to strive, to risk, and to explore—should always be balanced

by a return to a place of stillness and repose where we can integrate all we have learned.

There is an undeniable symmetry in this life focused on making graceful movements high above the ground. Studying the passage of light. Climbing stone walls, then returning to admire the cut glass water of a mountain stream. Chopping wood. Lighting a fire at twilight. Learning to live with skill and integrity in a vertical world.

I believe climbing is one of the most creative outlets possible for modern humans. Like dance, it is a performance art, a way to express all the joy of living in a powerful and ecstatic body. In a society ever more removed from anything lasting and authentic, it reconnects us to the real, existing world—plugging us directly into the primal juice of the earth that was buzzing long before Man came along, and that will continue long after we are gone. And like other spiritual practices like meditation, yoga, and the martial arts, climbing heals the rift between our bodies, which evolved 75,000 years ago in the Pleistocene Epoch and the distracted multitasking mind of today. Perhaps most important, climbing imbues life with meaning, passion, and purpose in a culture starved for all three.

Climbing's the vehicle to ride for a joy-filled, switched-on life.

What are you waiting for? Get on the bus!

Jay Smith, age 61, hiking the crux of *Voodoo Child* (11+), just one of nearly 1,500 new routes he's done worldwide

NOTES

THE WAY HOME

1 Reinhold Messner, *My Life at the Limit*, Mountaineers Books, 2014.
2 Hanshan, *A Full Load of Moonlight: Chinese Chan Buddhist Poems*, trans. Mary M. Y. Fung and David Lunde, Music Stone Culture, 2014.
3 Gary Snyder, *The Practice of the Wild*, North Point Press, 1990.
4 John Haines, *Living Off the Country*, University of Michigan Press, 1982.
5 Dan Froelich, *Rock & Ice #230*, November 2015, used with permission.
6 Gaston Rébuffat, *Starlight and Storm*, The Modern Library, New York, 1999.

GAME THEORY

1 In the first issue of the mountaineering anthology *Ascent*, which at that time was published by the Sierra Club.

THE HEROIC LIFE

1 Rébuffat, *Starlight and Storm*.
2 Kevin Crossley-Holland quoting H. R. Ellis Davidson, Introduction, *The Norse Myths*, Pantheon, 1981.
3 Shawn Achor, *The Happiness Advantage*, Crown Business, 2010.

SPIRIT MATTERS

1 *Alpinist* magazine 43, Summer 2013.
2 Diane Ackerman, *Deep Play*, Random House, 2000.

ALEX HONNOLD

1 Daniel Duane, "The Heart-Stopping Climbs of Alex Honnold," *NY Times Sunday Magazine*, March 12, 2015.

Rachel Melville setting out to *Ride the Lightning* (13b/c),
New River Gorge, West Virginia

Out at the end of a thousand dirt roads, rootless nomads searching for the next flash of backcountry satori. Modern climbers are the spiritual heirs of mountain hermits who left the world seeking simplicity.